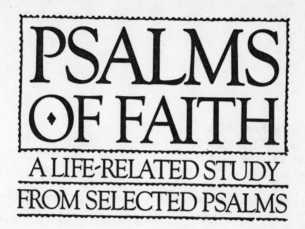

PSALMS OF FAITH

A LIFE-RELATED STUDY
FROM SELECTED PSALMS

Ray C. Stedman

GL

Regal Books

A Division of GL Publications
Ventura, California, U.S.A.

Published by Regal Books
A Division of GL Publications
Ventura, California 93006
Printed in U.S.A.

Library of Congress Cataloging-in-Publication data.

Stedman, Ray C.
    Psalms of faith : a life-related study from selected Psalms / Ray C. Stedman.
      p.   cm.—(Bible commentary for laymen)
    ISBN 0-8307-1324-7
    1. Bible. O.T. Psalms—Commentaries. I. Bible. O.T. Psalms. English. Selections.
1989. II. Title. III. Series.
BS1430.3.S74 1989
223″.207′7—dc19   88-28427
                                          CIP

1 2 3 4 5 6 7 8 9 10 / 92 91 90 89 88

Rights for publishing this book in other languages are contracted by Gospel Literature International (GLINT) foundation. GLINT also provides technical help for the adaptation, translation, and publishing of Bible study resources and books in scores of languages worldwide. For further information, contact GLINT, Post Office Box 488, Rosemead, California, 91770, U.S.A., or the publisher.

Dedicated to
my wife Elaine
and my four daughters
Sheila
Susan
Linda
Laurie
who have taught me much
and loved me more

Contents

A leader's guide for individual or group study with this book is
available from your church supplier.

Preface

For centuries the Psalms have been read and loved by people from many backgrounds and viewpoints, largely because, being poetry, they speak to the heart directly. They laugh, they sing, they weep, they rail, they cry out in pain, fright, derision, joy, and the sheer delight of life. Consequently, many read them solely to find an answering spirit to their own mood.

But the Psalms are much more than poetry. Many of them bear the title *Maskil* or teaching psalm. They are thus intended to instruct the mind as well as to encourage the heart. They are designed not only to reflect a mood, but to show us also how to handle that mood; how to escape from depression, or how to balance exaltation with wisdom. This quality is the mark of their divine character. They are not merely human folksongs, reflecting the common experience of men, but they relate also the wisdom and release that ensues when a hurt or a joy is laid at the feet of God.

It was a great personal joy to me to share these studies with the responsive congregation of the Peninsula Bible Church. I am delighted also that two of the studies—those on Psalms 23 and 34—are written by my gifted former colleague, David H. Roper, and reflect his careful and insightful exposition.

It is my prayer that God will use these studies to open many eyes to the beauty and help of the Psalms.

Ray C. Stedman

Introduction

The Psalms are particularly appropriate for our day because they relate the experiences of believers of the past, reflecting the emotional upsets, problems, and disturbances that saints of old have gone through. They are wonderful for helping us in our own emotional pressures.

There is no book like the Psalms to meet the need of the heart when it is discouraged and defeated, or when it is elated and encouraged. This book is absolutely without peer in expressing these emotional feelings. The Psalms are helpful simply because they teach us how to find our way through many types of problems. These marvelous folksongs are much like the ballad style of music that was so popular in the late '60s and early '70s, simply recounting what various men and women of the past have experienced.

Most of the Psalms were written by David. Others were written by his choir leaders in Jerusalem, and the names of Asaph, Jeduthun, Ethan, and others appearing in the Psalms are royal choirmasters. One or two were written by Moses, and one or two by King Solomon. There are several Psalms whose authors it is impossible to identify. The whole book is a collection that has been put together by the ancient Hebrews in order that we might understand what the people of God have gone through and how they found their way out of their troubles.

The Psalms divide into five books, which are similar in theme to the first five books of the Bible, the Pentateuch (Genesis, Exodus, Leviticus, Numbers, and Deuteronomy). The first book of Psalms ends with Psalm 41 and echoes the theme of Genesis, an introduction to human life and a revelation of the needs of the human heart. It is the book of foundations. The second book of Psalms begins with Psalm 42 and runs through Psalm 72. This corresponds to the book of Exodus. That is the book of redemption, the story of God's moving in human history to change and redeem people and save them from themselves.

The third book begins with Psalm 73 and goes through Psalm 89. It is like the book of Leviticus, the book in which Israel learned how to draw near to God, how to worship Him through the provision God made for His people, the tabernacle. Then Psalm 90 to Psalm 106 constitutes the fourth book, which goes along with the book of Numbers, the book of wilderness wandering, of testing and failure. Finally, the fifth book covers Psalm 107 to Psalm 150 and is like the book of Deuteronomy, the second law, i.e., the law of the Spirit of life in Christ Jesus, which sets us free from the law of sin and death (see Rom. 8:2). It describes the way by which God finally accomplishes the redemption and sanctification of His people, the changing of human beings into the kind of men and women He originally designed.

A Song of Foundations

Psalm 1 to 41 make up the first book of Psalms that parallels the first book of the Pentateuch, Genesis. This first book of Psalms records the beginnings of life and the basic needs of the human heart. Psalm 1 is a description of the wicked and the righteous. It describes both the God-centered life and the self-centered life.

When the psalms talks about the wicked it is not referring to murderers, rapists, or drug dealers, the kind of people we usually think of as wicked. We often think of some notorious person, such as a gangster or hoodlum, as being wicked. But the psalmist does not mean that.

The term really means the ungodly, the one who has little or no time for God in his life; someone who has ruled God out of his affairs and his thinking. God is the greatest Being in the universe, the One who makes sense out of life, the One around whom all of life revolves. To eliminate such a Being from one's thinking is to be wicked, or to be ungodly. But in contrast, the God-centered life is set before us, and the results that come from godliness. That is the simplest division of the psalm two balanced parts.

The God-Centered Life

Look at what is said about the God-centered life. David cries out:

> *Blessed is the man who walks not in the counsel of the wicked, nor stands in the way of sinners, nor sits in the seat of scoffers; but his delight is in the law of the Lord, and on his law he meditates day and night* (vv. 1,2).

That is a description of a life centered in God. Quite appropriately it begins with the word *happy*. In many versions the word is *blessed*, but *blessed* is one of those code words that only Christians use—it really means happy. Here, then, we have the secret of happiness.

You may recognize that word as the way the Lord Jesus began the greatest sermon ever uttered before men, the Sermon on the Mount. It begins with what we call the Beatitudes (another code word, which means "the Blessings"). These Beatitudes are the secret of blessing or happiness. So here in Psalm 1 the psalmist is giving us the clue to happiness. "Oh the blessedness," he says, "oh the happiness of the man who lives like this."

Walking, Standing, Sitting

Then he gives us a description of this man's life, both negatively and positively. First is the negative: "who walks not in the counsel of the wicked, nor stands in the way of sinners, nor sits in the seat of scoffers." He gathers up in three key words the varied aspects of life: who walks . . . who stands . . . who sits.

Notice also the progress of evil. He speaks of the wicked, of sinners, and of the scoffers. The psalmist is pointing out to us that the ungodly are characterized by a totally different way of life, which progresses from bad to worse.

To walk is a reference to the decisions that must be made all day long. We all know how it is. We take steps throughout each day, making decisions about all kinds of matters. Walking is taking a series of steps.

To stand is a picture of the commitments we make to various causes. We give ourselves to certain things, we take our stand upon certain important matters.

To sit is a picture of the settled attitude of the heart, the continuous disposition of a person's life.

Now, says the psalmist, the man who has found the secret of happiness can be recognized by the fact that he does not walk in the way of the wicked, i.e., he does not make decisions as do the ungodly. He has rejected the philosophy of the ungodly. What is that philosophy? Perhaps it can be put into three simple propositions: "Me first"; "Get it now"; "Nothing bad will happen." That is the counsel of the ungodly, the wicked. The man who has learned the secret of happiness rejects that. He does not make his decisions on that basis.

Second, he does not stand in the way of sinners. This word *sinners* is most interesting in the Hebrew. It is a word that means "to make a loud noise" or "to cause a tumult." It is the idea of provoking a riot, of creating a disturbance, making trouble. The psalmist says you can recognize the godly man in that he does not make trouble. He does not provoke riots, he is not at work causing disturbances; he is obedient to the laws of life and of the land.

He does not "stand in the way of" (does not identify with) those who live to cause trouble. He has rejected all that.

Third, he does not sit in the seat of the scornful, of those who blame everyone but themselves for what is wrong. We all know how easily that kind of attitude comes to our heart. If anything goes wrong, somebody else is always at fault, right? Parents blame the children, the children blame the parents, and they both blame the schools. The schools blame the parents and the government. One nation blames another nation. Everyone is blaming everyone else. That is the philosophy of the world, is it not? These are the scornful, the scoffers, the cynics, who cast a baleful eye at life in general and blame others for their problems.

A Positive Description
The godly man has rejected that attitude. On the contrary, his life is characterized by positive things. He is selfless in his motivations, obedient in his actions, obedient to law, and he does not adopt the role of the critic, but is cheerful and acceptant of whatever comes as coming from the hand of God. I love that description of a Christian, "A Christian is one who is completely fearless, continually cheerful, and constantly in trouble." This is exactly what the psalmist describes. It is an unusual life. I think most of us, hearing this, say to ourselves, "Do I meet that description?"

But that is the negative side. Now look at the positive side. "But his delight is in the law of the Lord, and on his law he meditates day and night" (v. 2). Here is the reason why this man is able to reject the world's philosophy. He has learned to delight in the law of the Lord. Now "the law of the Lord" is, in the Psalms, another name for the Scriptures. It means more than the Law of Moses; it includes the whole revelation of God. This godly person has learned that in the book of God he is given a completely different view of life than what he gets from the world.

In the book he is told the truth about life. He has learned to delight in this book, which tells him the truth and shows him a whole new way of life.

Discovering Truth and Appropriating Power

If this were the only description of the godly man, one might infer that this man thinks too much of himself; that he does not act like others because he thinks he is better than they are. But this second verse makes clear that this is not the reason why he lives the way he does. It is because he has discovered the truth about himself out of the law of God.

One Sunday morning a minister read the following verses from 1 Corinthians 6 to his congregation. "Do you not know that the unrighteous will not inherit the kingdom of God? Do not be deceived; neither the immoral, nor idolators, nor adulterers, nor homosexuals, nor thieves, nor the greedy, nor drunkards, nor revilers, nor robbers will inherit the kingdom of God. And such were some of you. But you were washed, you were sanctified, you were justified in the name of the Lord Jesus Christ and in the Spirit of our God" (1 Cor. 6:9-11).

Then he said to the congregation, "Now that is a description of the Christians in Corinth and the life they once had led. I would like to ask if there are any here who have had this kind of a background. How many in this congregation have done some of the things listed here?" He read the list again, "Immoral, idolators, adulterers, homosexuals, thieves, drunkards, greedy, revilers, and robbers." One by one, all over the congregation people began to stand to their feet until more than half the congregation was standing.

A young man was visiting the church for the first time that morning. He had recently become a Christian and had attended several churches looking for a fellowship where he could feel at home. He took one look at this great crowd and said, "These are my kind of people."

Yes, "Such were some of you. But you are washed, you are sanctified (made clean), you are justified in the name of the Lord Jesus Christ by the Spirit of our God." That is what the man of the first Psalm discovers when he reads the law of God. He learns not only that God demands a certain perfection, but also how that perfection is made possible through the Redeemer whom God will send, whose life he learns to share. By faith, he learns to appropriate the strength of that coming Lord.

He meditates on the law day and night. That does not mean he goes around thinking about Scriptures and repeating them over and over all day long. That is a mechanical understanding of this verse. Rather, this man has learned a wonderful new life made possible by God and available for any situation. He keeps appropriating it all day and all night, whenever he needs it.

He does not attempt to mobilize his human resources or to find some kind of encouragement from outsiders and thus to depend upon external circumstances for peace and rest; he learns to draw only upon the strength of God. This is the secret of the godly life. This is the only way any of us can learn to be selfless, obedient, and cheerful under every circumstance.

A "Deep-Rooted" Life

Now the psalmist goes on to give us the evaluation of this kind of life,

He is like a tree planted by streams of water, that yields its fruit in its season, and its leaf does not wither. In all that he does, he prospers (v. 3)

Many years ago when I was first beginning my ministry, we held a youth conference in the Sierra Nevada. There a young man came to me and took me aside. We stood together underneath a great Douglas fir and he said, "Pastor, I don't know what is the matter with me. I want to be a good Christian, and I try hard, but somehow I just never seem to make it. I'm always doing the wrong thing. I just can't live like a Christian."

I said to him, "Well, there may be several reasons for that, but let me ask you this: What about your private life with the Lord? How well do you know the Lord? How much do you delight in reading His Word and then spending time talking to Him? Because, after all, it's not the time spent in reading the Word that's important, but it's the time spent in enjoying the presence of God that strengthens you."

He hung his head and said, "Well, I admit I don't do very much of that."

Just then this very phrase from the Psalms flashed into my mind, "He shall be like a tree planted by rivers of water." I stepped back and said to him, "Look at this tree we're under. What does it remind you of? What are the qualities this tree suggests to you?"

He looked at the great Douglas fir, towering into the heavens above, and said, "Well, the first thing is, it's strong."

I said, "Yes. Anything else?"

"Well," he said, "it's beautiful."

Finding Beauty and Strength

I said, "Exactly! Beauty and strength. Those are the two things you admire about this tree. And those are exactly the two things you want in your own life, aren't they? Beauty and strength?"

He said, "Right."

T HE man who is godly has learned, in the hidden inner parts of his life, to draw upon the grace and glory and strength of God.

"Well," I said, "tell me this: What makes this tree beautiful and strong? Where does it get its beauty and its strength?"

He stopped for a moment and looked at the tree, then he said, "Well, from the roots, I guess."

I asked him, "Can you see the roots?"

"No," he said, "you can't." Then he said, "I get it! That is the hidden part of life, but it is the secret of this tree's beauty and strength, isn't it?"

That is what this psalmist is saying. The man who is godly has learned, in the hidden inner parts of his life, to draw upon the grace and glory and strength of God. His roots run deep into rich and moist soil, and this is what makes him beautiful and strong. He is like a tree planted by rivers of water.

Bringing Forth Fruit

And he is fruitful. "He brings forth fruit in its season." That is probably a reference to the fruit of the Spirit, which is described in the New Testament. It is the character of

God which is always the same in either the Old or the New Testament: love, joy, peace, patience, kindness, goodness, faithfulness, self-control.

"Its leaf does not wither." That means he is always vital, always an exciting kind of person. He is never dull, never dreary, never boring; he is an exciting, vital person because he is in touch with a vital God. Finally, all that he does prospers; he is effective. What he puts his hand to he accomplishes because he is not doing it in his own strength but in the strength of another, a hidden Other, from whose resources he is continuously drawing.

That, you see, is the godly life. The man who learns to live that way is a happy person. It does not make any difference what his outward circumstances may be, because happiness does not consist in the abundance of things that you possess, as Jesus tells us. This man is happy because he has learned the true secret of happiness. "In all that he does, he will prosper." That is God's promise.

The Ungodly Life

Now, more briefly, in contrast to this he describes the man who has no time for God.

> *The wicked are not so,*
> *but are like chaff*
> *which the wind drives away* (v. 4).

It takes two verses to describe the secret of the godly life; it only takes two words to describe the life of the ungodly: "not so." Everything that is said about the godly is "not so" for the ungodly. They believe in the philosophy of the world, the counsel of the ungodly. (Me first; Get it now; Nothing bad will happen.) They are involved in small or large acts of rebellion. They violate the fundamental laws of life, yet they blame everyone else for their troubles. "The ungodly are *not so*," not like the godly, "but," and here is the evaluation of their life, "are like the chaff which the wind drives away" (v. 4).

A Worthless Existence

I do not think city folks understand chaff. In Montana every fall we had harvesters who came around with a thrashing rig. The bundles of wheat would be thrown into this machine. The straw would be blown out onto the stack and the wheat would come dribbling out to be poured into trucks or wagons and taken away to the granary. But floating around in the air everywhere was chaff. It was the "awfullest stuff" you ever saw. It stuck to the skin wherever you were sweating—on the back of your neck and down your shirt. It created frightful itching. It was universally regarded as totally worthless.

Clear back in David's day, 1000 years before Christ, the only thing they could think of to do with chaff was to let the wind blow it away. And still, 2,000 years after Christ, the only thing we can do with chaff is to blow it away. The thrashing rig tries to blow it up onto the straw stack and get it out of the way, for it has no value at all.

And that is God's evaluation of the life that has no room for Him. It is like chaff. Oh, it may be very impressive in the eyes of the world. Such a man may have a beautiful home, drive several big cars, have many luxuries, and be regarded as a big wheel. But in God's evaluation, his life is worthless and he's only going around in circles. He has never fulfilled a single purpose for which God put him in this world. His life is so much wasted time as far as God is concerned. It is worthless, like the chaff that the wind drives away.

No Standing Before God

As a result, there are two things said of Him *"He shall not stand in the judgment."* That means the daily judgment of God, the evaluation that God constantly makes of our lives. This man has no standing in that at all. Everything he does is so much wasted labor. Nor will he be *"in the congregation of the righteous"* (v. 5). That is a reference to the final judgment. When all the redeemed are gathered together, this man will be absent. He may even have been religious. I rather think he was. But, you remember, Jesus said that, "Many shall say in that day, 'Lord, Lord, did we not prophesy in your name? And did we not do many mighty works and cast out demons in your name?" And he shall say, "Depart from me I never knew you" (see Matt. 7:22,23). I *never* knew you. This man shall not stand in the congregation of the righteous because he has never put God at the center of his life.

A Contrast of Good and Evil

Then the psalm concludes with a tremendous word of explanation. Why does all this happen in this way? Why is it that, though outwardly a man's life may be very impressive, inwardly it may be nothing but a hollow shell, empty and worthless? The answer is, *"The Lord knows the way of the righteous"* (Ps. 1:6). The Lord knows that path, He is watching over that man, guiding him, guarding him, and keeping him (or her). "But the way of the wicked (the ungodly) will perish" (v. 6). That means it will dribble out into nothing. "His lamp will be put out in utter darkness," says the proverb, a tremendous phrase (Prov. 20:20).

This has never been demonstrated more strikingly than in the days of the New Testament. There came a time when the apostle Paul stood as a prisoner before Nero Caesar. Nero was at that time a most dissolute, vain, cruel, inhuman, implacable monster. He is regarded now by historians as one of the most vile and contemptible rulers ever to sit upon a throne. He even commanded that the body of his own mother be ripped apart that he might see the womb that had borne him. He once saw a handsome young man in his court and he ordered him castrated and used him as a woman the rest of his life. Yet Nero's name was known all over the empire. He was Caesar. The whole of the Roman world bowed to his will. The life of that mighty empire revolved around this man, Nero Caesar.

Then there stood before him this obscure little Jew, Paul the apostle, from a despised Roman province. No one knew him. He had scarcely been heard of except in a few isolated places where he had caused certain troubles. He was a prisoner in chains, standing before this mighty emperor. Yet, as it has been often pointed out, today we name our sons Paul, and our dogs, Nero. "The Lord knows the way of the righteous, but the way of the ungodly shall perish."

Father, we cannot read these words without asking ourselves the question: Have we discovered the secret of happiness? Are we allowing this marvelous provision for producing godlikeness to be at work in us? Or does a great deal of our life still consist of ungodliness so that we are like the chaff the wind drives away? Are great areas of our life worthless and wasted because we are living on the principles and precepts of the world around us?

Lord, thank you for having come to teach us the way of godliness, and to show us how your life can be manifest in us. We pray that you will help us to lay hold more fully of this life, that our lives, in the Day of Judgment, will find value; that we shall stand in the congregation of the righteous; that we may live the remaining years of our life, under your eye, in your living care. This we ask in your name, Amen.

Man and God

The inscription of Psalm 8 states "To the choirmaster: according to the Gittith." The word *gittith* means a winepress but also designates a stringed instrument, which was shaped like a winepress. The Greeks took the word and the instrument that it represented and called it a *kithara*; from that comes the Spanish *guitarra* and from that the English *guitar*. We are therefore in the prophetic succession when we hear a guitar accompaniment to these psalms. They were designed to be sung to the music of a guitar.

The Majesty of God

The theme of Psalm 8 is given to us in the first and last verses,

*O Lord, Our Lord, how majestic is thy name in all
the earth!* (v. 1).

It is a psalm of David and most scholars feel that it
probably comes from the early part of David's ministry,
reflecting his experience as a shepherd boy alone at night
with his sheep on the hillsides of Judea, under the starlit
heavens. There he had ample opportunity to observe the
glories of God in nature. It is evident that the psalmist is
greatly impressed with the being of God. This psalm sets
forth what he has discovered about God that awes and
inspires him. He can only express it in these beautiful
words, "How majestic is thy name in all the earth!"

Many years ago, a young man came up to me at the
close of a service held at a beautiful conference grounds
high in the Cascade Mountains of northern Washington.
We had been discussing the greatness of God, the glory of
His person, the warmth of His compassion, and His
redemptive love for mankind. At the close of the service
this young man came up and, in contemporary words but
with utmost reverence, he said, "Man, God really swings,
doesn't He?" Surely that is something of what the psalmist
is saying here. What a tremendous God! How majestic!
How excellent is His name in all the earth!

The Simplicity of God

Verses 2 through 8 tell us why the psalmist came to this
conclusion, what it is about God that is so impressive. The
first thing is rather startling. It is God's simplicity. He puts
it this way:

*Thou whose glory above the heavens is chanted by the
mouths of babes and infants, thou hast founded a*

> *bulwark because of thy foes, to still [or silence] the*
> *enemy and the avenger* (v. 2).

What had impressed this man was that the transcendent glory of God, His greatness, which was far above all the heavens, could still be grasped and expressed by a child. Evidently he had often struggled to put into words the thoughts and ideas of his heart, but he found that his rationality, his intelligence, was challenged by such an attempt. Yet here is a God who can reveal himself in such marvelous ways that children, babes, infants even, can grasp what He means. They often understand more rapidly and more thoroughly than do the intelligentsia.

Out of the Mouths of Babes

The psalmist's observation is confirmed by an incident from the New Testament. In the twenty-first chapter of Matthew, the Lord Jesus quotes the words of this psalm on a certain occasion. Matthew tells us:

> *And the blind and the lame came to him in the temple, and he healed them. But when the chief priests and the scribes saw the wonderful things that he did, and the children crying out in the temple, "Hosanna to the Son of David!" they were indignant; and they said to him, "Do you hear what these are saying?" And Jesus said to them, "Yes; have you never read, 'Out of the mouth of babes and sucklings thou hast brought perfect praise'?"* (vv. 14-16).

These chief priests and scribes thought that Jesus should be offended by the fact that these street urchins, ragged and dirty, were crying out, "Hosanna to the Son of David!" This was not a children's choir trained by the temple leaders. It was merely a band of ordinary children who happened to be there at the time Jesus healed the blind and the lame. But when they saw these wonderful things, the children began to cry out, "Praise be to the Son of David! Hosanna to the Son of David!" The scribes and chief priests were indignant and thought Jesus ought to silence these ragamuffins.

Instead, He said, "They are the ones who have caught the truth, they are the ones who see. They understand that here is being manifested the healing power of God. It is all right in line with the prediction of David in the eighth Psalm that God's marvelous simplicity can be conveyed to a child much more easily than it can to an adult."

Remember that the apostle Paul says much the same thing in his opening words in 1 Corinthians. He declares that God has deliberately designed life in this way. God has chosen the weak things and the things that are not to set at naught, to show up, to expose the things that are—to convey His messages through weak, foolish and obscure things. Every now and then God seems to delight in taking some poor uneducated person and using him in great power to change a nation or the world. He has the ability to convey himself to the childlike mind. The reason for this of course is because children (and those who are childlike) are filled with humility. Pride blots out truth.

Any time you approach the Scriptures, regarding them as insignificant or thinking yourself superior to their wisdom so that you must correct them or sit in judgment over them, you will find that their pages are shut to you. You will never understand them at all. But if you look at them as a child looks at life, impressed by everything and listening to everything, not thinking that he knows all the answers but simply trying to observe, then you will find the truth begins to speak volumes to you and you will understand it.

Jesus prayed on one occasion, recorded in Matthew 11, "I thank thee, Father, Lord of heaven and earth, that thou hast hidden these things from the wise and understanding and revealed them to babes" (v. 25).

Confounding the "Wise"

Now, says the psalmist, this is not only the mark of the greatness of God, but it is also that which baffles the enemy. By means of His ability to convey truth to infants, God has founded a bulwark—erected a wall—"because of your foes, in order to silence the enemy and the avenger." That expresses the idea that when God speaks through children (and childlike persons) He often baffles the rational, the intelligent. Those who pride themselves upon their wisdom are frequently routed by the insight of someone they consider quite insignificant.

It is reported that on one occasion an infidel was lecturing against God. Again and again in his lecture he stated, "There is no God!" In the back of the room listening to the lecture was a rather simple individual who was a believer in God, a Christian. He raised his hand and when the lecturer recognized him, the Christian stood up and said, "Sir, the next time you say, 'There is no God' would you mind adding, 'as far as I know.'" With keen insight he had put his finger upon the logical fallacy of that lecturer. He was trying to defend a negative absolute. It is impossible to defend such. No one can ever prove that there is no God. This uneducated person saw the error and put his finger right on it. "You are limited by your own knowledge," he is saying. "You don't know enough yet. You can't know that there is no God, so don't speak out of your ignorance."

A liberal Sunday School teacher had a class of boys. He

was teaching the story of the feeding of the five thousand and said something like this: "You know, this isn't really a miracle. Jesus did no miracles. What really took place here was that when this crowd was hungry a little boy present there decided to share his lunch with Jesus. He brought his lunch to Jesus and Jesus commended him for this. When the crowd saw that, it suggested to them that if they would share the lunches they had brought, everybody would have enough. So they all began to share and there was plenty for everyone. If there was a miracle at all it was a miracle of sharing." He leaned back rather satisfied with himself on having explained away the miracle.

Then one little boy in his class said to him, "Sir, may I ask a question?"

The teacher said, "Yes."

And he said, "What did they fill the twelve baskets with afterwards?"

Thus God, in order to demonstrate His greatness, often uses children to teach truths adults will not face. Man is forever thinking that it takes vast education and profound knowledge to reach God. But God is forever trying to tell us that, although He is certainly in favor of knowledge, for He is a God of truth and knowledge, nevertheless knowledge is not the way man finds God. He finds Him by listening with the humility of a child. That is why Jesus said, "Except you become as little children you cannot enter the kingdom of heaven" (see Matt. 18:3).

An End to Uncleanness

One of the greatest saints of all time and one of the most profound theologians of the church was St. Augustine. He was a wild and profligate young man in his early days in

Rome, studying philosophy. He lived an immoral and lecherous life, carousing and reveling till all hours of the night. At last he became sick of his guilt, of his immorality, and in the *Confessions* tells of his conversion. He says:

"I flung myself under a fig tree and gave free course to my tears. I sent up these sorrowful cries, 'How long, how long? Tomorrow, and tomorrow? Why not now? Why is there not this hour an end to my uncleanness.?'

"I was saying these things and weeping in the most bitter contrition of my heart, when, lo, I heard the voice of a boy or a girl, I know not which, coming from a neighboring house, chanting, and oft repeating, 'Take up and read; take up and read.' Immediately I ceased weeping, and I began to consider whether it was usual for children in any kind of game to sing such words; for I could not remember ever having heard the like. I got to my feet, since I could not but think that this was a Divine command to open the Bible and to read the first passage I should light upon.

"I quickly returned to the bench where Alypius was sitting; for there I had put down the Apostle's book [the book of Romans] when I had left. I snatched it up, opened it, and in silence read the passage on which my eyes first fell—'Let us conduct ourselves becomingly as in the day, not in reveling and drunkenness, not in debauchery and licentiousness, not in quarreling and jealousy. But put on the Lord Jesus Christ, and make no provision for the flesh, to gratify its desires.' I wanted to read no further, nor did I need to; for instantly, as the sentence ended, there was infused in my heart something like the light of full certainty, and all the gloom of doubt vanished away."

What an impressive God, who is able to convey truth in such a simple way, through the lips of a child!

The Wisdom of God

The psalmist now turns to the second thing that has impressed him about God: His wisdom.

When I look at thy heavens, the work of thy fingers,
the moon and the stars which thou hast established;
what is man that thou art mindful of him, and the
son of man that thou dost care for him? (vv. 3,4).

Imagine the scene. Here is young David out under the stars at night watching his sheep. Of course, the air at that time and place was not darkened with smog or polluted

---

ALL the knowledge that has been gained about the universe in which we live only serves to deepen our impression of the tremendous wisdom and power of God.

---

with the irritants that fill the air today. The stars were brilliant, and the moon, in its full phase, was crossing the heavens. He felt, as we have all felt as we stood under the stars at night, something of mingled mystery and awe as he looked up into the star-spangled heavens. He considered the beauty of nature and its silent witness to the wisdom of God. He sees the ordered procession of the stars and, watching them through the night, sees how they wheel in silent courses through the heavens. He notices the varying glory of different stars, and the evident vast distances that are visible in the heavens. All the breathtaking beauty of this scene breaks upon his eyes as the sun sets. He is astonished at the greatness of a God who could create such things.

The interesting thing is that 30 centuries after David wrote these words we feel the same impression when we consider the starry heavens. Though we are now able to go to the moon, which David could only see, yet all the knowledge that has been gained about the universe in which we live only serves to deepen our impression of the tremendous wisdom and power of God. How vast is the universe in which we live! Incredible in its extent and out-reach, these vast distances are spanned only by the mea-surement of the speed of light—and even that is hardly adequate. These billions of galaxies whirl in their silent courses through the deepness of space. How tremendous is the power that sustains it all and keeps it operating as one harmonious unit! That is what impressed this psalm-ist.

The Significance of Man

Then he faces the inevitable question that comes to man whenever he contemplates God's greatness. "What is man that thou art mindful of him, and the son of man that thou dost care for him?" You will recognize that this is the ques-tion that cries for an answer in our day. What is man? Where did he come from? What is his purpose here? Why does he exist on this small planet in this vast universe? Is there meaning, is there significance, is there reason for his living?

Now there are basically only two answers that are being given. A mechanistic science looks out into the uni-verse using instruments of exploration such as the tele-scope and tells us that man is nothing but another creature like the animals; that he is the highest of the animals; having grown from animal stock, and that he is alone in the universe as an intelligent, rational being. There is nothing beyond the whirling stars; man is part of a great cosmic machine, which grinds on relentlessly; man is but an insignificant cog, hardly able, with the exercise of his utmost powers, to do anything at all about the universe in which he lives. The late Bertrand Russell, whom many regarded as the high priest of humanism, eloquently expressed it this way:

"The life of man is a long march through the night surrounded by invisible foes, tortured by weariness and pain, toward a goal that few can hope to reach and where none may tarry long. One by one as they march our comrades vanish from our sight, seized by the silent orders of omnipotent death.

"Brief and powerless is man's life. On him and all his race the slow sure doom falls pitiless and dark. Blind to good and evil, reckless of destruction, omnipotent matter rolls on its relentless way. For man, condemned today to lose his dearest, tomorrow himself to pass through the gate of darkness, it remains only to cherish, ere yet the blow falls, the lofty thoughts that ennoble his little day."

That philosophy is producing widespread despair in our world today. Everywhere, young men and women, boys and girls, are succumbing to an existentialist despair that says there is nothing permanent, life is futile, and we all live out our days in a hopeless tangle of meaninglessness. As Shakespeare put it, "Life is but a tale told by an idiot, full of sound and fury, signifying nothing." We see about us on every side violent attempts to grasp for the moment what life there is. An awful sense of frustration and meaninglessness, skyrocketing suicide rates, and dark despair and spreading a blanket of gloom across the peoples of earth as they face the growing, inexorable problems of our day.

God's Purpose for Man

But contrast that with the biblical view of man, for the psalmist goes on to answer his own question by the revelation of the program and purpose of God for man.

> *Yet thou hast made him little less than God, and dost crown him with glory and honor. Thou hast given him dominion over the works of thy hands; thou hast put all things under his feet, all sheep and oxen, and also the beasts of the field, the birds of the air, and the fish of the sea, whatever passes along the paths of the sea* (vv. 5-8).

The psalmist says that God's greatness is revealed in His purpose for man, which is two-fold. First, man has a unique relationship to God. He was made to be a little less than God himself. Some perhaps are startled by that translation, for the King James Version says, "a little lower than the angels." But it was the Septuagint, the Greek translation of the Old Testament that used the phrase, "the angels." The Hebrew actually says "little less than Elohim" (God).

The Expression of God

That remarkable expression is a revelation of God's purpose for man. According to the Bible, God made man to be the expression of His life, the means by which the invisible God would be made visible to His creatures. Man is to be the instrument by which God can do His work in the world. He is the creature nearest to God. Man is such a unique being, such a remarkable creature, that God Himself intends to live in him to be the glory of man's life. Man is the bearer of God.

What a great gulf there is between this and Bertrand Russell's view of man! What an infinite difference! This is why God loves man—even lost man. He sees in every man and woman His own image, that which was designed for Himself, that which He made to be the bearer of His glory. Thus every person is inexpressibly important to God. God longs to reach every man, woman, boy, girl, because each is made and designed for Himself.

The Dominion of Man

But further, says the psalmist, because of that unique relationship, man is designed to be in dominion over all other things. He is to rule the animal creation and all the natural forces in the world in which he lives, and to exercise that dominion in an effective way. We read "Thou hast put all things under his feet, all sheep and oxen, and also the beasts of the field," and we say, "Yes, that's true because man can assert his will over the animals of the world."

But that is not what this psalmist means. He is not talking about man's ability to force the animal creation to obey him. What he is describing is the relationship God intended in which the animals would willingly serve man.

In Hebrews 2 the writer quotes this passage and says two very significant things. First, "We do not yet see all creation in subjection to man" (see v. 8). That is clearly true. Here we are facing the fact that man has been so twisted and perverted by the Fall that instead of running the creation, he is ruining it. He is polluting the air and consuming natural resources at a prodigious rate. He is befouling the waters and the soil and making it almost impossible for human life to continue. We must face this.

There is no way out of it. It stares us in the face every time we turn around. Each time we take a breath we experience the terrible evidence for the truth of what the writer says in Hebrews, "We do not yet see all things in subjection to man." We find no way out.

The Fulfillment of Creation

But he also says something else. "But we see Jesus, who for a little while was made lower than the angels, crowned with glory and honor because of the suffering of death" (v. 9). Because of the suffering of death God has crowned Him with the glory and honor that He had intended for man at the beginning. In seeing Jesus, we see that God yet intends to fulfill His original creation.

Watch the Lord Jesus in the Gospel record. The first thing He does is to change water into wine at a wedding feast. He short-circuited the process that is taking place in every vineyard in California right at this moment and thus changed water into wine. But He did not do that as God, He did it as man, man as God intended man to be. When He quieted the winds and the waves with the words, "Peace, be still," and the wind whimpered and stopped its blowing and the waves quieted down, the disciples looked at one another and said, "What manner of man is this?" (see Matt. 8:26,27). They did not realize that what He had done was not done out of His inherent deity but as a man indwelt by God. As Jesus Himself said, "It is not I who do the works; it is the Father who dwells in me, He does the works" (see John 14:10). When He broke the loaves and fishes and fed the 5,000, He did not do that as God; He did that as man—man ruling over creation, man fulfilling the intention of God for man. All the other natural miracles that He performed He did not as God but as man. Thus the writer of Hebrews says, "We see Jesus"—the beginning of a new humanity God is building.

God's New Humanity

The ultimate question we are facing here is: What is the
purpose of life? What are you here for? Why do you go on
making money to buy food and other things year after
year? What is the reason for it all? The answer is, if you
have discovered Jesus Christ, you are a part of God's new
humanity. God is fulfilling His original intention for man
right now. He is beginning a new humanity and He is
teaching us lessons through the struggles and difficulties
of life that we could never learn in any other way.

Paul says in chapter 8 of Romans that the whole creation is eagerly looking forward to the day of the manifestation of the sons of God (see vv. 22,23). God is not going to
be defeated by the wickedness and foolishness of man.
Even though man is destroying the world in which he
lives, making it a mess in which he can no longer exist, yet
God will not be defeated. Amidst the increasing ravaging
of nature, God is doing something.

The exciting news of today is not what is recorded in
our newspaper headlines. The events that are reported in
the headlines will all be entombed in some dusty old history book or buried in a trash can in another 10 years.
They will be of little significance to any living being at that
time. But the exciting thing today is what is happening in
the new humanity that God is creating through the trials
and difficulties we are experiencing. These troubles are
transforming you and me who know Jesus Christ into sons
of God who are awaiting the day when the curtain is drawn
back and all the world shall see what God has been working on behind the scenes. In Romans 8 the apostle says, "I
know that the sufferings of this present time are not worth
being compared with the glory that is to be revealed" (see

v. 18). In 2 Corinthians he says, "For our light affliction, which is but for a moment, is working for us a far more exceeding and eternal weight of glory" (see 4:17).

A Purpose to Life

There is purpose to life—if you know Jesus Christ! There is no purpose outside of Christ. There is no real reason to live if you do not know Jesus Christ. But if you know Him you are part of a new creation that God is fashioning behind the scenes within the framework of history and one of these days it will be revealed. When the curtain is drawn back, all the world—and all the universe—will sing together the words of the last verse of this psalm.

> *O Lord, our Lord, how majestic is thy name in all earth!* (v. 9).

What a magnificent God who can work through babes and infants and who is deeply concerned about man. The one who created the heavens is concerned and compassionate toward men and ultimately will fulfill all the dreams of humanity. "O Lord, our Lord, how wonderful is thy name in all the earth!"

We bow before thee, our Father, and almost tremble because we are privileged to call you Father—such a great God, such a revelation of wisdom, greatness, power and strength and yet, *our* Father, *our* Lord, *our* God.

> "That thou shouldst so delight in me
> and be the God thou art;
> Is darkness to my intellect
> but sunshine to my heart."[1]

1. Author unknown, public domain.

Opening the Books

In 1968 the California State Board of education proposed a modification of its guidelines for textbook selection so that school faculties could have refereces from which to teach the theory of creation, along with the theory of evolution, (Darwinism) as an approach to understanding the origin and development of life on earth. This proposal evoked considerable reaction, both pro and con. The nineteenth psalm speaks right to the point of that controversy.

The basic issue behind all the arguments is whether or not it is right to acknowledge that God is involved in the universe. Does the study of nature and of science have a spiritual aspect? Are we confronted with God in these realms, we may be in the study of the social sciences like psychology and sociology, and in the humanities? These are really fundamental questions and this psalm deals directly with them.

The Book of Nature

The knowledge of God has been written for us in two volumes, and it takes both volumes to know God. There is a revelation in nature, and there is a revelation given in a Book, in the written Word. Both are essential to the knowledge and understanding ofGod declares this psalm. In the first part of this psalm the psalmist, David, sets forth the book of nature:

> *The heavens are telling the glory of God; and the firmament proclaims his handiwork. Day to day pours forth speech, and night to night declares knowledge. There is no speech, nor are there words; their voice is not heard; yet their voice goes out through all the earth, and their words to the end of the world* (vv. 1-4).

That is a declaration of the greatness of God as seen in the world of nature. Every night since time began the stars have come out, and they spell out to man the message of the power and wisdom of God. This is becoming especially vivid today. We are starting to read some of the fine print in this book of nature. We have now been able to step outside the envelope of atmosphere that surrounds the earth and see the stars in new glory. We have seen more of the orderliness of the universe, of the procession of the heavenly bodies, and of the marvelous mystery of gravitation, which holds the stars and planets in suspended balance with one another. All this is designed to speak of God and of His intelligence, wisdom and power.

The Story of the Heavens

In the first verse the clarity, the plainness of this revelation is underscored. Literally, "The heavens are 'narrating' the glory of God." They are telling forth a story which, when read, will reveal the glory of God. That is what they are for. And the firmament, the "stretched-out-ness" of space, the infinity of space, proclaims or "shouts about" His handiwork.

Speech and Knowledge

In verse 2 the abundance of this revelation is emphasized: "Day to day pours forth speech, and night to night declares knowledge."

The day pours out information about God and the night also spreads knowledge of God before us. In other words, truth about God is pouring in to us from all dimensions, if we only have eyes to see it. I never read this psalm without thinking of these words of Elizabeth Barrett Browning: "Earth's crammed with heaven, and every common bush aflame with God; but only those who see take off their shoes, the rest sit round it and pluck blackberries."

Having a "Seeing Eye"

It takes a *seeing* eye to perceive what God has said in nature, but that which can be seen is pouring in upon us. We have all felt it. It is why a hush falls upon a group of people who step out under the stars in a night sky, when the moon is riding high or the stars glow with glory. We feel the mystery of the infinite, reaching, calling out to our spirits, and a silence descends upon us. It is why men fall silent before the ebb and flow of the sea as they sense the restless, surging power of the sweeping tides. They understand something of the power of God in nature through that. It is why we feel a sense of loneliness and an intimation of infinity when we hear the wind howl, or we watch a storm rage, the thunder and lightning crashing around us. There is something of the voice of God that gets through to us on these occasions.

The Islamic prophet Mohammed wrote in the Koran about the God whom he saw in nature—out in the sands of Arabia, back in the sixth century:

"The marvels of the starry heavens, the day that follows the night, the rain that gives life to the dead earth, the ship that sunders the sea, the bird that flies, the horse that gallops, the motionless rose and the still stone, the winds, the clouds, the fire, water, the glance of a woman, the smile of a child, the palm tree that bends, the date that ripens; here, O believers, are the proofs of the power of God. The trees sing of his power, flowers waft their perfume towards him. He is the Lord of the pink morning, the white noon, and the blue evening."

This is the way it ought to be. No men live anywhere who have not been exposed to this witness of God in nature. God has designed that nature should teach man of His being, of His power and of His wisdom.

The Universality of Nature's Revelation

Verses 3 and 4 declare the universality of this revelation: "There is no speech, nor are there words; their voice is not heard [the message is not conveyed through actual words which can be heard]; yet their voice goes out through all the earth, and their words to the end of the world."

In the fourteenth chapter of Acts is the account of the apostle Paul and his traveling companion, Barnabas, coming into a pagan city and being received as gods because they performed a miracle. The people thought they were Jupiter and Mercury and began to worship them. Paul and Barnabas stopped the crowd and said, "Don't do that; we're nothing but men, just like you! But we have come to declare the true God unto you, the One who made heaven and earth. He does not need to dwell in temples of stone, and He rejects these idols. But He has not left Himself without a witness among you. He has given you rain and food, has done good to you" (see vv. 15-17). They were referring, of course, to the witness of nature, to its remarkable testimony that behind the universe is a Designer, a Planner, a great and wise Being of infinite power and might.

Clouds Block the Sun

Now, why is it that men do not get this message? Why is it obscured or distorted? In the next two verses the psalmist uses the sun to give us a specific illustration of this testimony of nature:

> In them he has set a tent for the sun, which comes forth like a bridegroom leaving his chamber, and like a strong man runs its course with joy. Its rising is from the end of the heavens, and its circuit to the end of them; and there is nothing hid from its heat
> (vv. 4-6).

To the observer on earth the sun appears to move across the sky. And as all men see it they are exposed to its testimony. But somehow that testimony has been clouded. Men do not see it clearly. They have missed the message. Instead of worshiping the God who made the sun, they worship the sun. Men have failed to see that just as the sun is needed to give light and strength to all living things on earth, so God is needed to give moral light and spiritual strength to men.

Worshiping Creation Rather than the Creator

I have a print in my study of a famous painting by the great cowboy artist, Charles M. Russell. It shows three Blackfoot indians facing the sun in the early morning and worshiping it. Why do men, especially children of nature like

> WHAT is desperately wrong is that Darwinism, as it is largely taught in our schools and our popular communications media today, is often a means of removing God from His creation.

these Indians, worship the sun? Because the message that comes to us in nature is clouded. Men do not understand it clearly. And, as a result, that which has been designed to teach the deity and the power of God is being missed, overlooked.

That is the great issue at stake in this controversy over creation and evolution. I have no quarrel with scientists who want to come up with hypotheses as to the processes by which the universe was formed and life was developed. This is perfectly proper and is their sphere. The theory of evolution is an attempt at this, based upon certain types of evidence, which have been construed to support it.

Removing God from His Creation

But what is desperately wrong is that Darwinism, as it is largely taught in our schools and our popular communications media today, is often a means of removing God from His creation. It is a way of teaching that this whole process just happened, apart from any exercise of creative intelligence. Thus, the testimony of nature is rendered silent, and the message, which God designed to speak to man, is not heard. Man does not know that there is a God in the universe. Thus man thinks God is dead, if indeed He ever existed at all. Darwinism is one of the major reasons why that idea has taken root in the late '60s and early '70s.

As a result something is happening to us as a people. In the first chapter of Romans the apostle Paul says that men are exposed to the truth about God evident in creation, but they deliberately reject it. Because they do, God lets certain things take place. Paul lists them for us. One is that because men do not like to retain God in their knowledge, He gives them over to a reprobate mind (see v. 28). Their thinking becomes distorted. That is what is producing the twisted applications of some of the discoveries of science, resulting in the tremendously complex, insoluble problems we are facing today.

Men do not want to retain God in their knowedge. There is a conspiracy of silence to eliminate God from His creation. Scientists are unwilling to acknowledge that God is in the laboratory as well as in the church building or in the home. Therefore, God gives men over to a demented science, which produces not only helpful technological achievements but also those which blast and ruin us. Science and technology, once regarded as our benefactors, are now appearing to us more and more as our destroyers, having polluted the atmosphere, ravaged the forests, and destroyed many forms of life. Now we are confronted with the possibility of the total pollution and destruction of our environment. That is the judgment of God upon a world that twists and distorts the revelation of nature.

Nature is designed to tell us not only *how* things happened but *who* is behind them. It is perfectly proper for a scientist to investigate the realm of nature. Man has made some wonderful discoveries about how God put things together. These discoveries are fascinating, exciting, opening up whole new vistas of life, and properly so. What is wrong is the attempt to exclude God from that realm and not to allow nature to bring us to the understanding that, behind this universe, behind ourselves and the mystery of our own being, is the great intelligence and wisdom and power of a living God. That is why we feel so lost and lonely, alienated and forsaken in a mechanistic universe.

The Book of His Word

But the book of nature is only volume I. There is also another book, volume II, designed to answer the other pressing questions we humans ask: "Why? What is behind all this? What is the meaning of it all? Where are we headed, and why are *we* involved in this whole process?" Nature can never answer those questions. Those who work exclusively in the realm of nature can never state a satisfactory purpose for life. Nature simply does not embody that knowledge. If this great, throbbing question "Why?" is ever to be answered, the answer must come from the lips of God Himself. So He has given us a Book, and now the psalmist presses on to that. In the next few verses he outlines for us the effect of the Word, the written revelation of God, and what it can do in human life:

> *The law of the Lord is perfect, reviving the soul; the testimony of the Lord is sure, making wise the simple; the precepts of the Lord are right, rejoicing the heart; the commandment of the Lord is pure, enlightening*

*the eyes; the fear of the Lord is clean, enduring for
ever; the ordinances of the Lord are true, and
righteous altogether. More to be desired are they than
gold, even much fine gold; sweeter also than honey
and drippings of the honeycomb. Moreover by them is
thy servant warned; in keeping them there is great
reward* (vv. 7-11).

Nature feeds, strengthens, and supports our outer
life. But here is the resource of God that touches the inner
life and makes for the conquest of that inner space, which
is so all-important to human life. The psalmist takes its
characteristics one by one and shows us what it can do.

The Law of the Lord

First, "the law of the Lord." That is the widest term for
the written revelation God has given us. "The law of the
Lord is perfect." It is complete, there is nothing left out. It
is comprehensive, it does everything that we need it to
do. There is no part of your life, no problem that you will
ever face in your life, no question with which you will ever
be troubled, that the Word of God does not speak to and
illuminate and meet. So it is perfect, "reviving the soul."
Remember that Jesus spoke of "rivers of living water,"
which would be available to buoy up the human spirit and
to meet its need. That is exactly what the Word of God is
designed to do for us.

The Testimony of the Lord

Second, "the testimony of the Lord is sure, making wise
the simple." *Sure* means "dependable, reliable." You can
count upon this word to be true. Therefore, you do not
need to know a lot about everything else. Now, the Word

of God is not against knowledge; it is only against knowledge that does not begin at the right place. But even if you do not have a lot of knowledge, evenif you are "simple" in terms of education, you can still be made wise by trusting Scripture because it is sure, it is reliable. So we are exhorted, "Trust in the Lord with all your heart, and do not rely on your own insight" (Prov. 3:5), and, "There is a way which seems right to a man, but its end is the way to death" (Prov. 14:12).

TO follow pleasure for pleasure's sake is the way of death, and it will lead you on to that.

You can be deluded and decieved by some of these alluring, gossamer philosophies that float around today, suggesting, for example, that pleasure is the reason for which you exist, that to enjoy yourself is the supreme object in life, that anything you do in the pursuit of pleasure is right. But the Word of God says, "No, that is not right!" God is the One who ultimately will give pleasure. It will be beyond anything you ever dreamed. But to follow pleasure for pleasure's sake is the way of death, and it will lead you on to that. The testimony, the Word, is sure.

The Precepts of the Lord

Then, "the precepts of the Lord are right, rejoicing the heart." Do you not rejoice in your heart to know that you are right about something? When you get into a controversy with somebody and he argues with you but you have the solid assurance that you are right—what a feeling! Well, that is the way it is with the Word of God. The glorious thing about His Book is that when the story is all told, when everything is said and done it will all end up just as it is written here. This Book is *right*, it is the way things really are.

The Commandment of the Lord

"The commandment of the Lord is pure, enlightening the eyes." The charge is sometimes made that the Bible is a dirty book because it speaks of incest and adultery and fornication and perversions like homosexuality and other ugly things. It also speaks of malice and bitterness and is filled with slaughter and bloodshed. It is often described as an immoral book, and there have been attempts to classify it with some of the immoral and obscene literature that is so widely available today.

However, there is one great difference. The Bible contains these things because it is a realistic book, which deals with life as it is. The one difference is that it never shows evil as though it were good. It never makes adultery look attractive. The Bible always shows adultery as it really is—sordid and shameful. The Bible never makes homosexuality appear to be inconsequential, but reveals it to be a terrible distortion of human nature. Those engaged in homosexuality are pathetic beings who need to be prayed for and helped and delivered from the awful hold over them, which is destroying their manhood or their womanhood. The Bible is honest about life, frank and forthright. It is pure, enlightening the eyes, showing you the truth. That is what David has found.

The Fear of the Lord

"The fear of the Lord is clean, enduring for ever." The word *fear* is sometimes read as though it meant cowering in terror before some awful being who is about to strike you dead. But that is not what this means at all. It means respect, honest respect for God, That, says the psalmist, is clean, and it will keep you clean, too. It is "enduring for ever." Once you enter into the fear of the Lord in its rightful sense you find that this produces a quality of life that keeps you from defiling yourself.

The Ordinances of the Lord

Then he sums them all up: "The ordinances of the Lord are true, and righteous altogether." They are also wealth-producing, enriching, "more to be desired than gold," he goes on to say. And they are wonderfully pleasant, marvelously pleasure-producing, "sweeter also than honey and drippings of the honeycomb. Moreover by them is thy servant warned; in keeping them there is great reward."

Channels to Find the Lord

"Well," you might say, "I don't see these things in the Bible. I read my Bible and it's supposed to do that for you, but when I read it I don't find these things." Do you know why? The psalmist will help us with this, too. We need to notice as we go through this list that when David talks about various aspects of revelation he always uses the phrase, "of the Lord. The law "of the Lord," the testimony "of the Lord," the precepts "of the Lord," the commandment "of the Lord"—all the way through.

This, of course, means that these aspects in themselves are not what we need; they are channels by which we find the Lord. It is God who does all these wonderful things for us. He forgives and revives and cleanses and enlightens and makes us to rejoice. It is as we find Him in the pages of Scripture that these wonderful things happen to us.

Discerning Our Errors

The only things that can interfere are given in the next few verses. David asks, "But who can discern his errors?" (v. 12). That is the problem. If you cannot read the book of nature, or you cannot read the book of the Word, it is not because there is anything wrong with either book. The reader is the problem. "Who can discern his error?" What a question that is! It indicates that we are all victims of hidden evil in our lives. If we examine ourselves we usually look fine in our own eyes. The very last verse in the book of Judges says that at one period of Israel's history, "Every man did what was right in his own eyes." That permitted just about anything and the chaos was terrible.

Everybody thinks that what he or she does is right. We cannot see our own errors. Yet these errors, these twists, these distortions of attitude and thought, are constantly affecting us so that we cannot see the truth the way it is. We do not understand it in nature and we do not understand it in the Word. We desperately need to be delivered from hidden errors. In the New Testament the apostle Peter says, "So put away all malice and all guile and insincerity and envy and all slander. [Then you will be] Like newborn babes [who] long for the pure spiritual milk [of the Word], that by it you may grow up to salvation" (1 Pet. 2:1,2).

Cleansing from Our Faults

What hinders our desire for the Word? These hidden errors. The psalmist faces the fact that something is wrong with the reader. So he concludes this psalm with a wonderful prayer:

Clear [or cleanse] thou me from hidden faults. Keep

*back thy servant also from presumptuous sins; let
them not have dominion over me! Then I shall be
blameless, and innocent of great transgression"*
(vv. 12,13).

"Cleanse thou me from hidden faults." Is that your prayer?
Do you know what will happen when you pray that way?
You might think that God will take a sponge and wipe
around inside you so you will not even know what those
hidden faults were. But God does not do that. His way of
dealing with hidden faults is either to send somebody to
point them out to you or to bring them out through some
circumstance in which you are suddenly confronted with
what you have done or said. You find it is ugly, and you do
not like it. That is the way God cleanses us from hidden
faults. He opens up the secret places.

Usually He does it through other people because, as
God well knows, we cannot see ourselves, but other people can see us. These faults are hidden to us but not to
others. They see them very plainly. And we can see their
hidden faults better than they can. You know that you can
see the faults of somebody you are thinking about right
now better than he can. You say, "I don't see how he can
be so blind." Well, someone is thinking that very same
way about you. We do not see ourselves. That is why it is
necessary to pray, "Lord, cleanse thou me from hidden
faults. Help me to see myself through the eyes of a friend
who loves me enough to tell me the truth."

And then, "Keep me back from presumptuous sins."
Presumptuous sins are those in which you are confident
that you have what it takes to do what God wants. Self-
confidence is presumption. God never asks us to do anything on that basis. If we depend upon ourselves we are
acting presumptuously, and any activity that stems from

self-confidence is a presumptuous sin. "Whatever does not proceed from faith is sin" (Rom. 14:23). For me to act as though there is anything that I can contribute that does not originate with God is to be guilty of this kind of sin. The cure for this is dependence upon the activity of God in you as a believer. So David is praying, "Lord, keep me back from presumptuous activity. Let me realize that without you I can do nothing. Help me to depend upon you to work through me. Then I will be blameless and innocent of great transgression."

Acceptable in His Sight

Then he closes with these often-quoted words, which are wonderfully, marvelously penetrating:

> *Let the words of my mouth and the meditation of my heart be acceptable in thy sight, O Lord, my rock and my redeemer"* (v. 14).

"Let the words of my mouth—what I say, and the meditation of my heart—what I think, be the kind of words and thoughts that have sat under the judgment of your Word, Father, reflecting the instruction, the light, and the love of your heart, so that what I am, both inside and outside, will be acceptable before you." That is a wonderful prayer, is it not? That is what opens the books. When you pray that kind of prayer before you read either the book of the Word or the book of nature, you will find that God will speak to you in a marvelous way.

George Washington Carver, that brilliant black scientist, was a warmhearted, humble Christian. He came to God and said, "Lord, there are so many secrets in the universe. Please show me your secrets." God said, "George, the universe is too big for you. I want you to take a peanut and start with that." So George Washington Carver prayerfully began to investigate the mysteries of the peanut. He discovered over 150 new uses for it and thereby revolutionized the technology of the South. He became a tremendous benefactor to mankind and was especially a blessing to the black people because he began with this prayer: "Let the words of my mouth and the meditation of my heart be acceptable in thy sight, O Lord, my rock and my redeemer."

Thank you, Father, for this word of instruction to our own hearts and lives. We pray that we may follow through on this truth and live in the humble understanding that you have revealed yourself to us, Lord. Let us be ready to listen and see, ready to search and find out and discover. We ask in your name, Amen.

Best Wishes for the Future

I never think of the future without a sense of adventure, and also an awareness of peril, of danger. I do not know how you feel, but I feel a little fear, as well as the thrill of excitement, as I look forward to the years ahead. Standing at the gateway of each new day or month or year makes us all feel very much like explorers entering an unknown land where we do not know what lies ahead— what perils may beset us, or what joys await us.

It seems that every problem the world could possibly face is fast coming to a head. Population explosion, world food shortages, lack of natural resources, air pollution— scientists tells us that these problems will have to be solved soon, or they will be unsolvable. It is an ominous picture.

The twentieth Psalm is wonderfully suitable for us at this point in history because it is a song that the people of Israel sang when the king went forth to battle. Before he went out to face the peril and uncertainty of war, they sang this psalm as a prayer for his safety and victory. It was not just a nice custom on their part. It was a genuine prayer, an expression of their faith, a song of trust in the power of the living God who would keep the king and his armies in the midst of desperate battle.

The psalm falls into three natural divisions. The first five verses are the people's prayer for the king. In verses 6 through 8 we have the king's response. Verse 9 is a shout of benediction by the people.

A Day of Trouble

You remember that the New Testament tells us that God has made every believer in Jesus Christ to be both a king and a priest (see 1 Pet. 2:9). So when we read Old Testament stories about kings and priests of old, we are perfectly justified in applying them to ourselves. They are designed to teach us how a king ought to act and how a priest ought to behave, to lead us through experiences that kings and priests have, and to show us the way out.

It opens with a very realistic recognition of the situation:

> *The Lord answer you in the day of trouble!*
> *The name of the God of Jacob protect you!* (v. 1).

Right from the start there is recognition that the king is heading into a day of trouble. It is not easy to fight battles, but this king had no choice but to do so.

We do not know what lies ahead, but we do know that

we have never faced such a time of peril and danger to the human race as we are facing today. What awaits us is no joke. It is going to be tough, really tough. A teenager I once knew put it this way in the opening paragraphs of an editorial published in his high school newspaper.

"Things are happening, and they're happening fast: at this very moment, millions are starving in Africa, India, and Asia . . . overpopulation is threatening every country in the world, including ours . . . . Violence is increasing by leaps and bounds . . . . Scientists predict that within the next few years, the world's food shortage will start affecting the United States seriously . . . . Man is now capable of completely wiping himself out hundreds of times over with the pushing of some buttons . . . . Pollution is very real—the history of the automobile in America can be read by the layers of lead from car exhaust in the remote snows of Greenland . . . . DDT has been found in seals from the far north . . . . Every year the risks of life become greater. We never know when the next international crisis could threaten the troubled tranquility of the world; tension over race relations, and economic hardship are always just below the surface . . . . Crime, and I'm talking about murders and rapes and stealing, is rapidly increasing."

Well, that is nothing new, is it? We know the problems that have been on the periphery of our nation and of our lives have now moved overhead. The dark clouds can no longer be avoided. And they are going to come home to us much more personally in the future than they ever have before.

The God of Jacob
How are you going to find your way through? Well, the

psalmist, David the king, gives us the answer. His day, too, was one of trouble: "The Lord answer you in the day of trouble! The name of the God of Jacob protect you!" There is where our refuge lies—in the name of the God of Jacob. Only God is adequate for the situation. Only He can tell what dangers lie ahead. Only He has the wisdom and foresight to steer a course through all the various perils. If you are not resting upon the God of Jacob, you will never make it. That is what this psalmist is saying, and he drew upon a wealth of personal experience.

Why does he say "the God of Jacob?" I am glad he chose that title. There are two men in the Bible who have always encouraged me greatly. In the New Testament it is Peter, with his handicap of congenital "foot-in-mouth" disease, because I suffer from the same malady. In the Old Testament it is Jacob——Jacob, the maneuverer, the manipulator, the wheeler-dealer, the big-time operator. He thought he had to maneuver everybody, to manipulate them, in order to bring a situation around to the way he wanted it. He depended upon his wits, his wisdom, his cunning to accomplish what he wanted. The result, for people like him, is that they are constantly short-changing themselves. The very thing they think they are protecting, they end up destroying. They find themselves coming out on the short end of the bargain because no man is adequate for that kind of living.

But God found a way to set Jacob free from that way of living. Jacob had a God who finally taught him, lesson after painful lesson through the years, to abandon the old way of life, his old way of thinking, and to come at last to trust and to worship. Hebrews 11 tells us that Jacob was one of the great heroes of faith because he finally learned to lean on the top of his staff and to worship (see v. 21). By then he did not feel he had to maneuver everything; he could wait on God and worship, while God acted. That is why God is called here "the God of Jacob."

What do you and I do when we face a day of trouble? We tend to panic, don't we? We cast about for some kind of maneuver to accomplish what we want. We tend immediately to start manipulating, bringing pressure, trying to finagle the situation—like Jacob, exactly. But the God of Jacob is our refuge. May the name of the God of Jacob protect you.

Help from the Sanctuary

In the second verse we have the procedure by which the help of the God of Jacob will come to us:

> *May he send you help from the sanctuary,*
> *and give you support from Zion!* (v. 2).

That is wonderful—"help from the Sanctuary." The sanctuary always pictures the place where we meet with God. In Israel it was the temple, the place where the Israelite came to get his thoughts straightened out. There he met with God, there he heard the word of God, the mind and the thoughts of God.

For us the sanctuary, obviously, is the Scriptures. There is where we get help. It is there that our minds are illuminated, that we begin to see the world the way it is, not the way it appears to be. There is not one of us who has not already learned that life is not the way it seems to be, that what looks to be the answer and what we are convinced at first is the way things are, often turns out to be exactly the opposite. Life is filled with illusion and deceit.

Doesn't your heart cry for somebody to tell you the truth, to tell you the way things really are, to open your eyes to what is going on? That is what the Bible is for. Unless you are in the Scriptures there is no help. This is the provision God has made for the help of the God of Jacob to come to you. "May you find help in the sanctuary, in the Scriptures," is the psalmist's prayer, "that your eyes might be enlightened and you might understand."

Unclaimed Promises

It always amazes me how many Christians fail to employ the Scriptures when they are in difficulty. If your television set breaks down, what do you do? You call for the repair man. You get him to come over promptly so you won't miss your favorite program. If your water pipes begin to leak, what do you do? You send for the plumber. If you are slapped with a lawsuit, you call up a lawyer. If your tooth begins to ache, you phone Dr. Paneless or, if it is bad enough, Dr. Extract—he'll pull it. We seem to know instinctively what to do when some of these physical things go wrong.

But people can have their hearts broken, they can be depressed of spirit, or sick with shame or guilt, or driven half mad with fear or worry, and their Bible lies unopened, it promises unclaimed, even unread. They desperately cast about for some kind of help, when the help already provided is ignored. Is that not amazing? Why do we live that way? Why do we act so stupidly in that area of our lives?

I am indebted to a friend for sending me a wonderful quotation from President Woodrow Wilson:

"I am sorry for men who do not read the Bible every day. I wonder why they deprive themselves of the strength and of the pleasure? It is one of the

most singular books in the world, for every time
you open it some old text that you have read a
score of times suddenly beams with new meaning.
There is no other book that I know of, of which this
is true. There is no other book that yields its meaning so personally, that seems to fit itself so intimately to the very spirit that is seeking its guid-
ance."

That is a wonderful word from the twenty-sixth president of the United States.

Support from Zion

Help from the sanctuary, and "support from Zion." Zion is
another name for Jerusalem, the capital of the kingdom,
the headquarters. In the Scriptures it stands as a symbol
for the invisible kingdom of God that surrounds us. It is
made up of angels sent forth to minister to those who are
to be the heirs of salvation. All the invisible help that God
can give you in the day of trouble, in the hour of pressure,
is made available from Zion.

Remember that in the garden of Gethsemane, as Jesus
was praying and sweating drops of blood, at the height of
His agony an angel appeared and ministered to Him and
strengthened Him. That angel was made visible to Him in
order that we might be taught a lesson of what happens
when we pray. I have never seen an angel, but I know that
I have experienced the ministry of angels. I have gone into
prayer depressed, downcast, discouraged, defeated.
While praying I have felt my spirits caught up, changed,
and strengthened. I came out calm, at rest, and at peace.
Why? Because I have received help from Zion, from the
invisible kingdom of angels waiting to minister to those

who are struggling through a time of trouble. Does that not encourage you in facing the future?

The Great Sacrifice

But that is not all the encouragement available. In verse 3 we have the basis and the guarantee upon which help rests.

> *May he remember all your offerings,*
> *and regard with favor your burnt sacrifices!*
> *Selah* (v. 3).

The offerings of Israel were the meal offerings, the cereal offerings, and the sacrifices of bulls, goats, lambs, calves, pigeons, and other animals. What did they mean? Well, those sacrifices, we well know, are pictures of the work of the Lord Jesus Christ. He is the *great* sacrifice. And these offerings speak of the basis that He has laid, and of the guarantee that basis gives us that our prayers will be answered. How do you know that God will help you in the reading of Scripture and in prayer? Because of the sacrifice of the Son of God.

He has given Himself in order to remove any hindrance to God's love toward us. In the sacrifice of the Lord Jesus our sins and our guilt were taken care of completely. So there is no hindrance at all to God's mercy and ministry to us. He can pour it out upon us without restraint, no matter what we have done, as we confess our sins and receive the forgiveness of His grace. That is wonderful. That is why the writer says "Selah" at this point. It means "Stop and think. Pause for a moment and think about this."

The apostle Paul puts it beautifully in Romans 8:32: "He who did not spare his own Son but gave him up for us all, will he not also give us all things with him?"

Is that not marvelous? There is your guarantee that God is with you. He who spared not His own Son but delivered Him up for us while we were yet enemies, will He not with Him freely give us all things now that we are His children, now that we are His friends?

You see, when you come to God in prayer on that basis, you are praying in Jesus' name. "In Jesus' name" is not a little magic formula you tack on at the end of a prayer to make it work. "In Jesus' name" means that you are praying on the basis of His sacrifice. You are resting on the finished work of the Lord Jesus Christ, and that is why you expect God to answer your prayers. That is why the psalmist says, "May he remember those sacrifices!"

Our Heart's Desire
In verse 4 we have the extent to which this help is available:

> *May he grant you your heart's desire,*
> *and fulfil all your plans!* (v. 4).

When our hearts have been cleansed by the Word of God and by prayer, then what is left is what God wants for us. Basically, every believer in Jesus Christ wants what God wants. We are one spirit with Him. And what do we want? If you were to put it into words, what do you want more deeply than anything else? Immediately, of course, you would eliminate from consideration all the *things* that you might like to have because they are not *really* what you want, are they? What you really want is to be a happy, whole person. You want to be confident, courageous, able to cope with situations, able to handle what comes, and to be trusting and loving. Is that not what you want? That is what I want. That is my heart's desire. And if I could read your hearts, I think I would see that this is the desire of your hearts, too.

Well, there is God's promise. He will grant you your heart's desire. And He will fulfill your plans. What are your plans? They are the ways by which you will achieve your heart's desire. These plans are really the day-by-day choices that you and I must make. They are not made at a crisis point but are the day-by-day carrying out of those basic decisions that may have been made in a moment of crisis. At some emotional point you may have taken a look at your life. You may have said, "Lord, there are some things in my life that I want to be different. I'm going to keep my temper. I'm going to be more outgoing toward others. I want to be more obedient to your will and your Word." You were caught up in the spirit of the moment and in the glory of it. And in the emotion of that moment you laid your life on the line again and said, "Lord, here I am, available to you."

Well, that is great. No one disparages the value of those moments. But that is not when your character is built. When you make a decision in a moment of crisis, that is just a beginning. When your character really begins to be built is the next morning when you wake up and you don't feel like you did when you made the big decision. You feel quite differently. You feel like being your same old nasty self. But then you remember your decision that you are going to commit yourself anew to the Lord, and so you do, right then, no matter how you feel. You do the same the next morning, and the next morning, and the next. And *that* is fulfilling your plans to achieve your heart's desire. That is what God is saying—that He will grant your desire by fulfilling your plans, by giving you the grace to present yourself to Him day by day.

The Fellowship of Rejoicing

In verse 5 we have the fellowship of rejoicing, which God's help always produces:

May we shout for joy over your victory,
and in the name of our God set up our banners!
(v. 5).

This is a gathering of believers. May *we* shout for joy over victory. Victory is never a one-man accomplishment. You do not win your victories by yourself. You might think you do, but you don't. Others have had a part in it. They have entered into the battle with you, sharing the blood,

---

A CHRISTIAN is one who is completely fearless, continually cheerful, and constantly in trouble!

---

sweat and tears. Therefore they have a right to share in the joy when victory comes. You are going to be fighting battles in the future, difficult ones—maybe all the more difficult because of the world situation. But remember this! Others who love you are going to be praying for you and with you in these battles, encouraging and strengthening you. So when you come to a victory, share it with them. Then all can rejoice together.

The psalmist pictures a group that has gathered together and "set up their banners." When I read that, I think immediately of the scenes at the Rose Bowl game every New Year's Day. Over on one side is a great crowd of partisans, who support one team. On the other side are those supporting the other team. They all have fancy little banners, pennants, and pom-poms, which they wave with great excitement, and they shout for joy whenever their side makes a gain down on the field. That is exactly what David is describing here. That is what a church meeting should be—a time when we set up our banners and rejoice with somebody who has gained a victory through Jesus Christ. Written on the banners of Israel were these words: **MAY THE LORD FULFILL ALL YOUR PETITIONS.** That is the sharing of the body of Christ.

Response of the Anointed

In verses 6 through 8 we have the response of the king. It opens with this note of sturdy confidence:

> *Now I know that the Lord will help his anointed;*
> *he will answer him from his holy heaven*
> *with mighty victories by his right hand* (v. 6).

Why, he has not even gone to battle yet, and here he is declaring with confidence what is going to happen! That is also the mark of a Christian. A Christian is one who is completely fearless, continually cheerful, and constantly in trouble! The king is declaring that he is not afraid. "Now I know," he says. "You have reminded me of all His promises, and now I know that the Lord will help His anointed." Now, that word *anointed* means the one anointed to be king. And since we are kings, *we* are God's anointed. It also is the very word that is translated "Messiah." You are God's messiah in this day. Did you ever think of yourself in that way? "We beseech you on behalf of Christ," says Paul, "be reconciled to God" (2 Cor. 5:20). Here is the confidence begotten by a reminder of these great promises of God.

I never tire of reading those wonderful words of Paul to his friends in Philippi. He is in prison and chained to a Roman guard. Things look discouraging because he has to appear before Nero. It does not look as if there is much chance that he will survive; nevertheless, he writes: "Yes, and I shall rejoice. For I know that through your prayers and the help of the Spirit of Jesus Christ this will turn out for my deliverance, as it is my eager expectation and hope that I shall not be at all ashamed, but that with full courage now as always Christ will be honored in my body, whether by life or by death" (Phil. 1:19,20).

Rejecting the False
What a marvelous sense of confidence the king has. Along with it he rejects the false:

> *Some boast of chariots, and some of horses;*
> *but we boast of the name of the Lord our God.*
> *They will collapse and fall;*
> *but we shall rise and stand upright"* (vv. 7,8).

The world has its sources of confidence, too. But they will not suffice. There is nothing wrong with them, as such, except that they are not adequate for the task. This psalmist well knew that horses and chariots are needed in battle, but he also knew that if they are all you are going to trust in, you will not have much of a chance. Horses and chariots are not enough without the Lord of glory behind them.

As you face the future, what do you trust in? What are you relying upon? There are many modern equivalents to these horses and chariots. You could say, "Some trust in missiles and tanks; but we shall rely upon the name of the Lord our God." "Some trust in ancestry and education; but I will rely on the Lord my God for power." "Some trust in tranquilizers and charm school; but I will rely upon the Lord my God." Here is the note of faith, the quiet, confident expression of a man who has learned where true power lies. And so he says, "I am not going to trust in anything secondary, but I will trust ultimately in the working of the Lord my God."

A Triumphant Shout

Finally we have the wonderful expression of benediction, a triumphant shout:

> *Give victory to the king, O Lord;*
> *answer us when we call* (v. 9).

We see here an implied promise of continued prayer. The people are saying, "Give victory to the king, as we keep calling upon you, O Lord." This is the promise to pray for one another. As we pray for one another, God will continue to supply us with that which is needed to take us through the problems, the perils, the dangers, and the battles of the years that lie ahead. Who knows what you are going to face? No one knows. But we know a God who hears and answers prayer. Therefore, pray for one another in this way.

The Lord answer you in the day of trouble! The name of the God of Jacob protect you! May He send you help from the sanctuary, and give you support from Zion! May He remember all your offerings, and regard with favor your burnt sacrifices! Selah

May He grant you your heart's desire, and fulfill all your plans! May we shout for joy over your victory, and in the name of God set up our banners! May the Lord fulfill all your petitions! Amen.

CHAPTER 5 / PSALM 22

The Suffering Savior

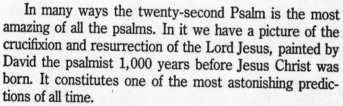

In many ways the twenty-second Psalm is the most amazing of all the psalms. In it we have a picture of the crucifixion and resurrection of the Lord Jesus, painted by David the psalmist 1,000 years before Jesus Christ was born. It constitutes one of the most astonishing predictions of all time.

At least nine specific events or aspects of the Crucifixion are described here in minute detail. All of them were fulfilled during the six hours in which Jesus hung upon the cross, from nine o'clock in the morning until three o'clock in the afternoon. Moreover, the latter part of the psalm clearly depicts the resurrection of Jesus from the dead. The probability that the predictions of these nine events would be fulfilled by chance in one person, on one afternoon, is inconceivably small. The chance that all this could occur by accident is beyond any realm of possibility our minds could imagine. Yet all was fulfilled as predicted in this psalm.

All the world knows that on November 22, 1963, President John F. Kennedy was assassinated in Dallas, Texas, while riding down a Dallas street in a motorcade. Suppose there had been in existence a document that predicted this event and that we knew to have been written in A.D. 963. That was about the time of the height of the Byzantine Empire, when most of the Western world was ruled from Constantinople, much of Europe was only sparsely inhabited by barbarian tribes, and America was not yet discovered.

Suppose this document predicted that a time would come when a man of great prominence, head of a great nation, would be riding down a street of a large city in a metal chariot not drawn by horses, and would suddenly and violently die from the penetration of his brain by a little piece of metal hurled from a weapon made of wood and iron, aimed at him from the window of a tall building, and that his death would have worldwide effect and cause worldwide mourning. You can imagine the awe with which such a document would be viewed today. That hypothetical prediction would have been made even before the invention of the automobile or of firearms, and 500 years before the discovery of America. It would be regarded as fantastically accurate. Yet such a prediction would only be similar to what we already have in Psalm 22.

The psalm has two major divisions. The first 21 verses recount for us the sufferings of an unknown person who is all alone and is crying out to God in his agony. Many scholars assert that these first 21 verses represent the thoughts that went through the mind of the Savior as He hung upon the cross. From verse 22 to the end the sufferer is no longer alone but is in the midst of a large company and is praising God and shouting in victory. It ends with His claiming the worship of the entire world.

A Cry of Abandonment

The best and simplest way to approach this psalm is simply to read it through, making certain observations. It is so clear, so unmistakable, that it hardly requires comment. It begins, very strikingly, with the words Jesus uttered on the cross:

> *My God, my God, why hast thou forsaken me?*
> *Why are thou so far from helping me,*
> *from the words of my groaning?*
> *O my God, I cry by day, but thou dost not answer;*
> *and by night, but find no rest* (vv. 1,2).

These opening words have been called "the cry of dereliction," that is, the cry of abandonment as the sufferer becomes aware that He is forsaken by His God. As we know from the New Testament, Jesus uttered these words at the end of a strange period of darkness, which had settled upon the land. For the first three hours as He hung upon the cross, the sun shone brightly and there was normal daylight. But at high noon a strange and disquieting darkness settled upon the whole land around Jerusalem. No one has ever been able to explain it. It lasted for three hours. It was not an eclipse of the sun, because eclipses do not last that long.

There have been similar periods at other times in history. In 1780, for instance, there was a strange dark day that settled upon the New England states when, for some still unexplained reason, the light of the sun failed in only that particular portion of earth so that it passed into a period of darkness in the middle of the day. Something like that happened at Jerusalem. Notice how the psalm reflects this. It says that the sufferer cries out in the day and in the night—in the light *and* in the dark—but still God does not answer.

Remembering God's Faithfulness

So here we have the strange mystery of the abandonment of the Son of God—what some have called "Immanuel's orphaned cry"—"My God, my God, why hast thou forsaken me?" Jesus actually spoke these words in Aramaic. Because He cried out with a loud voice, passersby misunderstood Him. He said, *"Eloi, Eloi, lama sabachthani?"* When the bystanders heard the words, *"Eloi, Eloi,"* they thought He was calling for Elijah. But He was calling out for God from the depths of His being because of His sense of abandonment. The strangeness of that rejection by God is highlighted for us by the sufferer's stated awareness of the faithful character of God:

> *Yet thou art holy,*
> > *enthroned on the praises of Israel.*
> *In thee our fathers trusted;*
> > *they trusted, and thou didst deliver them.*
> *To thee they cried, and were saved;*
> > *in thee they trusted, and were not disappointed*
> (vv.3-5).

He is remembering the history of men of faith in the past, and the fact that a faithful God never abandoned one of them. Even though they were sinful men, God saved them when they cried out to Him.

Treated Differently

"But," He says, "I am a worm, and no man." For some strange reason God is treating Him differently. Even the spectators reflect that difference of treatment:

> But I am a worm, and no man;
>> scorned by men, and despised by the people.
> All who see me mock at me,
>> they make mouths at me, they wag their heads;
> "He committed his cause to the Lord;
>> let him deliver him,
> let him rescue him, for he delights in
>> him!" (vv. 6-8).

He is treated like a despised and hated criminal, as though He had lost his right to live in human society. Matthew records for us the fact that the crowd actually used these very words. The unthinking multitude passing by, looking at the sufferer on the cross, said, "He trusts in God; let God deliver Him now" (see 27:43). What an

---

WE are faced with the strange mystery of why the Son of God was abandoned by His Father.

---

amazing prediction this is! The very words of a multitude, which could not have been controlled and had no intention of fulfilling prophecy, are clearly foretold.

No Grounds for Abandonment

We are faced with the strange mystery of why the Son of God was abandoned by His Father. He goes on to press the point Himself. He shows us that there are no grounds for abandonment in Himself:

> *Yet thou art he who took me from the womb;*
> *thou didst keep me safe upon my mother's breasts.*
> *Upon thee was I cast from my birth,*
> *and since my mother bore me thou hast been my*
> *God.*
> *Be not far from me,*
> *for trouble is near*
> *and there is none to help* (vv. 9-11).

How utterly forsaken He is! His friends have rejected Him and fled. His disciples and family have left Him alone; all have gone. Only God is left and now He senses that God Himself is forsaking Him. He knows no explanation for this. He says that from the very moment of His birth He was in fellowship with God. He was always the delight of God's heart, kept by His Father right from birth. And, you recall from the New Testament, as He began His public ministry the Father spoke from heaven and put His seal of approval upon His life, saying, "This is my beloved Son, with whom I am well pleased" (Matt. 3:17). There is absolutely nothing in Himself to merit abandonment, and yet here He is, forsaken.

In His human weakness He does not understand it, and so He cries out in this strange cry of dereliction, "My God, my God, why hast thou forsaken me?" Now, we know, of course, that it was because He was being made an offering for the sins of the world. All the ugliness and meanness and defilement and filth of our sin was laid upon Him. "But he was wounded for our transgressions, he was bruised for our iniquities; upon him was the chastisement that made us whole, and with his stripes we are healed" (Isa. 53:5).

Scene from the Cross

He goes on to describe the scene from the cross:

> *Many bulls encompass me,*
> *strong bulls of Bashan surround me;*
> *they open wide their mouths at me,*
> *like a ravening and roaring lion* (vv. 12, 13).

In the beautiful method of the Old Testament poets, He uses these figures to describe the onlookers. Like bulls, powerful, unopposable, they seem to be strong. Remember that Jesus said to His enemies at that very time, "This is your hour, and the power of darkness" (Luke 22:53). They seemed to be irresistible, like great, powerful bulls. Then He changes the figure and says they are like lions, fierce, ravening, threatening, their fangs dripping with anxiety to be at Him and tear Him apart. He is surrounded by His enemies.

Physical Reactions

Then He describes His own reaction:

> *I am poured out like water,*
> *and all my bones are out of joint;*
> *my heart is like wax,*
> *it is melted within my breast;*

> *my strength is dried up like a potsherd,*
> *and my tongue cleaves to my jaws;*
> *thou dost lay me in the dust of death*

(vv. 14,15).

What a clear description of the exhaustion of the Cross! Having hung there for five to six hours, His body suspended by the nails in His hands and feet, His bones are pulled out of joint. There is an awful sense of weariness and fatigue. His heart feels like melted wax within Him. His body, dehydrated in the hot sun of that spring day, is gripped now by a terrible, ravaging thirst. He cries out from the cross, "I thirst."

Death by Crucifixion

Then we have a most amazing and unmistakable description of death by crucifixion. This was set down when no one, so far as history tells us, put anyone to death by crucifixion. Certainly the Jews did not, for their method of execution was to stone someone to death. But here is One who clearly describes His own crucifixion.

> *Yea, dogs are round about me;*
> *a company of evildoers encircle me;*
> *they have pierced my hands and feet—*
> *I can count all my bones—*
> *they stare and gloat over me;*
> *they divide my garments among them,*
> *and for my raiment they cast lots* (vv.16-18).

It is absolutely impossible to explain that verse on any natural basis. It is clearly a God-given picture of the Crucifixion. The psalmist says that the sufferer is surrounded by "dogs." This was the common Jewish term for Gentiles, and especially for the Romans. Roman executioners are all around the cross here. He decries the fact that He is surrounded by these alien people. They have stripped Him; He is naked. He can see all His bones and, worse yet, He can feel them.

And the crowning indignity is that at the foot of the cross they are actually casting lots for His garments. The calloused, hardened Roman soldiers were trying to divide the spoil of His clothing. Because they did not want to rip His seamless robe apart, they cast lots for it. It is impossible that this could have been fulfilled by the collusion of the Roman soldiers. Yet here it is, clearly described 1,000 years before, so that Jesus' death by crucifixion is unquestionably in view.

Crying Out to God

Now we hear the final prayer of this sufferer:

> *But thou, O Lord, be not far off!*
> *O thou my help, hasten to my aid!*
> *Deliver my soul from the sword,*
> *my life from the power of the dog!*
> *Save me from the mouth of the lion,*
> *my afflicted soul from the horns of the wild*
> *oxen!* (vv. 19-21).

The "sword" would be a symbol for the authority of the Roman government. The "mouth of the lion" would picture the invisible powers, the Satanic forces. In the figure of the "horns of the wild oxen" it is as though He were impaled upon two great, widespread horns, and He is crying out now in final extremity for help from God. You will recall this is exactly what the Savior did in His last words as He hung upon the cross. He cried out, "Father, into thy hands I commit my spirit!" (Luke 23:46). "If anyone is going to save me, it has to be you, Father. If anyone is going to lift me out of the dust of death, raise me up again, it will be you. I trust myself to you." And so, in this closing prayer, we have reflected His commitment at last to the hands of the Father.

Made Perfect Through Suffering

Verse 22 constitutes a clear change. Without a word of explanation the same speaker goes on and says:

> *I will tell of thy name to my brethren;*
> *in the midst of the congregation I will praise*
> *thee* (v. 22).

What is this? Here, unquestionably, is the Resurrection. The same One who has just suffered and died is now in the midst of a company whom He calls His brethren. The writer of Hebrews picks up this theme. In Hebrews 2 he applies these very words to Jesus. He says that it was the will and purpose of God the Father to bring many sons to glory, and that it was fitting that He should make the captain of their salvation perfect through suffering. And, he continues, "That is why he is not ashamed to call them brethren, saying, 'I will proclaim thy name to my brethren, in the midst of the congregation I will praise thee'" Heb. 2:11,12).

Result of the Resurrection

What a wonderful picture of the result of the

Resurrection—the calling out of the people of God who are one with Him, and who are joint heirs with Christ, members, like Him, of the family of God. And so He says to them,

> *You who fear the Lord, praise him!*
> *all you sons of Jacob, glorify him,*
> *and stand in awe of him, all you sons of Israel!*
> (v. 23).

Why? Because this is the One who has answered the prayer of a dead man and raised Him from the dead. The Resurrection is the ground of Christian worship. He says:

> *For he has not despised or abhorred*
> *the affliction of the afflicted;*
> *and he has not hid his face from him,*
> *but has heard, when he cried to him* (v. 24).

Again, the writer of Hebrews says to us, at the end of his letter, "Now may the God of peace who brought again from the dead our Lord Jesus, the great shepherd of the sheep, by the blood of the eternal covenant, equip you with everything good that you may do his will" (Heb. 13:20,21).

A Living Lord

This is what constitutes the ground of praise for all Christians: we have a *living* Lord who has been raised from the dead and whose life is now shared with us so that His life is ours, and ours belongs to Him. He goes on to tell us just that:

From thee comes my praise in the great
   congregation;
   my vows I will pay before those who fear him
(v. 25).

That is, "I will fulfill my word to them. I will do for them what I have promised to do." What is that?

The afflicted shall eat and be satisfied;
   those who seek him shall praise the Lord!
   May your hearts live for ever! (v. 26).

Is that not great? His promise is that, out of the resurrected power that He holds, He will give us everything we need. So we will be satisfied. And, as Peter puts it in his second letter, "His divine power has granted to us all things that pertain to life and godliness" (2 Pet. 1:3) There is not one thing more that we need than what already has been made available. Thus it is true, as Hebrew 7:25 tells us, "He is able for all time to save those who draw near to God through him, since he always lives to make intercession for them."

The Great Commission

The next verse in the psalm goes on to trace the effect of this power as it moves out across the face of the whole earth.

All the ends of the earth shall remember
   and turn to the Lord;
and all the families of the nations
   shall worship before him.

For dominion belongs to the Lord,
and he rules over the nations (vv. 27,28).

It is the fulfillment of Jesus' great commission that His gospel shall be preached to all nations. And out of every tribe and nation shall come those who respond, who fear Him, because God is the ruler of all and He will see to it that His message reaches all men. We are living in the very days when men from every tribe and nation are coming to Christ.

It Is Finished

The final picture encompasses the utter subjection to Him of all people and all creatures everywhere in the universe:

Yea, to him shall all the proud of the earth
bow down;
before him shall bow all who go down to the dust,
and he who cannot keep himself alive [that is, the
poor, obscure, weak, and helpless].
Posterity shall serve him;
men shall tell of the Lord to the coming generation,
and proclaim his deliverance to a people yet
unborn,
that he has wrought it (vv. 29-31).

Those last words are amazing! In the Hebrew the last phrase is literally, "It is finished." So the verse really says, "There shall be proclaimed deliverance to a people yet unborn, that it is finished." It is striking that this psalm both opens and closes with a word of Jesus from the cross. "My God, my God, why hast thou forsaken me?" And, as He cried with a loud voice just before He died, "It is finished." All is done. There is nothing left to do.

Is that not tremendous? What a psalm! What an anticipation, and what a fulfillment of this amazing event!

Our Father, we can only bow in worship and adoration
of a God who plans like this, and who carries through His
plans against all the opposition of men and devils, who fulfills in history what He has predicted long before and
brings to pass all His words. And we, who have been made
the recipients of this amazing work of grace, who have
profited by the death and the resurrection life of the Son of
God, give thanks to you out of the fulness of gratitude in
our hearts for all that has been given to us. In His name,
Amen.

CHAPTER 6 / PSALM 23

The Shepherd Psalm*

Because many of us have memorized the twenty-third Psalm as small children, we often neglect the opportunity to study it in detail in our adult life. Yet it is a great psalm. It ministers to our deepest spiritual needs.

This, of course, is a psalm of David. We know something of the circumstances of its composition. In the fifteenth chapter of 2 Samuel there is recorded the instance in David's life when his own son, Absalom, rebelled against him and toppled him from the throne. David was forced to flee into the Judean wilderness with his family and servants, and for a period of time he was unable to reclaim his throne. His life was in jeopardy and he was hunted and hounded for a number of months. Perhaps, because so much of his early life had been spent as a shepherd in that same wilderness, the circumstances reminded him of his shepherd life. That could be why the images in this psalm are drawn right out of his experience as a young shepherd.

This is a psalm for people who, like David, are experiencing a major upheaval in life. Perhaps you too have children who are rebelling, or your home is in turmoil, or some long-standing relationship in your life is breaking up. This psalm is written for you. It is a psalm for people who are shaken and in turmoil.

We Shall Not Want

David begins with a statement of the theme of the entire passage:

The Lord is my shepherd, I shall not want (v. 1).

Because the Lord is my Shepherd, I will not lack anything. He satisfies my needs. That is the place to which God wants to bring us. He wants us to be independently dependent upon Him, to need Him alone. There are really only two options in life. If the Lord is my Shepherd, then I shall not want; but if I am in want, then it is obvious that the Lord is not my Shepherd. It is that simple. If there is emptiness and loneliness and despair and frustration in our lives, then the Lord is not our Shepherd.

Or, if anyone or anything else is shepherding us, we are never satisfied. If our vocation shepherds us, then there is restlessness and feverish activity and frustration. If education is our shepherd, then we are constantly being disillusioned. If another person is our shepherd, we are always disappointed and ultimately we are left empty. If alcohol or drugs is our shepherd, as one rock artist said recently, then "we are wasted." But if the Lord is our Shepherd, David says we shall not want.

It occurs to me that if Jehovah is to be our Shepherd, then we have to begin by recognizing that we are sheep. I don't like that analogy, frankly, because I don't like sheep. I come by my dislike honestly. I used to raise sheep. In high school I was in the 4-H club, and I had a herd of sheep and goats. Now, goats I can abide, because they may be obnoxious, but at least they're smart. Sheep are, beyond question, the most stupid animals on the face of the earth. They are dumb and they are dirty and they are timid and defenseless and helpless. Mine were always getting lost and hurt and snakebitten. They literally do not know enough to come in out of the rain. I look back on my shepherding days with a great deal of disgust. Sheep are miserable creatures.

And then to have God tell me that I am one! That hurts my feelings. But if I am really honest with myself I know it is true. I know that I lack wisdom and strength. I'm inclined to be self-destructive. As the hymn says, "I'm prone to wander." Isaiah said it best: "All we like sheep have gone astray; we have turned every one to his own way" (53:6). I know my tendency toward self-indulgent individualism, going my own way and doing my own thing. That's me. I'm a sheep. And if Jesus Christ is to be my Shepherd, I have to admit that I need Him. It is difficult, but that is where we must start. Once we admit that need we discover the truth of what David is saying. We shall not want.

Nourishment for the Inner Man

In this psalm David enumerates the ways in which the Good Shepherd meets our needs. The first is found in verse 2 and part of verse 3:

He makes me lie down in green pastures.
He leads me beside still waters;
he restores my soul (vv. 2,3).

The first thing He does is to meet the needs of the inner man, the basic needs that we have for nourishment within. The basic needs of a flock of sheep are grass and water. Here is the very picturesque scene of sheep bedded down in grassy meadows, having eaten their fill and now feeling totally satisfied, and then being led by still

---

A S we feed upon Him. As we come to know Him, believe what He says, and act on His Word, we discover that the inner man is fed.

---

waters. Sheep are afraid of running water; they will drink only from a quiet pool. A good shepherd, particularly in a semi-arid region such as Palestine, knows where the watering holes are. He knows where the grassy meadows are. And so he leads the sheep into places where they can feed and drink, and where they can rest. The picture is one of calm and tranquility, because the basic needs of the sheep are met.

The counterpart in our lives is obvious. It is God who restores the inner man through His Word. As we feed upon the Word of God we see the Lord Jesus there. We draw upon Him and our inner man is satisfied. "Beyond the sacred page," the hymn says, "we see thee, Lord." We see Him, and we eat and drink of Him, and we discover Him to be the resource that we need. As Paul says, "Though the outward man perishes, the inward man is renewed day by day" (see 2 Cor. 4:16). Our souls are restored. How? As we feed upon Him. As we come to know Him, believe what He says, and act on His Word, we discover that the inner man is fed.

I once had a Bible study Wednesday nights in a fraternity house at Stanford University. Our basic assumption there was that the Bible is the authority. No one really taught the class; we simply opened up the Word and the men in the group made observations. One night a student from Austria sat in with us, a fine young law student who was traveling in this country and visiting Stanford for a few weeks. He shared some of his thinking with us and made a real contribution to the group. Afterward, as we were leaving, he made this comment: "I'm so thankful I could be here tonight, because I discovered that you men have found direct access to God through this Book."

Have you discovered that access? In times of deep, dire need, when we cast about for help, it is no further away than God's Word. Everything we need to nourish the inner man is right there. Everything we need, which relates to life and to living godly lives in the world, is available in the Word.

Direction in Life

The second thing the Good Shepherd does is to give direction in life:

He leads me in paths of righteousness
for his name's sake (v. 3).

Or, as an alternate reading indicates, "he leads me in right paths." The Hebrew word translated "paths" means a well-defined, well-worn trail. That indicates again how stupid sheep are because, even when the trail is well laid out, they still need a shepherd. They are still inclined to wander away, no matter how obvious the path. The shepherd knows the trails. He has been there before, and the sheep trust him.

Making Decisions

The most anxiety-producing factor in the world today is uncertainty about the future. What is going to happen tomorrow, and the next day? There are decisionswe must make, which bear, not only upon our own lives, but upon the lives of everyone with whom we are associated. My life touches my family and my neighbors and my business associates; so does yours. We are constantly making decisions. How do we know that we are making the right ones? Decisions can be crucial, and frustrating!

There is a classic story about a man undergoing basic training in the army. He was pulling KP and was given the assignment of sorting potatoes. There was a huge mound of them and the mess sergeant told him to put all the bad ones in one bin, and all the good ones in the other bin. He came back about two hours later to find the man just looking at one potato. There was nothing in the bins. The sergeant said, "What's the matter, don't you like the work?" The soldier said, "It's not the work; it's the decisions that are killing me."

We have to make countless decisions, day after day, which touch the lives of our children and our wives and husbands. We need wisdom. We need a shepherd. We need someone who knows the trails, someone whom we can trust.

Discovering the Right Paths
Now, the Lord knows the way. But the question arises,

"How can I discover His will for my life?" May I suggest these steps: First, submit wholeheartedly to the leadership of the Shepherd. That is the basic attitude we must maintain. Unless we are willing to admit that we don't know the way through the wilderness, we will never find the way.

Jesus said, "If your eye is sound, your whole body will be full of light; but if your eye is not sound [evil], then your whole body will be full of darkness. If then the light in you is darkness, how great is the darkness!" (Matt. 6:22,23). He is saying, in a very picturesque way, that if our eye is fastened on Jesus Christ, if our eye is "sound" [single], then our whole body will be full of light. We will know what to do. We will know the truth, and we'll act on it. We'll have understanding and wisdom. But if we have one eye on Christ and the other on the world or on our circumstances or our boyfriend or girlfriend or whatever, if the eye is "not sound" [dual], how great is that darkness! We never know where we are to go. We will have no sense of direction, and will wander in darkness.

We have to be willing to submit wholeheartedly to the leadership of the Shepherd. We must be willing to say, "I'll go anywhere. I'll do anything. I'll be anything. I'll carry any load, live any place you want me to live, do anything you want me to do." Once we're willing to say that, then God can reveal His will. Paul said it another way: "Present your bodies as a living sacrifice, holy and acceptable to God, which is your spiritual worship . . . that you may prove what is the will of God" (See Rom. 12:1,2).

Following the Right Paths
The second thing we must do is to obey what we know now to be God's will for us. Probably 95 percent of God's will is already revealed in His Word. We have to begin by

obeying the truth that we have. If we are disobedient to our parents, we cannot expect God to give us wisdom concerning our next step. If we are not raising our children in the nurture and admonition of Christ, we cannot expect God to direct us. If we as men are not loving our wives as Christ loved the church, the Lord will not reveal more of His will. If you wives are not in submission to your husbands, God's leadership will not come to you. But when we obey the 95 percent of the truth that we have, then the 5 percent that is indefinite simply follows along as a matter of course.

Now, that does not mean that we have to be sinless, because who of us is? But it does mean we have to be willing to face and put away sin as God points it out to us. If we are willing to be brought into conformity to Jesus Christ in every area of our life, and if we are allowing Him freedom to work, then He will reveal more truth to us. But He won't if we are consciously holding out and defending sin. He reveals additional truth only to men and women with open, obedient hearts.

The Peace of God

But what about other areas of life where the Scriptures do not give specific information? There we are led through the *peace of God*. As we spend time in prayer and waiting upon God there comes the sense of peace, an inner conviction, about the correctness of a certain direction. The peace of God will umpire in our life and will let us know what to do. I have discovered that we can trust that peace. When we move out on the basis of it we discover that God supports and undergirds our actions and, through confirming circumstances, further strengthens our sense of peace.

Now, having stepped out in faith, we sometimes discover that things don't work out as we had anticipated. But even at that point we can't second-guess God. We cannot say that He did not give us wisdom. James says, "If any of you lacks wisdom, let him ask God who gives to all men generously" (1:5). We can believe that His wisdom will be given. There is often a tendency to second-guess ourselves and to think that perhaps we missed God's will if things don't go as we had planned. But God wants us to know His will even more than we do. He is not trying to play games with us. He is not trying to be obscure and to hide the truth from us. He wants us to know. And as we step out on the basis of His peace, we can believe that this is the direction God wants us to go.

In a small way I was once tempted to second-guess myself in a decision I had made a few weeks before. My Volkswagen was totally wrecked in an accident and I had to replace it. The insurance company gave me a generous settlement and I went out to purchase another car. I didn't want to spend much time because I didn't have any. In the newspapers about 40 Volkswagens were advertised for sale. I knew that I couldn't look at every one, and so my wife, Carolyn, and I prayed together, "Lord, we've got to find a car. It's your car, and so we're not going to worry about it; please lead us to the right situation."

After looking at half-a-dozen or so, we finally settled on one. It seemed good. I'm not much of a mechanic but I kicked the tires and slammed the doors and it seemed all right to me. I talked to the owner. He seemed ethical and claimed he'd just rebuilt the engine. So I bought the car and brought it home. Now we've discovered that it has a lot of problems. It's using oil and a number of other things are wrong. It's going to cost money to fix it up. My first thought was, "Oops, the Lord led me astray." But then I had to remember that we prayed for wisdom, and James says if we pray for wisdom we'll receive it. We acted on that promise when we bought the car. I don't know what God has in store for me in this matter, but I know that car is God's will for my life right now.

That is what I mean by confidence in God's ability to lead us. David says that He will lead us in the right path. That is a promise! And He does this for His name's sake. It isn't our name that is at stake, it is *His* name. It's His character, His reputation that is at stake. He has promised to give us wisdom. I believe that; I act. You believe it; you act. And it *has* to be true. God must fulfill His promise, otherwise His own reputation is impugned. His name is Faithful, and He has promised that He will lead us in the right paths. To me that is a tremendous source of encouragement. I know that the decisions I make today and tomorrow, as I walk under His shepherding will be correct. Even though the events that follow may not necessarily be all that I expect, the decisions will be right. That is His promise, and we can count on it.

Providing Protection

The third thing David says that a good shepherd does is to provide protection:

> *Even though I walk through the valley of the*
> *shadow of death,*
> *I fear no evil;*
> *for thou art with me;*
> *thy rod and thy staff,*
> *they comfort me* (v. 4).

This again is a very picturesque scene. The shepherd is leading the sheep back home at evening. As they go down through a narrow gorge the long shadows lie across the trail. In the Hebrew this is a "valley of deep shadows." The sheep, because they are so timid and defenseless, are frightened by their experience. But they trust the shepherd, and therefore they are comforted. They will fear no evil, because the shepherd is with them.

No Reason to Fear

We are reminded of the Lord's words quoted in the book of Hebrews, "I will never fail you nor forsake you" (13:5). Hence we can confidently say, "The Lord is my helper; I will not fear what man can do to me." I do not know what

---

HE reproves, corrects, encourages, and instructs in righteousness, dealing with us firmly and gently.

---

your experience has been, but whenever I'm in a situation like this, when there is a great deal of pressure, I begin to wonder if the Lord hasn't abandoned me. But He says He never fails us, never forsakes us. He is always there. Therefore, we have no reason to fear. That is a great comfort.

Discipline with Love

And then David writes, "Your rod and staff comfort me." The rod was a club that was used to drive off wild animals. It was never used *on* the sheep but was a heavy instrument used *to protect* the sheep from marauding predators. The staff was a slender pole with a little crook on the end. It was used to aid the sheep. The crook could be hooked around the leg of a sheep to pull him from harm. Or it could be used as an instrument to direct and, occasionally, to discipline the sheep with taps on the side of the body.

Understanding how the shepherd tends his sheep has helped me so much in understanding the character of God. When I go wandering away He doesn't say, "There goes that stupid sheep, Dave Roper!" and —WHAP!—down comes that big club! No. His attitude is, "Well, there's Dave, wandering away again. How can I help him? How can I move in to bring him back into line? How can I comfort him, and supply what he needs?" He may have to discipline, but He always does it in love. He reproves, corrects, encourages, and instructs in righteousness, dealing with us firmly and gently.

The rod and staff are also used against the two greatest enemies we have to face. The rod is for the outside enemy, Satan, who is working through the world system to destroy us. Jesus said, "He is a liar and a murderer" (see John 8:44). He's out to devour us, and so the Lord uses the club on him. But the other enemy is me, the enemy within. In the immortal words of Pogo, "We have met the enemy, and he is us." I know that. The shepherd's staff is used to chasten, and to subdue the enemy within. But the confidence He gives is that I have nothing to fear, either from the enemy without, or from the enemy within.

The Gracious Host

In verses 5 and 6 David changes the metaphor a bit—from the good shepherd to the gracious host:

> *Thou preparest a table before me*
> *in the presence of my enemies;*
> *thou anointest my head with oil,*
> *my cup overflows.*
> *Surely goodness and mercy shall follow me*

all the days of my life;
and I shall dwell in the house of the Lord
for ever (vv. 5,6).

Jehovah spreads a sumptuous meal before him, a great banquet, in the presence of his enemies. This figure encompasses all the figures David has used before. That God feeds and provides, leads and protects, is all bound up in this symbol of a gracious host.

Interestingly enough, this figure grows right out of the historical situation in which David wrote. When David was driven into the wilderness by his son's rebellion, he found himself out in the desert, hungry and weary, his army in disarray. As recorded in 2 Samuel 17, three men who were not even Israelites, Shobi, Machir, and Barzillai, "brought beds, basins [so they could wash and refresh themselves], and earthen vessels, wheat, barley, meal, parched grain, beans and lentils, honey and curds and sheep and cheese from the herd, for David and the people with him to eat; for they said, 'The people are hungry and weary and thirsty in the wilderness'" (vv. 28,29). David saw that God, as a gracious host, was preparing a table before him in the presence of his enemies. Paul said it this way: "My God will supply every need of yours according to his riches in glory in Christ Jesus" (Phil. 4:19).

A final note is that the word *follow*, in Psalm 23:6, literally means "pursue." David says that God's goodness and mercy shall pursue him, in contrast to the pursuit of his enemies who are out to dethrone and destroy him. David's desire was to go back to the tabernacle and to worship there. God's mercy and kindness ought to evoke the same response from us. We worship, not in a tabernacle, but, as Jesus said, "in spirit and in truth" (see John 4:23). We worship in the inner man, where God dwells. When we see that the Good Shepherd does feed us and does lead us and does protect us, our response ought to be worship—a recognition of all that Jehovah is, a word of thanks for what He has done, and the statement, "Here is more of myself for you to put to your intended purpose." That is true worship.

Our Father, we realize that the only reasonable act of worship is for us to present our bodies as a living sacrifice. It is the only response we can make to your goodness. You are the Good Shepherd. You are utterly trustworthy. We discover that you do feed us continually, you do lead us, you do guard us and protect us, and we want to say thank you for that. We want to say again that our bodies are yours to fill and use. This is the only reasonable thing that we can do. We thank you for all that you are to us, in Jesus' name, Amen.

*This study is by David H. Roper, once associate pastor at the Peninsula Bible Church, Palo Alto, California, now pastor of Cole Community Church, Boise, Idaho.

CHAPTER 7 / PSALM 34

Facing Fear*

I once worked with college students. The more time I spent with these people and came to love them and to understand them, the more I became convinced that their greatest needs are not intellectual, but emotional. As they honestly shared their hearts with me without trying to pretend anything, I sensed that what really bothered them were problems of guilt, fear, loneliness, and lack of motivation and real direction in life. In thinking back on my contacts with students I would conclude that the greatest dilemma they eventually have to face is how to handle their fears.

Someone has said that the generation of young people today is a fear-ridden generation. They are afraid of themselves and afraid of other people. Yet this is not something that is unique only among students. We can all identify with them because we are there ourselves. Many in the world are turning to encounter techniques and T-groups to try to get rid of their fears. But, as is so often the case with the world's attempts to deal with fear, they treat just the symptoms. Their approach is superficial and short-range and it does not meet the deep needs of the heart. Only the Word of God speaks to the real needs of people and that is why I turn your attention to this psalm.

In this psalm David teaches us a way to face fear—fearful circumstances in our lives and the emotions of fear that are a consequence of those circumstances.

The title of this psalm gives us the occasion for its writing, "A Psalm of David, when he feigned madness before Abimelech, so that he drove him out, and he went away."

The historical background of this psalm is found in 1 Samuel 21. The setting is in David's life when he was a part of King Saul's court before he himself became king. Some jealousy broke out between Saul and David. People were beginning to think that David was the greater person. They were writing folksongs about him, saying, "Saul has slain his thousands, and David his ten thousands." Saul became so jealous that he tried to kill David. So David fled south, from the frying pan right into the fire, into the country of the Philistines where he was captured. The Philistines recognized him immediately as their enemy who had killed Goliath. He was dragged before King Achish (in the title of the psalm he is called Abimelech, the traditional name for the Philistine kings, but his personal name was Achish). At this point, David was fearing for his life. In order to escape, he pretended to be mad by falling down and groveling in the dirt, drooling down the front of his beard and making a fool of himself. Evidently Achish was touched with pity for this man or he thought he already had enough madmen around him, so he drove David away. David then went down into the wilderness where he found a cave, the cave of Adullam, and hid there for a number of months until his mighty men joined him.

It was a time of intense loneliness and fear for David. He had been anointed king, but was unable to sit on the throne. He had been abandoned by his own people as well as by his enemies. Here he was hiding in a cave, frustrated, discouraged—and scared to death. These were the experiences that produced this psalm, which is his account of what he learned about facing fears.

The psalm is one of the seven acrostics in the book of Psalms. Each verse is based on a different Hebrew letter, from the first letter of the Hebrew alphabet, *Aleph*, to the last, *Taw*, in verse 21. Verse 22 is just a postscript. An acrostic evidently was easier to remember as people worshiped in public or meditated on it in private. In times of difficult circumstances they could reflect back on the ideas expressed here, and the alphabetical order would help them remember the sequence of thoughts.

Yielding to His Authority

Now let's look at the psalm itself. David begins with a call to united expression of praise for his deliverance. In the opening phrase, "I will bless the Lord at all times," the words are literally, "bless the Lord *in* all times"—in that circumstance, in this frightening situation, standing before the face of King Achish.

> *I will bless the Lord at all times;*
> *his praise shall continually be in*
> *my mouth.*

My soul makes its boast in the Lord;
*   let the afflicted hear and be glad.*
O magnify the Lord with me,
*   and let us exalt his name together!* (vv.1-3).

Our English word for blessing usually means to confer benefit on another person or to praise Him. But the Hebrew word for blessing is taken from the word for knee and means literally to bend the knee. So what David is saying is, "In this frightening situation, I will bend the knee to Jehovah. I will acknowledge Him as Lord. I will yield to His

> E VEN the most terrifying circum-
> stances come to us not just as acts of
> chance but as events strained through the
> fine screen of the love of the Father.

authority in my life. I will accept this circumstance not as something capricious that has happened to me but as a part of His right to rule in my life. I will acknowledge His lordship and yield to Him." He emphasizes the depth of this attitude in the answering refrain of verse 1, "his praise shall continually be in my mouth."

Acknowledging His Lordship

The overall message of the psalm and the key to deliverance is, first of all, to acknowledge the lordship of Jehovah God in our lives. Have we learned to accept any circumstance in our life as from the hand of the Father? Even the most terrifying circumstances come to us not just as acts of chance but as events strained through the fine screen of the love of the Father. They happen because God wants them to happen. We experience them because God wants us to experience them. He expects us to acknowledge His right to do as He pleases in our lives. This is where we have to begin. Paul says in Philippians 4, "Rejoice in the Lord always; again I will say, Rejoice. Let all men know your forbearance [or patience]. The Lord is at hand" (vv. 4,5). This realization that the Lord is present in every circumstance is what makes it all work. He has not abandoned us. We are not shut up to our own resourses. We are to acknowledge His presence, His sovereignty in our lives.

A Lord of Compassion
Now why do we do this? Because of who the Lord is. What kind of a Lord do we have? What kind of Lord did David have? Well, the Scriptures are very clear. He is a Lord of compassion, and He understands us. He knows our circumstances much better than we do. He knows our hearts. He knows our fears, He knows our feelings of frustration, and He is infinitely merciful and compassionate. He is a Lord of power, able to act. He is not immobilized by my fears. I may be, but he's not. He is not inhibited in any way by my circumstances or by my fears. And if I turn away from myself and my own attempts to be something before God and lay hold of Him, then I discover that He is there to deliver.

The writer of Hebrews says that we do not have a high priest who is unable to be touched by the feelings of our weaknesses but was in every respect tempted as we are yet without sin (see Heb. 4:15). In the garden of Gethsemane Jesus faced fear. He was emotionally shaken, He was tempted to give way to fear and to abandon the Father's purpose and will for His life and to turn from the cross. Therefore, it does not embarrass Him that I am afraid. He does not reject me; He has been there Himself. The passage in Hebrews goes on to say that because we have this kind of high priest, we can come confidently to the throne of grace (*throne* here refers to the power of God; *grace* refers to compassion), that we may receive mercy and find grace to help in time of need (see Heb. 4:16). There is all the power that we need. When we understand God to be like this, we can yield to His authority and acknowledge His lordship in every circumstance. We know that He loves us, that He seeks the best for us above all else, and that He has the power to act on our behalf.

Thanksgiving to God

In the latter part of verse 2 David states the purpose of the psalm: that "the afflicted hear and be glad." That is the way the Word ought to work in our lives. It is intended to be life-changing; not something just to be read and forgotten or held theoretically. The psalmist says that understanding these principles will set us free to be glad instead of depressed and inhibited by our fears. The final result is a unified exaltation of His name, as all the body of Christ together expresses a thanksgiving to God because of what He has done. In summary that is the psalm.

Responding to Our Needs

We want to look at it in detail beginning with the next paragraph, verses 4 through 7. This is a paragraph where David recounts his experience.

> *I sought the Lord, and he answered me,*
> *and delivered me from all my fears* (v. 4).

He is saying he longed for God and sought Him desperately. And God answered him and delivered him from fear. And we can expect this, can't we, from a Lord such as ours? He will hear us. He will respond. He is not powerless or unable to move. I know from my own experience in our family that when one of our three boys cries out in the night, either my wife or I will get out of bed and hit that cold floor and go in to see what's wrong. Now certainly, with all our limitations and weaknesses as parents, if we're willing to do that, how much more our loving heavenly Father, who never sleeps, is ready at any moment to respond to our need?

Exposing Our Fears

Through the rest of the paragraph David spells out the three-step process of deliverance. The first is in verse 5, the second in verse 6, and the third in verse 7.

> *Look to him, and be radiant;*
>   *so your faces shall never be*
>   *ashamed* (v. 5).

The original language actually says, "so *their* faces shall never be ashamed." I think the psalmist is personifying his fears here, and that the verse ought to be translated like this: "He delivered me from all my fears; in looking to Him they (my fears) were enlightened, and their faces shall never be ashamed (or literally, I will never put a veil over the face of my fears. I will never try to hide them.)" I think David is saying, "I took my fears and exposed them to God, and He shed light on them. And now I'll never again be ashamed of my fear. I'll never try to cover it up again. I'll never try to appear to be something that I'm not in the face of others or in the face of God. I'm willing to admit that I'm fearful." David discovered that the key to deliverance was in acknowledging his fear. And that is the first step in the process.

I don't like to acknowledge my weaknesses and I suspect that you don't either. Most of us are ashamed of our fears. We like to appear poised and cool. In our fantasies we are always the ones who will do the thing right when everybody else is falling to pieces. Yet we know that we don't have what it takes to be poised, but we don't want people to know that.

I will never forget an experience that my friend, Coach Jim Shofner, and I had in the Zeta Psi house at Stanford one year. We were going in for a meeting and Jim and I were both scared but we wouldn't admit it to each other. I had worked out my talk and it was going to be a masterpiece. I was going to boldly stand up at dinner and tell these men what was on my heart.

We got into the house and discovered that they had just lost the intramural football championship and practically everybody in the house was drunk. We walked into the dining room where they were throwing half-gallons of milk all over the room. As we sat down, the president of the house stood up, three sheets to the wind, leaning about 15 degrees to the left, hanging onto the edge of the table. We had coached him very carefully on what to say, but when he got up he couldn't remember what we'd told him. So he said, "There are two men here who are going to talk about God." And then he sat down. There was a stony silence in the room as I got up and everything that I had planned to say just vanished. To this day, I don't know what I said, but I do know that my voice was quivering and my hands were shaking the whole time. When it was over, I sat down in relief. I walked away from there feeling embarrassed and convinced that I had failed. Fortunately, God overruled, but it was a good lesson for me.

Why was I so embarrassed? Because I didn't want those men to see that I was weak. I wanted to be a strong man, but God wants us to acknowledge our weakness at the very outset because weakness is the key to strength. Only the fearful and the weak and the helpless ultimately

---

THE extent that we admit our weakness in a situation is the extent that we have God's ability for that situation.

---

have the power of God. Paul stated the paradox in 2 Corinthians 12. He is talking about his thorn in the flesh, this physical affliction that was given to him. He calls it a messenger of Satan to harass him and keep him from being too elated.

He writes, "Three times I besought the Lord about this, that it should leave me; but he said to me, 'My grace is sufficient for you, for my power is made perfect in weakness.' I will all the more gladly boast of my weaknesses, that the power of Christ may rest upon me. For the sake of Christ, then, I am content with weaknesses, insults, hardships, persecutions, and calamities; for when I am weak, then I am strong" (2 Cor. 12:8-10).

Recognizing Our Poverty

When we are weak and fearful, God is able to speak through us. The extent that we admit our weakness in a situation is the extent that we have God's ability for that situation. David picks this up in verse 6 by referring to himself as "this poor man"—not this strong man, not this resourceful man, but this poor man—this man who recognizes his poverty in the face of these circumstances.

> *This poor man cried, and the Lord heard him,*
> *and saved him out of all his troubles* (v. 6).

The second step in the process of deliverance from fear is appropriating the power of God for fearful situations. It is not enough just to admit our weakness. We also have to appropriate His power. C. S. Lewis has said, "Down through the ages whenever men might need courage they might cry out, 'Billy Budd, help me!' and nothing very significant happens. But for nineteen hundred years whenever men have needed courage and have cried out, 'Lord Jesus, help me!' something has happened." They have laid hold of the resurrection power of Jesus Christ and His ability there to meet any demand.

There is an interesting word here in the sixth verse. The word translated "troubles" means to be restricted and tied up, to be limited, inhibited. That is exactly what fear does to us. It ties us into knots or, as we say, it hangs us up and robs us of our freedom. But in laying hold of Christ we are freed from our inhibitions. He sets us free and makes us whole men. That's the kind of Lord we have.

Fortified for Battle

The third step in the process of deliverance from fear is shown in verse 7.

> *The angel of the Lord encamps around those*
> *who fear him, and delivers them.*

Literally the verse implies that He equips them for war, He fortifies them. When we acknowledge our weakness (step 1) and we lay hold of Jesus Christ (step 2) He fortifies us (step 3). That is an interesting figure of speech. The "angel of the Lord" encamping "around those that fear him" speaks of God's omnipresence, His presence with us in any situation, no matter how potentially fearful or threatening it may be. Encamping around us means to fortify us, to deliver us.

Now the emotional symptoms of fear may continue. We may quake and shake and we may not have the poise before people that we would like to have, but we are not paralyzed by fear. We can move through any situation with inner security and confidence because God delivers His power to accomplish the task He has laid out before us.

Laying Hold of the Truth

In verses 8 through 10 David turns from his own experience to encourage others to lay hold of this truth.

> O taste and see that the Lord is good!
>   Happy is the man who takes refuge in him!
> O fear the Lord, you his saints,
>   for those who fear him have no want!
> The young lions suffer want and hunger;
>   but those who seek the Lord lack
>   no good thing.

"O taste and see that the Lord is good." God wants us to taste His goodness and experience it, because experience in the Christian life is what leads to knowledge. And we can never really know the goodness of God until we step out on the basis of the knowledge that we have. We may have "knowledge" in our mind, but it is never really ours until we have stepped out by faith expecting God to act and we discover that He is true, that we can trust Him. Then we can truly say that we know. So the next time you are tempted to be fearful, don't call your psychiatrist, don't take a tranquilizer, don't take to your bed; taste and see that the Lord is good. Act on His principle and see if God does not set you free.

David says in verse 9 that those who fear the Lord have no want. "The lions suffer want and hunger"; he is speaking metaphorically here of those who rely on their own strength and brute force. "Those who rely on themselves will suffer want and hunger; but those who seek the Lord lack no good thing." God's promise is that we will lack nothing. Self-confident man finds himself in desperate need, but God's man never does. One of the best illustrations for this is from the life of the apostle Peter. He is a perfect illustration of the self-confident man. The Lord challenges Peter with the possibility of his falling away. Peter says, "Not I, Lord. I'll never forsake you!" And yet, when he was confronted by a little girl beside a fire, he forsook the Lord (see Matt. 26:34,74,75). He was the "young lion" counting on his own resources, and he suffered hunger. He didn't have what it took to face that situation. But if we seek the Lord and rely upon Him, we lack no good thing.

Excited About Life

Verses 11 through 18 are a teaching section very reminiscent of the book of Proverbs. David uses contrast to reiterate these same principles.

What man is there who desires life,

and covets many days, that he may
enjoy good? (v. 12).

What man is there who delights in life—who doesn't just exist but is excited about his life and its challenges. He is the person who sees every day as an adventure, and every challenge as an opportunity to be ventured into with confidence in God. That is the way it should be with us. We need never arise in the morning overwhelmed and discouraged by the responsibilities of the day. There may be fearful things coming up in our schedules and who of us knows the unforeseen events that lie ahead every morning. But despite the uncertainty of our futures, we have certainty in the adequacy of Jesus Christ for our lives. This security frees us to be excited about the next 24-hour period or the next year.

If we want to look at life this way, says the psalmist in verse 13, we are to keep our tongues from evil, and our lips from speaking deceit. We are to depart from evil and do good; we're to seek peace and pursue it. How do we usually react to fear? Very often with frustration and anger, grumbling and complaining, we lash out at people and circumstances. Or we become deceitful. When someone asks us to do something that is potentially frightening, we think of some other "appointment" for that particular time instead of laying hold of the power of Christ to get us through. But David said to depart from all of these things. Don't let your tongue speak evil and your lips speak deceit or lie. Put away the inner rebellion in your life and acknowledge the lordship of Jesus Christ.

Help for the Helpless

Why? Well, in verse 15 he says, "The eyes of the Lord are

toward the righteous, and his ears toward their cry." God sees us—He's aware of our need. He hears us—He's aware of our circumstances.

> *The face of the Lord is against evildoers*
> *[those who are fretting and complaining],*
> > *to cut off the remembrance of them*
> > *from the earth.*
> *When the righteous cry for help,*
> > *the Lord hears,*
> > *and delivers them out of all their troubles.*
> *The Lord is near to the brokenhearted,*
> > *and saves the crushed in spirit* (vv. 16-18).

This reminds me of Isaiah's great words in Isaiah 66:1-2 "Thus says the Lord: 'Heaven is my throne and the earth is my footstool; what is the house which you would build for me, and what is the place of my rest? All these things my hand has made, and so all these things are mine, says the Lord. But this is the man to whom I will look, he that is humble and contrite in spirit, and trembles at my word.'"

God is not impressed by our bravado, by our assertions that we have what it takes, by our attempts to face into the wind alone. Heaven does not help those who help themselves; heaven helps the helpless. Heaven helps the man who is crushed in spirit, who is brokenhearted, who is not counting on himself; heaven helps the one who is willing to expose his fears and be what he is—a weak, fragile vessel greatly in need of the power of God in his life.

God's Deliverance

Now, there is a final section from verses 19 through 22, a

series of promises that again are variations of the same theme.

Many are the afflictions of the righteous;
  but the Lord delivers him out of them all (v. 19).

Both of those are promises. We can expect to be afflicted if we want to be men and women of God. That is SOP—Standard Operating Procedure. Paul said, "For it has been granted to you that for the sake of Christ you should not only believe in him but also suffer for his sake" (Phil. 1:29). If you are going to be God's man or God's woman you can expect God to put you in the forefront of the action. You're going to be out where everyone is shooting at you. You're going to find yourself in terrifying circumstances. You're going to be where everything that is happening will test your strength. The righteous will be afflicted, but "the Lord delivers him out of them all." Three times in this chapter we find this refrain reiterating deliverance: in verse 4, deliverance from fear; and in verse 17, deliverance from troubles; and again in verse 19, deliverance from all afflictions.

The point is clear: as far as God is concerned, there is no such thing as a hopeless situation.

Dominated by Fear

He keeps all his bones;
  not one of them is broken.
Evil shall slay the wicked;
  and those who hate the righteous
  will be condemned (vv. 20,21).

Verse 20 is a prophecy that came true at the crucifixion of our Lord. Verse 21 is simply statements of fact. The evil man, in the context of this chapter, is the one dominated by his fears. His own fears slay him. They are the things that frustrate him and inhibit him and keep him from realizing his manhood. Those who hate the righteous way—the way of total abandonment to the Lord—will be condemned to a life of fear and frustration and uselessness.

Freedom from Fear

Verse 22 is a postscript to the entire chapter.

> *The Lord redeems the life of his servants;*
> *none of those who take refuge in him*
> *will be condemned* (v. 22)

A literal translation of this would read, "The Lord keeps on redeeming the life of His servants." He keeps buying us up, replenishing us, filling us, flooding us, supplying everything that we need. He keeps redeeming the life of His servants; and the final promise is that we will never be paralyzed or dominated by fear.

One day I was driving to get our baby-sitter. My young son, Brian, was with me. Since it was a warm evening, he had short pants on and no shoes. As we came walking up to the house, there was a dog lying by the door. Without any warning, when I rang the doorbell, the dog jumped up, grabbed me by the right leg, and proceeded to gnaw away on my shinbone, while Brian started climbing up my left leg. You can imagine the predicament I was in, trying to get Brian around in back of me while, at the same time, trying to kick the dog. Brian, of course, realized that when the dog finished with me he was going to start on his bare leg, and he was really frightened.

Later on, after we finally got rid of the dog, I was sitting in the car driving home when Brian said, "Daddy, I'll go anywhere with you!" And I thought, "Boy, *that's* misplaced confidence. I'm never going back to that place again!" But I couldn't help but think how true it is of our heavenly Father, that He really is not afraid to go anywhere. I can honestly say I'll go anywhere with Him. I'm a very shy, timid person by nature. But I know from knowledge and experience that He is able, and I can trust Him to be the One I need in the most fearful circumstances.

Father, how thankful we are that you're the One we can count on. We have learned to distrust ourselves, that we're not the people we want to be. We've learned to rely upon your strength, to lay hold of you and thus discover that in your power we can be all that you ever intended us to be. And we thank you that we have tasted and that we can see that you are infinitely good. Thank you for that. And now as we look into the future, with all of its challenges and all the potentially frightening circumstances and all the good things that may come, although we don't know what is ahead, we know that you hold the future in your hands. And we know that as we walk with you, we can go anywhere. We thank you for that. In Jesus' name, Amen.

*This study is also by David H. Roper, one-time associate pastor at the Peninsula Bible Church, Palo Alto, California, now of Boise, Idaho.

Lo, I Come

One of the strange paradoxes about Jesus Christ is that, though He has been the subject of more books than any other person who has ever lived, He never left us a single written word from His hand. Others wrote down His sayings and recorded them for us, but He Himself left no written record of His life. Perhaps that is because, in some sense, the record had already been written. The Messianic psalms, those psalms that predict the coming of the Messiah, are often presented in the first person, where the Messiah Himself is speaking. That is the case in this fortieth Psalm, which is an account from the lips of the Messiah of His coming, His experiences, His reactions, and His motives in entering into this world to accomplish the work of redemption.

Like all of these psalms, this one arose out of a historic

occasion. There was some local situation to which this psalm applied, and some experience of deliverance on the part of the psalmist. The Holy Spirit in a marvelous way spoke through this man as he recorded his own experiences and caused him to express truths that were beyond his experience. His language grew greater than the event he was trying to describe. The only ultimate fulfillment was to be in those coming days when the Messiah would appear among men in the flesh. This fortieth Psalm, is, in a sense, our Lord's own autobiography. He Himself tells us why He came to earth, what was accomplished, and what His experiences were.

Now, as happens in some of the other psalms, this one begins with the conclusion. The writer gives us the position to which he comes, and then describes how he got there. Modern writers are learning this technique. Many people have gotten in the habit of reading the last chapter of a book first. Some of you do that because you cannot wait to find out how the story ends. So now writers have learned to put the last chapter first. They tell you how it turns out, and then they tell you how it happened, which holds your interest almost as well. That is what this psalm does.

A Song of Resurrection

It begins with a cry, a song of resurrection, as the Messiah here describes His experience in resurrection. Notice these first three verses:

> *I waited patiently for the Lord;*
>   *he inclined to me and heard my cry.*
> *He drew me up from the desolate pit,*
>   *out of the miry bog,*

> *and set my feet upon a rock,*
> *making my steps secure.*
> *He put a new song in my mouth,*
> *a song of praise to our God.*
> *Many will see and fear,*
> *and put their trust in the Lord* (vv. 1-3).

That is a description of resurrection. "He drew me up out of a deep and desolate pit" or, as the Hebrew has it, "out of the pit of tumult," out of a terrible experience, out of a place of desolation and despair and death.

Waiting Patiently for the Lord

His testimony begins, you will note, with a wait and a cry—"I waited patiently for the Lord." In terms of the experience of Jesus, this was a wait that occupied His entire life. At the age of 12, He came down from Nazareth to Jerusalem with His parents and went into the Temple to speak with the doctors and the scribes there and answer their questions. They were amazed at the answers He gave. When His parents missed Him and came and found Him at last in the Temple, He said, to them, "Do you not know that I must be about my Father's business?" (see Luke 2:49). Jesus was saying, "I am operating on the program my Father is unfolding before me. I am waiting patiently for Him as He unfolds the program and I move along in it." Do you remember that many times during His ministry He said to His disciples, "My hour is not yet come." I am waiting for something. My hour is not yet come. All that waiting was an experience of tumult and of desolation and of death in the midst of life.

Many Forms of Death

Life is often filled with death. Every experience that is

opposite to what God has designed for us is an experience of death. Bitterness and shame and sorrow, hate and greed and loneliness, are all forms of death that come into our lives right now. That is what our Lord was experiencing. He understands these things because He has been through them Himself. Ultimately they led Him, as they will lead us, to that final moment when life ends and death is before us, the deep, dark, desolation of death. But, He says, the Lord drew me out of that. He lifted me up from a desolate pit, out of a miry bog, and set my feet upon a rock, and made my steps secure.

First-Born from the Dead

That is a beautiful description of the experience of resurrection. None of us has ever been resurrected, and nobody before Jesus had ever been resurrected. There is a great difference between what happened to Lazarus and what happened to Jesus. Lazarus was really resuscitated; he was restored to this life almost as though he had been given mouth-to-mouth resuscitation. But Jesus was raised to a higher level of life. He was resurrected. He was the first born from the dead. He stepped into a whole new experience of life that God had designed from the beginning for mankind, an experience in which the body would be equal to the demands of the spirit. That is what the Messiah is describing here. The result is, "He put a new song in my mouth, a song of praise to our God" (v. 3).

A new song describes a new experience. When God does something great for you, you do not sit down and recite a proverb or compose a paragraph or devise a recipe. You write a song because singing is one of the best ways we have of expressing what is happening to us. And so He has a new song to celebrate a new kind of living, resurrected life. The effect of that resurrection life, He tells us, is going to be widespread. "Many will see and fear, and put their trust in the Lord" (v. 3). The effect of the resurrection of Jesus was that the story of Christianity, the message of the Christian gospel, exploded in the Roman world as the church literally thrust out in every direction and shook the world of that day.

During Jesus' lifetime many of the Jews said to Him, "Show us a sign that you are the Messiah." Now that was ridiculous, because every day that He ministered was a sign that He was the Messiah; the lame were made to walk, the eyes of the blind were opened, the dead were being raised to life, the captives were being set free. Yet these people came and said to Him, "Show us a sign." Finally, He said to them, "There will no sign be given you except the sign of the prophet Jonah." What did He mean? He went on to explain, "As Jonah was three days and three nights in the belly of the whale, so the son of man shall be three days and three nights in the depths of the earth" (see Matt. 12:38-40). In other words, "You will not believe until you hear of the Resurrection. When you learn that I have been raised from the dead, then your unbelief will flee. Then you will know—then you will *know* that what I have said is true." Our whole Christian faith has been grounded upon that basic rock of the resurrection of the Lord Jesus.

A New Song

You could put quotation marks around verses 4 and 5 in your Bible, because these are the words of the new song.

Blessed is the man who makes the Lord
his trust,
who does not turn to the proud,

to those who go astray after
false gods!
Thou hast multiplied, O Lord my God,
thy wondrous deeds and thy thoughts
toward us; none can compare with thee!
Were I to proclaim and tell of them,
they would be more than can be
numbered (vv. 4,5).

The Secret of Happiness

This song of resurrection has two elements that make it the new song. First is the secret of happiness. That word *blessed* is really the word *happy*. "Happy is the man,

---

HOW many today are being drawn away from the truth by the false belief that you can find in yourself all you need for living.

---

blessed is the man who makes the Lord his trust." One of the big lies of all history is the lie you hear on every side today: that man has hidden powers and abilities, which will be revealed if he just takes the right course or buys the right salve or uses the right cream. He will then be able to operate as he was intended to operate. That is a lie.

We were made to trust God, not ourselves. We were made to be dependent upon His activity in us. Blessed is the man who learns that secret. Happy is the man or woman who allows God to work through him or her. That is putting it positively. And then the negative: "who does not turn to the proud, to those who go astray after false gods!" (v. 4).

Oh, the lure of the false today! How many today are

being drawn away from the truth by the false belief that you can find in yourself all you need for living. "Do your own thing!" we are being told today. "Discover your own personality." I flicked on my car radio one day and a young female nightclub entertainer was being interviewed. The interviewer said to her, "Are you interested in getting married?" She said, "No, I'm not." He said, "Why not?" This was her reply: "Because I don't wish to share my life; I wish to be what I am." My heart sank for her when I heard those words because that is the philosophy which leads to despair. That is the philosophy which, in December of 1968, caused a leading socialite of San Francisco, a lineal descendant of President John Adams with all the wealth, influence, and power he ever wanted at his command, to take his own life in despair. But the song of resurrection is the song of those who have learned to trust in God.

All that God Offers

The second element of the song tells of the splendor of God's thoughts and His deeds toward man. As the writer says, "Thou has multiplied, O Lord my God, thy wondrous deeds and thy thoughts toward us; none can compare with thee!" (v. 5). The quality of this life is simply incomparable. It will do for you what nothing else will do. It will bring you into a level of existence you did not dream you could experience. Those are not mere words. This is not so much theological twaddle. It is actual, it is real. The New Testament promises: "Now to him who by the power at work within us is able to do far more abundantly than all we ask or think . . . " (Eph. 3:20). That is what God invites you to discover. All that God offers is simply beyond man's capacity to explore fully: "Were I to proclaim and tell of them, they would be more than can be numbered" (v. 5).

I am often struck by what Dr. John McIntyre, Professor of Nuclear Physics at Texas A & M University, said about studying the Bible. "We physicists have discovered many tremendously intriguing truths about nature, and the result has been an explosion of knowledge such as the world has never seen. Ah, but everyone of us is aware that, in the words of Sir Isaac Newton, 'We're but dabbling in the shallows of a vast ocean of knowledge that stretches unexplored before us.' And you know," he said, "that's the way I feel about the Bible. It's a vast revelation, which I've only begun to explore. And I can say, after 30 years of Bible study, there are times when I am simply dumbfounded with amazement at how much is in this book and how little I know of it. How vast is this unexplored area which breaks upon my astonished gaze to tell me more about who I am as a man, who God is, and how I'm related to Him." That is the resurrection of life.

Pathway to a Great Experience

Now beginning with verse 6 there is a sudden change in this psalm. We have covered the conclusion, the resurrection, and the life to which it brings us, but now the writer begins to trace for us the pathway to this great experience. Looking back now, tracing the course of Christ's experience, the psalmist begins, not on earth as we might expect, but in heaven. Verses 6 through 8 represent the words of the Messiah before He came to earth. These words are quoted in the tenth chapter of Hebrews, beginning with verse 5, where we are told definitely that Christ spoke these words as He stood on the threshold of time, about to step from heaven to earth, to the manger at Bethlehem. This is what he said.

Sacrifice and offering thou dost not desire;
but thou hast given me an open ear.
Burnt offering and sin offering
thou hast not required.
Then I said, "Lo, I come;
in the roll of the book it is written of me;
I delight to do thy will, O my God;
thy law is within my heart" (vv. 6-8).

The Fulness of Time

Have you ever thought of what was going on in heaven before the Lord Jesus was born on earth? Earth was wrapped in apathy and indifference. Nobody was ready for the coming of the King. A pagan emperor had sent forth a command for all the world to be enrolled. Men were busy with their own affairs, sunk in pagan darkness with very few gleams of light. But in heaven everything was aglow and abuzz with anticipation and excitement. The fulness of time had come. The angels understood. God was to bring forth His Son, born of a woman, made under the Law. In another part of Hebrews the writer tells us that when He brought His firstborn Son into the world, He cried, "Let all God's angels worship him" (Heb. 1:6). What a tremendous scene there must have been in heaven before Jesus came to earth, when the vast uncounted multitudes of angels were gathered in adoring worship of the Son of God.

An Open Ear

And why were they worshiping Him? Because of two things that He understood and was ready to fulfil. One, He knew something. He expresses it in these words: "Sacrifice and offering thou dost not desire." Put the next few words in parentheses and leave out the word *but*, "Thou hast given me an open ear." He goes on to say, "Burnt offering and sin offering thou hast not required."

Let me deal with the parenthetical phrase first. When He says, "Thou hast given me an open ear," He is referring to His readiness to hear, readiness to understand and learn. Isaiah gives us a beautiful picture of this same thing in the 50th chapter, another passage that points to the Messiah:

> *The Lord God has given me*
> *the tongue of those who are taught,*
> *that I may know how to sustain with a word*
> *him that is weary.*
> *Morning by morning he wakens,*
> *he wakens my ear*
> *to hear as those who are taught.*
> *The Lord God has opened my ear,*
> *and I was not rebellious,*
> *I turned not backward.*
> *I gave my back to the smiters,*
> *and my cheeks to those who pulled out the beard;*
> *I hid not my face*
> *from shame and spitting"* (vv. 4-6).

Understanding Humanity

Isn't that beautiful? The Messiah came with the tongue of a learner that He might know how to sustain with a word those who were weary. You see, He understood something about humanity. He understood that God did not want sacrifices of lambs and bulls and goats, and all the blood offerings. That was not what He was really after.

> *"Not all the blood of beasts*
> *On Jewish altars slain,*

Could give the guilty conscience peace
Or wash away the stain" (Isaac Watts, Public domain).

Jesus understood that God had given these sacrifices to teach men something.

Every time a man took a lamb and slit its throat so the warm blood ran out and the little lamb died so as to be offered on an altar as a sacrifice, God was saying something to humanity in very graphic terms, something that men ought not to have forgotten. He was telling us that the sickness that grips mankind, the awful power within that twists and distorts and wrecks and ruins our humanity cannot be dealt with lightly. It cannot be handled with but a few resolutions or with an earnest attempt to try to be better. It cannot be taken care of by some religious abracadabra. This sickness is deeper than that. It took the death of an innocent substitute, One who was Himself part of mankind, to cure the rotten core of our humanity.

There are many analyses offered today of the problems we are facing, and in many cases, I think, the analyses are right. You can hear people telling us in loud and clamant terms that what we ought to do is to love one another. And they are right. We desperately need above everything else to act in love toward one another. But the problem of love can never be solved by a few slogans and placards and songs. It is one thing to know what to do; it is another thing to do it. And that is where the rub lies. How can you love when irritations come and selfishness arises and you find yourself caught up in a "me first" philosophy. How do you love one another then?

The Only Solution
The Lord Jesus understood that this problem could never

be solved until the life of sin-bedeviled humanity was somehow poured out in death. And, understanding that, He said, "Lo, I have come to do thy will, O God, [to give up my life that humanity might be free] as it is written of me in the roll of the book [it has been predicted that I would come]" (Heb. 10:7; also see Isa. 61:1-3). To this day there is no other solution to the problems that grip

---

HE came to tell men that, despite all their evil, all the strife, the sin, the agony, the filth, the despair, and the shame of which humanity was guilty, God loved this lost and struggling world.

---

humanity. The only solution is in delighting to do the will of God. Jesus came fulfilling the Father's will; He came to make Himself wholly available to God to show mankind how it could be done. Throughout the record of those marvelous 33 years, Jesus was instantly and constantly available for the Father to express His life through the Son. There was never a moment when the Lord Jesus stepped out of that relationship.

The Love of God

The following words describe what happened after He came. First He gave a proclamation:

> I have told the glad news of deliverance
>   in the great congregation;
> lo, I have not restrained my lips,

as thou knowest, O Lord.
I have not hid thy saving help within
my heart,
I have spoken of thy faithfulness
and thy salvation;
I have not concealed thy steadfast
love and thy faithfulness
from the great congregation (vv. 9,10).

What was the heart of His message? Why, it was the love of God! He came to tell men that, despite all their evil, all the strife, the sin, the agony, the filth, the despair, and the shame of which humanity was guilty, God loved this lost and struggling world. He came to tell men of a faithful love, a steadfast love and a saving help that could set men free. He came not only to speak these gracious words, but also to demonstrate God's love. As John tells us in the opening words of his Gospel, "In the beginning was the Word, and the Word was with God, and the Word was God . . . . And the Word became flesh and dwelt among us, full of grace and truth; we have beheld his glory, glory as of the only Son from the Father" (John 1:1,14).

Grace and truth are the two attributes reflected in this psalm. Watch the Lord Jesus and see the graciousness of His words. He teaches the disciples by setting a little child in their midst. He shows grace toward the afflicted, and toward those who were caught in the act of sin. Read through your New Testament and find one place were Jesus Christ ever spoke harshly to a man or woman caught in an act of sin. He spoke harshly to the hypocrites, those who would not acknowledge their guilt, but you will never find one occasion where He condemned the one who had been caught red-handed.

He also spoke words of truth. There is a hint in these last words of verse 10 that it was sometimes difficult for Him to speak the truth. "I have not concealed thy steadfast love and thy faithfulness . . . " He was under pressure to conceal it at times. He spoke the truth even when the truth hurt. There were some who hated Him and they took counsel together to put Him to death because He told them the truth about themselves. Nevertheless, He was always the faithful witness speaking words of grace and words of truth.

A Cry for Mercy

Then, beginning with verse 11 on through 17, we read the description of His suffering, the infinite character of His suffering. This passage, by the way, is the cry that He speaks of in verse 1, a cry that arose from the very edge of the grave.

> *Do not thou, O Lord, withhold thy mercy*
> *from me,*
> *let thy steadfast love and thy faithfulness*
> *ever preserve me!*
> *For evils have encompasssed me without*
> *number;*
> *my iniquities have overtaken me,*
> *till I cannot see;*
> *they are more than the hairs of my head;*
> *my heart fails me* (vv. 11,12).

How could he say "my iniquities have overtaken me"? He had no iniquities. It is true that these words, growing out of the historical situation, did apply originally to a man who was guilty of iniquity. But in the application to the Messiah these words become the confession of sins of which He Himself was not a part, but which He had made His own at the cross. We are dealing here with that mystery, strange beyond any explanation. Paul described it in 2 Corinthians when he said, "For our sake he made him to be sin who knew no sin, so that in him we might become the righteousness of God" (2 Cor. 5:21). And from Isaiah 53 come those amazing words: "But he was wounded for our transgressions, he was bruised for our iniquities; the chastisement of our peace was upon him; and with his stripes we are healed" (v. 5, *KJV*).

A Prayer for His Enemies

Then the Messiah goes on to pray for His enemies. Remember how He prayed from the cross, "Father, forgive them; for they know not what they do" (Luke 23:34). You get the elements of that prayer in verses 13 through 15:

> *Be pleased, O Lord, to deliver me!*
> *O Lord, make haste to help me!*
> *Let them be put to shame and confusion*
> *altogether who seek to snatch away my life;*
> *let them be turned back and brought*
> *to dishonor who desire my hurt!*
> *Let them be appalled because of their*
> *shame who say to me, "Aha, Aha!"* (vv. 13-15).

"Well," you say, "that doesn't sound like forgiveness to me. He's praying that they be put to shame, and that they be turned back and brought to dishonor." But think a minute. What is necessary to experience forgiveness? You must admit that you need to be forgiven, otherwise you cannot experience forgiveness. That is what our Lord is praying for here. He is asking that God will arrest His enemies in the progress of their evil. "Stop them," He says. "Bring them to shame and confusion so they will not go on any further. And then open their eyes to the reality of what they are doing. Make them in their shame, in their understanding of the terrible deed they are doing, become aware of their guilt and their folly. And then, Father, extend to them that forgiveness that awaits the confession of a guilty heart."

A Prayer for His Friends

In verse 16 He is praying for His friends,

> But may all who seek thee rejoice
>   and be glad in thee;
> may those who love thy salvation
>   say continually, "Great is the Lord!" (v. 17).

The Infinite Mystery of the Incarnation

The final verse is the cry of agony from His heart. The wheel has come full circle now, and when He has explained to us how He came at last to the place of resurrection, He cries out,

> As for me, I am poor and needy;
>   but the Lord takes thought for me.
> Thou art my help and my deliverer;
>   do not tarry, O my God! (v. 17).

That, He says, is the way I came to the place where I could sing,

> *He drew me up from the desolate pit,*
> *out of the miry bog,*
> *and set my feet upon a rock,*
> *making my steps secure.*
> *He put a new song in my mouth,*
> *a song of praise to our God* (vv. 2,3).

There is the infinite mystery of the incarnation.

Isn't it marvelous that these words were written 1000 years before our Lord ever came to earth, yet they outline so clearly and so accurately the course that He would follow when He came. And today, 2000 years this side of the cross, we are faced with the marvel of the infinite God becoming a finite man. The Word that was with God, and was God, became flesh and dwelt among us in order to reveal what God was like. And the message of that revelation is unquestionable and clear today. There is no other hope for mankind but in Him.

No Other Hope

You and I are living now in a day when men are afraid of what is coming to pass. The greatest thinkers of our time are looking forward, faced with the insuperable problems that this world has produced, and they are giving us little hope. They are saying, "If we don't find a way out of this mess soon, it's hopeless! We'll never solve the problems that are facing us now!" They are telling us the problems that face the individual are beyond his ability to solve on his own—the bitterness, the boredom, the emptiness, the meaninglessness of life. All of this simply bears confirmation in our day and to our hearts personally that this psalm is telling us truth.

There is no other hope for mankind than the gospel of

Jesus Christ—no way out of darkness. There is no way to break the power and the grip of this evil sickness that has seized our race. The gospel has no rivals; it is absolutely without peer. It is the one way by which we can find what God intended man to have. Hear these words of the nineteenth century poet Christina Rossetti:

> *"None other Lamb! none other name!*
> *None other hope in heaven, or earth, or sea!*
> *None other hiding-place for sin and shame!*
> *None beside Thee!*
>
> *"My faith burns low; my hope burns low;*
> *Only my soul's deep need comes out in me*
> *By the deep thunder of its wants and woe,*
> *Calls out to Thee.*
>
> *"Lord, Thou art life though I be dead!*
> *Love's Flame art Thou, however cold I be!*
> *Nor heavens have I, nor place to lay my head,*
> *Nor home, but Thee."*

How we ought to give thanks, our Father, for this wonderful message. In the infinite mystery of your workings, He, who is greater than all the world, all of time, all of history, became a man in history, became a babe, "a tiny baby-thing that made a mother cry." Our Father, we pray that we may see that it was done deliberately, voluntarily, with understanding, because He knew what we were facing and He knew there was no other way to work out our salvation. "For there is none other name under heaven given among men, whereby we must be saved" (Acts 4:12, *KJV*) but Jesus' name. It was well said to Joseph and Mary, "Thou shalt call his name Jesus: for he shall save his people from their sins" (Matt. 1:21, *KJV*). We thank you, Father, in His name, Amen.

A Song of Confidence

As we have seen earlier, the book of Psalms falls into five different divisions, which correspond to the five opening books of the Bible: Genesis, Exodus, Leviticus, Numbers, Deuteronomy. These five books of Moses spell out the pattern of God's working with men.

The book of Genesis is the book of foundations. It is fittingly introduced by the first Psalm, which sets forth the only two ways of life: the godly versus the ungodly. The second book of the Psalms begins with Psalm 42 and corresponds with the book of Exodus, the story of redemption. It tells of God calling Israel out of Egypt and redeeming them by the blood of the Passover lamb. It is the story, in other words, of the work of God on behalf of man. It is most fittingly introduced by the forty-second Psalm, which is an expression of the confidence of man in God in a time of trouble. Since we all have troubles, this is a very appropriate psalm at any stage of life.

We need only to read Psalm 43 to see that it belongs with Psalm 42. Once these were probably one psalm but they were divided somehow into two, although they clearly belong together. We will handle Psalms 42 and 43 as one. The key to this psalm is found in the repeated refrain, which is found in 42:5,11 and 43:5.

Handling Our Blue Moods

Why are you cast down, O my soul,
  and why are you disquieted within me?
Hope in God; for I shall again praise Him,
  my help and my God (v. 5).

If you refer to the inscription that introduces this psalm you will note it is addressed to the choirmaster, and is called a Maskil of the Sons of Korah. These inscriptions are part of the inspired record; they belong with the psalm and indicate something vital about it. *Maskil* is the Hebrew word for teaching. This psalm is intended to teach something to us. What? Judging by the repeated refrain, it is intended to teach us how to handle our blue moods, those times when we get up in the morning and say, "Why are you cast down, O my soul, and why are you disquieted within me?"

Hope in God
We all know there are some mornings when we spring out of bed, bright-eyed and bushy-tailed, and say, "Good morning, God." There are other mornings when we only

manage to pry open our eyelids, sit dejectedly on the side of the bed and say, "Good God, it's morning." These are the mornings that are in view here. The answer to each blue mood is, "Hope thou in God," wait for God. He is working out His purposes and if you hang on you will yet praise Him.

Just a further word on the inscriptions. The Sons of Korah were a family of singers in Israel who passed along their musical office from generation to generation, and were noted as an outstanding family of musicians. Several of the psalms come from them. The experience, which this psalm reflects, was unquestionably David's, but it was put to music by the Korah Family Singers and dedicated to the Chief Musician, or the Royal Choirmaster. Most of us believe that the blues songs began with "The St. Louis Blues" but actually they began in Jerusalem with "The King David Blues." Here is one of The King David Blues.

Some scholars feel that the occasion reflected in this psalm was when David was excluded from the Temple at the time of Absalom's rebellion. Late in David's reign Absalom took over the kingdom temporarily and David was driven into exile outside Jerusalem. There is no mention of this in the psalm, but it clearly reflects a time of depression and frustration. But David does not accept that blue mood, that depression of spirit, as inevitable. He does something about it.

A Common Experience

None of us need think that because we are Christians we shall escape times of depression; they will come. But when they come, we ought to do something about them. I am afraid most Christians simply succumb to them. They go along making everybody around them miserable because they are passing through a time of depression. They are in a bad mood, and they wait for it to pass but do nothing about it.

Lest you think that some of the great saints have never had this kind of trouble, let me share with you a quotation from an outstanding theologian and preacher of the nineteenth century, Dr. John Henry Jowett. He once wrote to a friend:

> "I wish you wouldn't think I'm such a saint. You seem to imagine that I have no ups-and-downs but just a level and lofty stretch of spiritual attainment with unbroken joy and equanimity. By no means. I am often perfectly wretched, and everything appears most murky. I often feel as though my religious life had only just begun and that I am in the kindergarten age. But I can usually trace these miserable seasons to some personal cause, and the first thing to do is to attend to that cause and get it into the sunshine again" (source unknown).

Look for the Sun

This psalm attempts to teach us how to get into the sunshine again. As we look at it you will note that it traces three stages of the psalmist's experience, and at the end of each stage there comes the refrain that describes what brought him through, "Hope in God; for I shall again praise him, my help and my God."

Yearning for God

Now the first stage is one of intense longing and desire.

> *As a hart longs for flowing streams,*
> *so longs my soul for thee, O God.*
> *My soul thirsts for God,*
> *for the living God.*
> *When shall I come and behold*
> *the face of God?* (vv. 1,2).

How beautifully he puts that! As the deer running through the woods longs for water, so his soul is thirsting after God. He has reached the place in his experience where he knows only God can meet his need. He longs to come into a relationship of freshness and revitalizing fellowship that will quench his soul-thirst.

We learn why he so thirsts in the question he asks at the close of verse 2, "When shall I come and behold the face of God?" In other words, he is experiencing a sense of God's delay. There is no doubt in his heart but that there is help for him in God. He expects to find it. He knows God has met his need in the past and he expects Him to meet it again. But for some reason that help is delayed and this is hard for him to bear.

When God immediately answers your prayer and buoys up your dejected spirit and you find yourself strengthened, it is wonderful. This is the common, usual experience of most Christians. But there will also be times when God apparently does nothing. There will be times when He lets you wait. Those times of delay are the times that threaten and test our faith. That is what David is experiencing here.

Recalling the Past

It was made worse by the present taunts of his enemies and the thoughts of past experiences of joy.

My tears have been my food day and night,
while men say to me continually,
    "Where is your God?"
These things I remember,
    as I pour out my soul:
how I went with the throng,
    and led them in procession to the house
    of God,
with glad shouts and songs of thanksgiving,
    a multitude keeping festival (vv. 3,4).

He cannot sleep or eat because of his sorrow, his long-ing for God. He starts recalling the past. In the Hebrew it says, "I *will* remember." This is a strong expression of determination. He is determined to remember how God has helped him in the past. That is one of the greatest things to do when you begin to experience depression of spirit. Think back to what God has done for you in the past. Remember! Some people have a habit of remember-ing only the bad things. They date everything by these. "That was the day the garage caught on fire." "Oh, yes, I remember. That was the day when the baby fell in the gar-bage can." Everything is dated from unhappy circum-stances. "I remember that week! That was the week when the boss came to work with a hangover."

But here the psalmist is showing us that memory can be an important aid to thinking of the positive experiences of God's blessing. "I will remember," he says, "the times when God caused my heart to exult with joy, and shut the mouth of all my taunting enemies by answering in such a way that everyone could see that it was God's hand at work."

A Time of Testing

Several years ago I was in Tyler, Texas, accompanied on my speaking schedule by Mr. Ed Murphy of Overseas Crusades. I have known Ed for a number of years but I had never heard the full story of his Christian experience till he told it there. It was thrilling. He had been raised in a Roman Catholic family in the New England area. He was 14 years old before he even saw a Protestant. When he saw his first one he expected to see horns sprouting from his head and a tail waving around behind. Through a remarkable experience where God put him in a lonely lumber camp with a Christian boy, Ed came to know the Lord Jesus Christ. This lad gave him a New Testament and, through the reading of that New Testament, Ed Murphy's soul was captured for Christ.

Some time afterward he determined to obey God's call to go to a mission field, and he enrolled in Biola College. When his Catholic family heard that he was planning to go to Bible school they called him in and told him that if he went there he could never be their son again. His mother was particularly opposed to it and told him that if he went he was never to come home again. But Ed felt led of God and so he went to Bible school. When he drew near the close of the first year he had a job lined up for the summer to meet his expenses but he was lacking $60 to pay the final bills for the current semester. Before he took his final exam, it was required that he pay this money. He tried every way he knew to raise the money, but he couldn't.

Finally, in desperation, he wrote his mother saying, "Mother, I know you don't like what I'm doing, but I feel led of God to do it. I have now come to a difficult time. I lack $60 of my school expenses and I have to pay it before I take my final exam. You've helped me in other matters in the past and I just wondered if perhaps you might relent and help me again. I'll pay you back this summer."

His mother wrote back, "Son, when you left this house to go to a Protestant Bible college, I told you that you were never to come back again. I wanted nothing to do with you as long as you continued in the Protestant faith. You told me at that time that your God would take care of you but now that you come to a time of trouble you run back to me. If your God is really the God you say He is, then let Him take care of you. I will be in Los Angeles this next weekend. You tell me that if you haven't received this money you will have to drop out of school. I'll be at this address and if you want to come home with me, come there, and I'll know that you've dropped all this foolishness."

It was a great time of testing for Ed. He prayed about it, asked God again to supply, but the day came on which he had to take the exams and there was no money. So he packed his bags, called his mother and told her he would meet her to go home with her. Just as he was going out the door with his bags the Dean of Education stopped him and asked him to come into the office for a moment.

Ed went in and the Dean said, "How much is it that you owe the school?"

Ed said, "Sixty dollars."

The Dean said, "Well, it's strange. Just as you were going down the hall I was reading this slip with your name on it, which says you have $40 to your credit."

Ed said, "There must be some mistake. I don't know anything about that. I only know I owe the $60."

So the Dean called to check it out and it turned out that someone that very morning, quite anonymously, had sent in $100, credited to the account of Ed Murphy.

Sharing Our Testimony

When he went to meet his mother she said, "Well, son, you've given up your Protestant faith, have you?"

He said, "No, mother, I haven't."

She said, "But you can't go back to school."

He said, "Yes, I can. God has supplied and given me not only the $60 but $40 in addition."

His mother did not say a word. She turned around, went out the door, and went home. But two weeks later she wrote to him, "Ed, I want to know this kind of a God." That incident has been a source of strength to Ed Murphy through the years. Whenever he is discouraged he looks back to the time when God dealt with him in this remarkable way.

Remembering His Faithfulness

And that is what this psalmist is doing. He is looking back and remembering the times when God has so remarkably delivered him that his soul was filled with exultation and joy. He is obviously hoping that this will relieve his fears now, but it does not. So he reminds himself in the refrain,

> *Why are you cast down, O my soul,*
> *and why are you disquieted within me?*
> *Hope in God; for I shall again praise him,*
> *my help and my God* (v. 5).

Learning from Nature

But his trial is not over. He has reached a second stage and he tries another tactic. He says,

> *My soul is cast down within me,*
> *therefore I remember thee*

from the land of Jordan and of Hermon,
from Mount Mizar.
Deep calls to deep
at the thunder of thy cataracts;
all thy waves and thy billows
have gone over me.
By day the Lord commands his steadfast love;
and at night his song is with me,
a prayer to the God of my life (vv. 6-8).

He is still despondent. His remembering of the past has not worked. Usually it does. Usually this is enough to deliver us from this nagging fear that God is not going to do anything at all. But now it does not, and so he tries to

---

THE nature of God is linked up to the nature of the believer and that relationship never changes.

---

help by remembering something else: an experience that he had when he was in the northern part of Israel near Mount Hermon, at the head of the Jordan River, on a peak of the range where Mount Hermon is located, called Mount Mizar (which, incidentally, means "little mountain"). On that occasion he could hear the waterfalls of that mountainous region, the thundering cataracts. He became aware of how they seemed to be calling to one another, "deep calling unto deep," and it reminded him that the deeps in God call out to the deeps in man.

One of the amazing things about nature is the silent voices that call to one another across vast spaces. The moon calls to the deeps in the sea, raising the tides. Twice a day the waters rise in tides across the earth, because of the moon calling to the ocean. You know how the sun and the rain call to the deeps in a seed, causing it to stir with life and to spring up and grow. There are vast distances that call to the deeps in wild birds, causing them to wing their way across trackless wastes to lay their eggs; there are voices that call to certain fish, sending them across the seas to spawn.

In this way the psalmist is reminded that God also calls to man. There are deeps in God that correspond with deeps in man and He calls to them. The psalmist specifically names two here; the deeps of the love of God, and the joy of God, calling out to the corresponding deeps of prayer in the believer.

His Steadfast Love

By day the Lord commands his steadfast love;
and at night his song is with me,
a prayer to the God of my life (v. 8).

The love and joy of God call out from this man a prayer to the God of his life. This helps him. He is remembering that the nature of God is linked up to the nature of the believer and that relationship never changes. Even though he does not feel anything, they are there; these silent deeps in God calling out to the deeps in man. This usually steadies him, strengthens him and helps him. It is an excellent way to dispel the blues. Remember that what God has said about you, and therefore what is true about you, does not change. There are deep ties that are never broken between the believer and his God.

Has God Forgotten?

But this time even that does not work for the psalmist. He expresses his reaction in verses 9 and 10.

> *I say to God, my rock;*
>   *"Why hast thou forgotten me?*
> *Why go I mourning*
>   *because of the oppression of the enemy?"*
> *As with a deadly wound in my body,*
>   *my adversaries taunt me,*
> *while they say to me continually,*
>   *"Where is your God?"* (vv. 9,10).

He is still deeply troubled. The two usual means for dispelling depression have not helped him this time. He has not been able to shake his sense of God's untimely delay, and now it has grown into a nagging, torturing doubt: "Why hast thou forgotten me?"

One Sunday morning after the service I left for home by myself. My little seven-year-old daughter, Laurie, was in children's church. I thought she was with her mother. Her mother thought she was with me. So Laurie was left behind. Of course, as soon as we reached home we missed her, and I came right back. I found her waiting for me, tears standing in her eyes, and with the utmost reproach in her voice, she said, "Daddy, you forgot me!"

What a horrible feeling it is to be forgotten! It did not hurt her that she was a little late; it was just that she thought we had all forgotten her. That is the feeling expressed here, and what a terrible feeling it is. David says, "My enemies taunt me with this, and it is like a deadly wound in my body, like a dagger in the heart."

Actually the Hebrew is even stronger, *"As with murder in my bones,* my adversaries taunt me continually, saying, 'Where is your God?'" Faith can only reply,

> *Hope in God; for I shall again praise him,*
> *my help and my God* (v. 11).

A Place of Despair

Then we reach the third phase of his experience. The psalmist cries out now in desperation,

> *Vindicate me, O God, and defend my cause*
> *against an ungodly people;*
> *from deceitful and unjust men*
> *deliver me!* (43:1).

A Gross Injustice

We all know something of this problem. Men have betrayed him, mistreated him; it is a gross injustice. How common that is. How many times do we feel that those whom we have trusted have betrayed us, have deceived us, taken advantage of us. He cries out,

> *For thou art the God in whom I take refuge;*
> *why hast thou cast me off?*
> *Why go I mourning*
> *because of the oppression of the enemy?* (v. 2).

This time his question reveals he has reached the place of despair. "Why have you abandoned me? Why have you cast me off? I've taken refuge in you, God, and yet you do nothing, absolutely nothing. You have abandoned me, cast me away. I feel utterly forsaken." Have you ever felt that God has totally abandoned you? It is the greatest test of faith when the God to whom you cry apparently does nothing.

The Ultimate Refuge

But now he realizes, at last, the way out.

> *Oh send out thy light and thy truth;*
> *let them lead me,*
> *let them bring me to thy holy hill*
> *and to thy dwelling!*
> *Then I will go to the altar of God,*
> *to God my exceeding joy;*
> *and I will praise thee with the lyre,*
> *O God, my God* (v. 3,4).

What a word of final triumph! Now he understands that God is driving him step by step to the ultimate refuge of any believer in any time of testing: the truth of God coupled with the light. The truth is God's Word; the light is your understanding of it. He is crying out for an understanding of the Word as he reads it; light, breaking out of these marvelous promises, to encourage and strengthen his heart. He says, "If you will do that, God, then my heart will be filled with joy and with gladness, and I will praise you with the harp; for you, O God, are my God, my personal God." What a comfort that is.

There comes a time in each of our lives when we discover for ourselves that the ultimate refuge of any believer is in the Word of God, in what God has said. I remember such a time in my early ministry. I had just begun my work at Peninsula Bible Church when there came to me a young man who was having severe marital problems. He was in his 20s, and his wife had just divorced him. He was left with a boy about five years of age. He came to me for help, and I tried to help him as best I could and, through the circumstances, led him to Christ.

For a few weeks there was a real change in this young man's life. He gained firm hold on God. But, as often happens, there came a time of testing of his faith, and he was plunged into despair. One Sunday morning he called me up just before church and asked me over the phone for help and prayer. I counseled with him and we prayed together. I told him that as soon as the church service was over I would come to see him. When the service ended I went up to the house and knocked but there was no answer. I knew he should be there, so I knocked again, but still no answer. Finally, I tried the door, saw it was open, and went in. He was nowhere to be found until I went into the bedroom. There I found him lying in a spreading pool of blood, dead by his own hand.

It was a shock, a most terrible shock. I called the police and made arrangements, and then went home. The rest of the day I was shaken, unnerved, and did not know what to do. I was experiencing a combination of the emotions of fear, anger, sorrow, and grief. I was upset, and did not know whether I wanted to continue in the ministry; it seemed so senseless and useless. I tried every way to find help. I prayed, but it did not seem to relieve me. I talked with others, tried to keep busy, but nothing worked.

Finally, that night, fearing that I would lie sleepless all night long, my wife and I together took our Bibles and began to read. To this day I do not know what we read, but I remember that every word came like balm, like healing salve, to my heart. I have thought since of that marvelous phrase in Psalm 107, "He sent forth his word, and healed them" (v. 20). In that time of deep, dark despair and frustration, the reading of the Word healed my heart.

Stand Upon His Word

That is what this psalmist is saying. When you can't shake the blues, and you have a depression of spirit that nothing seems to relieve; when you have tried to remember the past, and tried to recall the unshakable, unchangeable relationships that exist between you and God, but nothing helps; then there is nothing left but to rest upon His Word, His truth, and to allow that to heal the heart. So the psalmist closes again with the refrain that catches up the whole meaning of this song,

> *Why are you cast down, O my soul,*
> *and why are you disquieted within me?*
> *Hope in God; for I shall again*
> *praise him,*
> *my help and my God* (v. 5).

Yes, hope in God, for He is working out His purposes. That is what the New Testament means when it says, "Having done all, stand" (see Eph. 6:13). Stand upon His Word.

Our Father, how grateful we are for this remarkable psalm and its help to our hearts in times of depression. Help us, Lord, to lay hold of it and use it in our lives, knowing this was written for our instruction, upon whom the ends of the age have come. We thank you in Jesus' name, Amen.

The King in His Beauty

Before getting into our study of Psalm 45, it is fitting that we should take a broad look at some of the psalms that are called the Messianic psalms, that is, the psalms that look forward to the coming of the Messiah. There are a number of them in these songs of faith. Both Jewish and Christian commentators agree that several of these psalms do portray the coming of the Messiah.

Some of them are well known. They cover various facets of the life and ministry of the Messiah. Psalm 22, as we have already discovered, is one of the most striking and graphic descriptions we have in the whole of the Bible of the crucifixion of Jesus Christ. Psalm 16 describes the resurrection of Jesus. On the Day of Pentecost, when the apostle Peter stood up and spoke to the gathered multitudes after the manifestation of the Holy Spirit's presence among them, he used the sixteenth Psalm to prove to his audience that the Scriptures had foretold Jesus' resurrection from the dead. Psalm 69 describes the betrayal of Judas, and how the Lord would react to that betrayal. Psalm 110 is a wonderful description of His present ministry with us, what the book of Hebrews calls the Melchizedek priesthood of Jesus. These Messianic psalms give us facts about the ministry of Christ that we would not have known otherwise, even from the Gospels.

Jesus Himself said that the Scriptures spoke of Him. In the twenty-fourth chapter of Luke's Gospel, as Jesus appeared to the disciples in the Upper Room after His resurrection, He said to them, "These are my words which I spoke to you, while I was still with you, that everything written about me in the law of Moses and the prophets and the psalms must be fulfilled" (v. 44). As He read the psalms He noted in them various things concerning Himself, and these were all fulfilled in His ministry.

There are three psalms that picture Jesus as King. Psalm 2 is a picture of the King in His authority: "Why do the nations conspire, and the peoples plot in vain?" (v. 1). Here the nations of the world are upset and God says in the midst of their confusion, "I have set my king on Zion, my holy hill" (v. 2:6). And He warns the nations, "Kiss his feet, lest . . . you perish in the way" (v. 11).

Then in Psalm 72 we have another beautiful description of Messiah as the king. This is a wonderful picture of the day that is coming when Messiah shall reign throughout the earth. The earth shall be restored in beauty and splendor, and peace shall fill the earth as the waters fill the sea.

A Song of Love to the King

In Psalm 45 we are looking at the king in his beauty. It is a glimpse of the character, beauty and the perfections of Jesus Christ. Evidently this psalm was originally written to commemorate the marriage of a king, probably King Solomon, at the time of his marriage to the daughter of the king of Tyre, which is mentioned in the book of Chronicles. But here is a description that goes far beyond the earthly wedding service. These words could never be limited to an earthly king. Even the Jewish commentators on this passage recognize that this is a picture of the Messiah in His coming. The first nine verses describe to us the King in His beauty, and it opens with a personal note from the author.

> *My heart overflows with a goodly theme;*
> *I address my verses to the king;*
> *my tongue is like the pen of a*
> *ready scribe* (v. 1).

This is clearly what the inscription of the psalm says, a love song. It is inspired by the love of this writer for the King, whom he sees. And as the inscription also tells us, it is a Maskil, or a teaching psalm. It is designed to teach us something about the beauty of the King. There is no other way to interpret this than to see it as applying to and being fulfilled in the ministry of the Lord Jesus Christ.

This writer confesses an eagerness to write. Words flow easily. "My tongue," he says, "is like a pen of a ready writer." That is what love does to you. It makes you ready to write. Years ago when my son-in-law left for Vietnam just one week after his marriage to my daughter, we started receiving letters. They came every day. Day after

day, week after week, there came a letter from him.
Unfortunately they were not addressed to the family so I
don't know what was in them. But I was struck by a
remarkable phenomenon. He had never been a letter
writer before, but suddenly the words just flowed from his
pen. That is what love does to you.

Fairer than the Sons of Men

Here is one who has fallen in love with the King in His
beauty and he describes Him to us. First of all there is the
general impression created by the King.

> *You are the fairest of the sons of men;*
> *grace is poured upon your lips;*
> *therefore God has blessed you for ever* (v. 2).

What an incomparable person this is, says this writer.
There is no one like Him. No one can compare to Him. He
is fairer than the sons of men.

I think we get a hint here of the physical appearance of
Jesus Christ. I know there are many who have tried to
guess what Jesus looked like, and it is amazing that in the
Gospels we are never given a hint of His physical appearance. Many painters have tried to portray how He looked.
Some have felt that perhaps He was very ugly, marred,
disfigured, and unattractive. They draw that from the
words in Isaiah 52, "As many were astonished at him—his
appearance was so marred, beyond human semblance, and
his form beyond that of the sons of men—" (v. 14). And in
Isaiah 53 we read, "He was despised and rejected by
men . . . " (v. 3). I have never belonged to that school of
thought because I feel those words in Isaiah 52 and 53 are
a description of what happened to Him on the cross. Our
Lord in His lifetime was evidently a most attractive per-

son. Everywhere He went children flocked to Him and the multitudes followed Him, not only to hang upon His words, but drawn by His beauty. As this writer says, "He is the fairest of sons of men." I think we capture this in that favorite hymn of many, "Fairest Lord Jesus, Ruler of all nature."

Words of Grace

Even more impressive and remarkable than His appearance, says this writer, are the words that came from His lips:

> *Grace is poured upon your lips;*
> *therefore God has blessed you for ever* (v. 2).

Luke tells us that on one occasion Jesus went into the synagogue in Nazareth, His hometown, and there among the people who had watched Him grow up as a boy, He stood up and asked for the scroll of the prophet Isaiah. He opened it and read to them the words from the sixty-first chapter that are predictive of Him and His ministry, "The Spirit of the Lord is upon me, because he has anointed me to preach good news to the poor. He has sent me to proclaim release to the captives and recovering of sight to the blind, to set at liberty those who are oppressed, to proclaim the acceptable year of the Lord" (Luke 4:18,19). Then He closed the roll and said, "Today this scripture has been fulfilled in your hearing" (v. 21).

Setting People Free

At the close of the message, after He had preached other things, it is recorded that "all spoke well of him, and wondered at the gracious words which proceeded out of his mouth" (v. 22). His words captivated people as they saw that here was One who knew the secrets of life. The crowds followed Him and the multitudes sought Him out, forgetting their work, their lunch, and everything else in order that they might hang upon these words. No wonder they said of Him, "Never did man speak like this man!" (see John 7:46). He Himself said that His words would have this power. He said to His disciples, "If you continue in my words, then you shall be my disciples indeed. You shall know the truth and the truth will set you free" (see John 8:31,32). That has been the experience of many hundreds of thousands through the generations as they have listened to the words of Jesus and have been set free to become the men and women God intended them to be.

Amazing Accomplishments

A number of writers have tried to capture in one way or another the incomparable character of Jesus Christ and to put it down in writing. I have seen several attempts on this, but here is one that has always struck me as being very realistic and true.

"More than 1900 years ago there was a man born contrary to the laws of life. This man lived in poverty and was reared in obscurity. He did not travel extensively. Only once did he cross the boundary of the country in which he lived and that was during his exile in childhood. He possessed neither wealth nor influence. His relatives were inconspicuous and had neither training nor formal education.

"Yet in infancy he startled a king; in childhood he puzzled doctors; in manhood he ruled the course of nature, walked upon the billows as if pavements and hushed the sea to sleep. He healed the multitudes without medicine and made no charge for his service.

"He never wrote a book, yet all the libraries of the country could not hold the books that have been written about him. He never wrote a song, and yet he's furnished the theme for more songs than all the songwriters combined. He never founded a college, but all the schools put together cannot boast of having so many students. He never marshalled an army nor drafted a soldier nor fired a gun, and yet no leader ever had more volunteers who have, under his orders, made more rebels stack their arms and surrender without a shot fired. He never practiced psychiatry, and yet he has healed more broken hearts than all the doctors far and near.

"He stands forth upon the highest pinnacle of heaven's glory, proclaimed of God, acknowledged by angels, adored by saints, feared by devils, as the living personal Lord Jesus Christ my Lord and Savior" (source unknown).

Victories of the King

Next the writer goes on to give us a picture of the victories of the king.

> *Gird your sword upon your thigh,*
> *O mighty one,*
> *in your glory and majesty!*
> *In your majesty ride forth victoriously*
> *for the cause of truth and to defend*
> *the right;*
> *let your right hand teach you*
> *dread deeds!*
> *Your arrows are sharp in the heart*
> *of the king's enemies;*
> *the peoples fall under you* (vv. 3-5).

This seems to be a complete right-about-face. Here is one who has been extolled as gracious in His words and now He is pictured as mighty in His enmity as He fights and destroys all His enemies. But we must remember that in these psalms we have figurative language. This is not a description of actual bloody warfare. The enemies spoken of here are not flesh and blood. The apostle Paul reminds us in Ephesians 6 that we are not wrestling "against flesh and blood, but against the principalities, against the powers, against the world rulers of this present darkness, against the spiritual hosts of wickedness in the heavenly places" (v. 12), who hold humanity enslaved.

Weapons of Truth and Righteousness

When this writer is picturing the victories of the King, he is not talking about battles won and bodies slain; he is talking about powers destroyed, and forces made to loosen their grasp, and powers of darkness driven back, and men and women set free. These are the victories of the King. He accomplishes them with the weapons of truth and righteousness. "In your majesty ride forth victoriously for the cause of truth and to defend the right" (v. 4). Literally, this part should read: "ride forth victoriously—by means of the truth and humble righteousness."

Humble righteousness is meekness, the primary quality of Jesus Christ. But there is another kind of righteousness. There is self-righteousness. Jesus never had that. But here the writer talks about that unselfish righteousness, which Jesus always manifested, that never made anybody feel uneasy or feel that he was "holier than thou," but which was perfectly right and true to the character and the being of God. Truth and humble righteousness are the weapons with which the King destroys His enemies.

Living "Between the Times"

How fearful men are today! In any business gathering men say they are afraid of what is happening in the world. They do not understand why people act the way they do. They can no longer account for the behavior of people, in public or in private, on the basis of the old explanations. Why is this? It is because, as Paul says, we do not wrestle against flesh and blood, but we are striking out against those dark powers that enslave humanity. Dr. Charles Malik, former president of the General Assembly of the United Nations, said, "We must remember that we are still living, as the Germans say *zwischen den zeiten* (between the times), when demonic forces can quickly soar very high, and can bring about conditions where men are no longer able to control the events of their lives."

That is what we are facing. The writer is celebrating the mighty power of Jesus to open men's eyes and to strike them free from the shackles that bind them—illusions that have an iron grip on the minds and hearts of young and old alike, holding them in enslavement to things that destroy themselves and others. They can seemingly do nothing about it. They do not even see how mixed up their thinking is, how confused they are. What a King this is who rides out in majesty to the destruction of powerful enemies and to the deliverance of their captives.

An Everlasting Throne

The next section describes the nature that He possesses.

> *Your divine throne endures for ever*
> *and ever.*
> *Your royal scepter is a scepter*
> *of equity;*

you love righteousness and hate wickedness.
Therefore God, your God, has anointed you
with the oil of gladness above your
fellows (vv.6,7).

These verses are quoted in the opening chapter of Hebrews to prove the deity of the Lord Jesus Christ and His superiority to any of the angels. He is not an angel. He is not the highest of the created beings. He Himself is God, God become man.

The Hebrew here reads "Your throne, O God, endures for ever and ever." The reason it is not rendered literally in the *RSV* is not because the revisers were trying to destroy the deity of Jesus. Rather, they were seeking to use language that they felt would fit the human situation from which this psalm arose. No Jew would have ever addressed a king as "Your throne, O God" and so in order to tone down the language to fit the human situation they translated it "Your divine throne." But this is a feature of the psalms that we need to remember. Oftentimes the language moves beyond any possible application to an earthly being and then it must be translated exactly the way it is. Here it is "Your throne, O God." The King is addressed as God.

Anointed by God

Yet in the very next sentence the text says, "Therefore God, your God, has anointed you." Here is One who is both God and yet has a God. The secret of His incarnation is thus recorded for us 1000 years before He appeared on earth. Here shines that marvelous mystery that caused the shepherds to whisper awe-struck wonder on the occasion of His birth in Bethlehem, "Immanuel, God with us."

Think of the wonder of this Person who was Himself the mighty God and yet became flesh. This moves the apostle Paul to cry out, "O great is the mystery of our faith, that God became flesh and dwelt among us!" (see 1 Tim. 3:16). It is what moved the hymn writers of the Christian faith to write their songs.

What an amazing mystery this is. "The Son of God appears!" "Veiled in flesh the Godhead see!" All these phrases center on this amazing, remarkable secret that One appears who blended together the natures of man and God.

Prophet, Priest and King

As He lived among us, His Godhead was there, hidden away, but He seldom acted or spoke from that. He relied, as we must rely, upon the imparted life of the Father dwelling within Him. And yet He Himself was God the Son. It is a mystery that defies all possible explanation; we cannot grasp it. He was the Messiah, the Anointed One, who fulfilled all the offices for which an anointing was required in the Old Testament that of prophet, of priest, and of king.

As a prophet He spoke the words of God in a way that has never been equalled. As a priest He offered Himself as a sacrifice. As a king He ruled the course of nature and came rising up from the dead. Death could not hold Him because He was anointed of God. "Therefore God, your God, has anointed you with the oil of gladness above your fellows." That beautiful phrase, "the oil of gladness," describes the Holy Spirit. The Spirit creates gladness in the human heart. All who come to know the Son of God share with Him in the heritage of this anointing with the oil of gladness.

Longing for His Bride

The final section of this division sets before us the relationship that the King desires. What is this all about? Why this marvelous story of One who is fairer than the sons of men, whose lips are filled with gracious words, who is able to set people free and strike the shackles of slavery from them, who combines in His own Being the character of God and man in a marvelous mystery of union? What is He after, what does He want? Well, the psalmist tells us. He has come to get married, He has come for a bride:

> *Your robes are all fragrant with myrrh*
> *and aloes and cassia.*
> *From ivory palaces stringed instruments*
> *make you glad;*
> *daughters of kings are among your*
> *ladies of honor;*
> *at your right hand stands the queen*
> *in gold of Ophir* (vv. 8,9).

Preparing Himself

This clearly describes a marriage service. It is most remarkable because we have traced here a line of preparation. First, the King has prepared Himself. The writer says, "Your robes are all fragrant with myrrh and aloes and cassia." Now these are burial spices. Remember that when the women went to the tomb on Easter Sunday morning, they carried with them a certain quantity of spices, myrrh and aloes, in order to encase the body of the Lord and preserve it in death. Yet here these burial spices are present at a wedding. What does it mean?

Surely it means that this marriage is made possible out of death, that somehow out of death comes this fragrant incense that makes glorious the scene of the wedding. It is easy to see how beautifully this fits with what the apostle Paul describes for us in Ephesians when he said that Christ loved the Church and gave Himself for it. He died for it. He went into the bonds of death for us. Why? In order that He might present to Himself a glorious church, a beautiful bride without spot or blemish or any such thing. That is what He is after.

A Wedding Place

Then He has prepared a place. We now find out where this wedding is to take place. "From ivory palaces stringed instruments make you glad; daughters of kings are among your ladies of honor." This beautiful picture reminds us immediately of Jesus' words to His disciples before the cross when He said to them, "I am going away. I am going to prepare a place for you. But if I go and prepare a place I will come again and receive you unto myself that where I am there you may be also" (see John 14:3). That place is being prepared now. It is a place of beauty and glory beyond description. The terms used here are simply a way of suggesting to us what it is like—ivory palaces, beautiful places filled with music and gladness with a rejoicing company around.

A Privileged Bride

And finally the bride herself is prepared: "At your right hand stands the queen in gold of Ophir." This golden dress was always presented to the queen by the bridegroom himself. He paid for the golden dress.

I've been interested for some time in trying to reestablish scriptural methods of wedding services here in the Western world. It is right for the *groom* to pay all the expenses, as He did here! Having four daughters, you can understand my feelings in this respect. But it is also a wonderful picture for us, is it not?

Who is it that is preparing us for this day, for this sharing of life together? There is a sense in which we have already entered into this relationship with the Lord, if we belong to His bride, the church of Jesus Christ. But it is He who is preparing us. He has clothed us with His own righteousness, our golden robe. Gold in Scripture pictures deity, and this hints at what Peter speaks of when he says, "We are made partakers of the divine nature" (see 2 Peter. 1:4).

JESUS Christ is blending our lives with His and giving us His position and His privileges and His power as well as His interests and His problems, so that all that belongs to Him belongs to us.

Do you really grasp this? Have you ever really thought that these words are not merely magic poetry? This is true. Jesus Christ is blending our lives with His and giving us His position and His privileges and His power as well as His interests and His problems, so that all that belongs to Him belongs to us. How easily we forget the privileges that we have. Yet here stands the bride, ready to join Him, dressed in gold, which He has provided.

Seek the Heavenly Bridegroom

This next section is addressed to the bride. If anything is significant for us in this psalm it is this section right here. Here are the words to the bride:

> *Hear, O daughter, consider, and incline*
> *your ear;*
> *forget your people and your father's house;*
> *and the king will desire your beauty.*
> *Since he is your lord, bow to him;*
> *the people of Tyre will sue your favor*
> *with gifts,*
> *the richest of the people with all kinds of*
> *wealth"* (vv. 10-13).

Reject the Past

He says two things to the queen. First, "consider, incline your ear, and forget your people and your father's house." Now what does that mean for us today? What is he saying when he exhorts us as Christians to forget our people and our father's house? What is our father's house? It is the old nature, the place where we were born. It is the Adamic life, the flesh, the self-centered life with which we started, the life of depending upon self. Forget this, turn from it, reject it, "forget your people and your father's house; and . . . "—and what?—"the king will desire your beauty." Isn't that encouraging?

Have you ever thought that when the Lord Jesus, through the Scriptures, is exhorting you to give yourself to Him, to forget your old selfish, self-centered ways of life and to make yourself available to Him, an instrument of His workings, you are arousing a desire and a hunger in His heart for you? Can you believe that Jesus desires *your* beauty? It is true!

Worship Him

And the second thing: "Since he is your lord, bow to him; the people of Tyre will sue your favor with gifts, the richest of the people." Throughout the Scriptures the city of Tyre is used as a picture of the world. He is saying here that if the Church begins to worship its Lord as it should, the world will start coming to our door asking for help. One of the problems with our present situation is that the Church has stopped worshiping its Lord. We do not often bow to Him anymore, we do not acknowledge Him. He is no longer King in our hearts; He is more like a constitutional monarch, a sort of figurehead, to whom we pay a homage now and then. Once in a while we toss Him a token or two to keep Him happy. But we do not follow Him, we do not obey Him.

That is why the world looks at the Church as an irrelevant and foolish waste of time. But when the Church begins to worship its Lord again, and to glory in His being, and to count on the riches of His grace, and to honor and exalt and obey Him, then the people of the world will court the favor of the Church and come again looking for wisdom and help and light to find a way out of their darkness.

Celebrate the Wedding

The rest of this section describes a beautiful wedding. I have chosen to quote an alternate reading for verse 13, which is more accurate to the original Hebrew.

> *All glorious is the princess within,*
> *gold embroidery is her clothing;*
> *in many-colored robes she is led to the king,*
> *with her virgin companions, her escort,*
> *in her train.*
> *With joy and gladness they are led along*
> *as they enter the palace of the king* (vv. 13-15).

This is but another way of describing that coming event Paul speaks of in Romans 8. There he says the whole creation is now held in bondage and travail, groaning in pain, waiting for the day when all that God is doing through this present age will suddenly be unveiled and the sons of God will stand forth in full manifestation. In that day the whole creation will be delivered from bondage; it will shout and sing, delivered from its curse, as in a great wedding celebration. Then the bride of Christ will be claimed in open acknowledgement of what she is, having been fashioned through this period of time. The psalmist says that the bride's inner life will be right ("all glorious is the princess within"). Her outer life will be attractive and spotless ("gold embroidery is her clothing"). God is at work now, cleansing and perfecting that Church.

The events recorded in our newspapers are not really the important events of the day. The most staggering significant events are taking place "behind the scenes," in the hearts of God's people. Changes of attitudes, deliverance from various bad habits, freedom to be what you ought to be, love beginning to fill your homes until you are no longer reacting in resentment and bitterness toward one another—these are events that will be valued throughout eternity. When you learn how to show forth the love of God as it is shed abroad in your hearts by the Holy Spirit, then there is real reason to celebrate.

Sons of the King

The psalm concludes with two verses that are the promise of God toward this might king.

Instead of your fathers shall be your sons;
you will make them princes in all the earth.

I will cause your name to be celebrated
in all generations;
therefore the peoples will praise you
for ever and ever (vv. 16,17).

Instead of the Davidic line, instead of emphasis upon human ancestry, the emphasis in that day will be upon those who are linked with the King as sons. The book of Hebrews says that the Father is in the process of bringing many sons to glory. That is what He is doing right now.

"I will cause your name to be celebrated in all generations." Is that not another way of saying what Paul wrote to the Philippians? "Therefore God has highly exalted him and bestowed on him the name which is above every name, that at the name of Jesus every knee should bow, in heaven and on earth and under the earth, and every tongue confess that Jesus Christ is Lord, to the glory of God the Father" (Phil. 2:9-11).

What a King! The King in all His beauty!

Our Father, we thank you for this glimpse through this Old Testament psalmist of the beauty of the Lord Jesus Christ. How our hearts are stirred again at this story of One who left heaven's glory and came to be among us in all the bondage, coldness, and enslavement of earth that we might be free to be with Him some day, sharing the glory of His Being for all eternity. How tremendous this is, Lord. What purpose and meaning it gives to life. Help us to rejoice in it this day, we pray in His name, Amen.

Here Comes the Judge

In looking together at these psalms we are sharing the experiences of men and women of the past who have found their way through difficulties and troubles, through trials and heartaches, by faith in a living God who has delivered them. To help others they have put their experiences into song and thus we have the psalms. How helpful these can be when we are going through times of difficulty! But they tell not only of times of difficulty but also of times of rejoicing, and they express beautifully the exaltation of the soul that has found deliverance in God.

The theme of Psalm 50 is a familiar one. If you remember the ballads and folksongs of America, you know that they frequently center around courtrooms, trials, juries (rigged or otherwise), prisons, policemen, and judges.

You get a great deal of this in folksongs and it is the theme also of this fiftieth Psalm. In this courtroom scene the psalmist is recreating his experience of God's judgment. If we were to put this in the street jargon of today we should title it, "When God Busted Me."

The Summons

Notice that it is inscribed as a psalm of Asaph. Asaph was the sweet singer who put these songs to music and sang in David's court. This psalm is from his pen though it reflects the experience of many believers. Like all courtroom scenes it begins with a summons.

> *The Mighty One, God the Lord,*
> *speaks and summons the earth* (v. 1).

Some time ago my doorbell rang on a Saturday morning. When I went to the door there stood a man I had never seen before. He did not say a word but handed me a piece of paper, turned around, and walked down the driveway. I stood there with the paper in my hands not knowing quite what it was all about. When I went inside and opened the paper I saw that it was a summons to appear in court. It affected me strangely. I was not quite sure what to do. I felt a mingled sense of fear and awe. I wanted to hide and wondered if it would not be better just to go back to bed and start all over again.

God Is the Judge

Perhaps this was the reaction of the psalmist when this great summons rang out. The scene is awesome and impressive as the psalmist pictures a courtroom where the

Judge enters and the people are summoned to the bar.

> *Out of Zion, the perfection of beauty,*
> *God shines forth.*
> *Our God comes, he does not keep silence,*
> *before him is a devouring fire,*
> *round about him a mighty tempest.*
> *He calls to the heavens above*
> *and to the earth, that he may judge his people:*
> *"Gather to me my faithful ones,*
> *who made a covenant with me by sacrifice!"*
> *The heavens declare his righteousness,*
> *for God himself is judge! Selah* (vv. 2-6).

"God Himself is judge!" This is a courtroom in which God sits to judge His people. In verse one He describes Himself in a three-fold way: the Mighty One, God, the Lord. In Hebrew they are three names: El, Elohim, Yahweh. These three names are most impressive for they gather up the major characteristics of God. He is first, El, the Mighty One, the All-powerful One, the One of authority and strength. Then He is Elohim, the One of majesty, of greatness, the Supreme One, sovereign over all else. But as Yahweh He is the God of mercy, the One who graciously enters into full understanding of His people's needs. Thus in this scene we have God the Judge introducing Himself to us as God of Might, Majesty, and Mercy, holding all three characteristics in perfect balance. He is the One of authority, of sovereignty and majesty, but also the One of grace, love, and tender concern.

Out of Zion

Now it is important to note that this Judge comes not from

Sinai but from Zion. "Out of Zion, the perfection of beauty, God shines forth." Sinai, of course, was where the Law was given. It was accompanied with thunderous judgment, with lightnings and the voice of a trumpet, which waxed louder and louder until the people could not stand it. They cried out to Moses, "You speak to us, but let not God speak to us lest we die!" (see Exod. 20:19). But here it is no longer Sinai but Zion. Zion is Jerusalem and stands for the mercy of God, the redemptive love of God, the grace of God. God is judging, but He is judging in mercy. It is well to remember as we go on into this psalm that the judgment will be realistic, but it will not be harsh.

Because Zion refers to Jerusalem some commentators have taken this psalm to be a description of the Second Coming when the Lord Jesus Christ shall return to earth in power and great glory (as He Himself described it in Matthew 25), and will sit on His throne and gather the nations before Him to judge them. Now it is true that Jesus is going to return to earth. When He came the first time He came in weakness and humility, born in a cold and dirty cave on the side of a hill in Bethlehem. There was no pomp, no circumstance, no power, But when He comes again He will come in great glory to judge the peoples of earth as they are summoned before Him. This psalm is, in my judgment, a very beautiful description in the Old Testament of the very event, which is recorded in the New Testament.

But it would be a great mistake to take the psalm as limited only to that event. As often happens with many scriptural passages, we have here a dual application. It not only looks forward to the time when literally and physically, Christ will return to judge His people, but it also describes a judgment that is going on right now. This is indicated for us in verse 1 by these words. "The Mighty

One, God the Lord, speaks and summons the earth *from the rising of the sun to its setting*" (italics added). The sun rises every morning and sets every evening. Thus this phrase indicates something that goes on daily. God is *daily* judging His people. He is sitting among them as a Redeemer/Judge. In verse 3 the Hebrew says, "Our God comes." Not "is coming" in the future but "keeps coming." He is always coming. We are always living in the presence of God and in the coming of God. "Our God comes, he does not keep silence."

Fire and Wind

Then the psalmist goes on to describe the character of the God who comes to judge His people. Two symbols mark the characteristics of judgment: fire and wind. "Before him is a devouring fire, round about him a mighty tempest." In the New Testament these two symbols are often used to describe God. "Our God is a consuming fire," says the writer to the Hebrews (see 12:29). And the Spirit of God is described in Acts as a mighty rushing wind (see 2:2). "The wind blows where it desires," said Jesus to Nicodemus, "and you hear the sound thereof, but you cannot tell where it has come from or where it is going. So is he who is born of the Spirit" (see John 3:8). These are highly suggestive symbols. Fire is that which purifies. Fire destroys all waste and trash, the garbage of life. As fire God will burn the dross, waste, and trash of our lives, the garbage of the soul.

But He is also wind. Wind is, in some ways, the mightiest force in nature. Some time ago I saw a picture taken after a tornado in the Southwest. It showed straw that had been caught up in the wind and driven entirely through a telephone pole. If I gave you a weak piece of straw and told you to drive it through a telephone pole you would look at me in amazement. You do not drive straw through a telephone pole. But this straw had been driven through by the force of a mighty wind. On the day of Pentecost, when the disciples were gathered, there was suddenly the sound of a mighty rushing wind. Caught up in the power of that wind the disciples did things they had never done before. Empowered by the wind of God they went out to do and say things that upset the world of their day. They startled and astonished men by the power that was evidence among them.

A New Covenant

The psalmist is telling us that when God judges He will do two things: He will burn up the trash and garbage of life, and then He will empower us. He will catch us up in the greatness of His strength, and we will be able to do things we never could do before. Notice in verses 4 and 5 who is particularly subject to this judgment. "He calls to the heavens above and to the earth, that he may judge his people: 'Gather to me my faithful ones, who made a covenant with me by sacrifice!'" We are his people, are we not? Of old it was Israel. They are the ones who made a covenant with God by sacrifice. Of course, He is referring to the animal sacrifices that Israel offered day by day. These were to reflect the relationship God had with His people. It was a covenant made in blood; in other words, a life had been poured out on their behalf. But all these Old Testament sacrifices were but a picture of the sacrifice of the Lord Jesus Christ. Each one was, in a sense, Christ being offered.

In Christ we are the people who have made a covenant with God by sacrifice. We have entered into the benefit of the new arrangement for living made through the sacrifice of the Lord Jesus Christ. This psalm then is really describing what is going on right now. It pictures God among His people and He has something to say to us. The God who comes from Zion, the God who loves and who sees things the way they are, desires to speak to us. That is why this section ends with the little word, *Selah*. It means, pause, stop, look, listen, think! God the Judge, is in our midst, God is judging His people.

God's Desire

Now the Judge speaks:

> *"Hear, O my people, and I will speak, O Israel,*
> *I will testify against you. I am God, your God.*
> *I do not reprove you for your sacrifices;*
> *your burnt offerings are continually before me.*
> *I will accept no bull from your house,*
> *nor he-goat from your folds.*
> *For every beast of the forest is mine,*
> *the cattle on a thousand hills.*
> *I know all the birds of the air,*
> *and all that moves in the field is mine.*
> *If I were hungry, I would not tell you;*
> *for the world and all that is in it is mine.*
> *Do I eat the flesh of bulls,*
> *or drink the blook of goats?"* (vv. 7-13).

What a remarkable piece of irony! This passage has a sardonic twist to it. God is saying, first, "I do not reprove you for your sacrifices," that is, "There are certain things you are doing that are right." Israel brought every day, punctiliously, the sacrifices that the Law prescribed. "I do not reprove you for that," God says, "there are certain things you are doing that are fundamentally right." But what was wrong was that they thought the act of sacrificing was all God wanted, that for some reason He needed bulls' flesh and goats' blood. They were displaying a grossly low concept of God.

God is saying to them, "How absurd can you get? Do you really think I am that kind of a God? Do you think I need flesh and blood? Why, I own the cattle on a thousand hills. I own the wild beasts of the forests, the elk, the bison, and all the other animals. Also, I know all the birds of the air. They're all mine and I can do with them as I will. If hunger were my motive in asking you to bring sacrifices, then I could heap up mountains of flesh. What do you take me for, anyway? A kind of cosmic Meat Grinder?"

A Parallel Today

Do you see the parallel to this today? Many people come to church and think that God wants them to sing hymns, bow in prayer, utter certain words and go through certain forms, and that is all He is after. How absurd! It is all perfectly right, there is nothing wrong with it, but that is not what He wants. It is not what God desires.

A young pastor came to me to talk about his ministry. He said, "Tell me, what is wrong with the evangelical church today, anyhow?" I have been trying to answer that question for quite a while but, being challenged to put it in a brief form, I had to think it through. I said finally that I thought two things were wrong with the evangelical church. There is a lot right about it. Our doctrine is right, it is scriptural. Our emphasis upon the authority of Scripture is right, it is good, it is solid. Our concern lest we get away from the authority of the Bible and the teaching of the Scripture is right. There is nothing wrong with that.

No Real Life

But the average evangelical church is dead! Many evangelical Christians are not demonstrating real life. Their words are wonderful but their lives leave something greatly to be desired. Years ago, when Averill Harriman was first appointed ambassador to France, someone said to him, "How's your French?" He said, "Oh, my French is excellent; all but the verbs!" That is a good description of evangelical Christianity. We have wonderful nouns: joy, peace, faith, redemption, salvation, justification. Oh, these nouns! But the verbs—loving, forgiving, healing, restoring—that is where we are weak, are we not? That is what God is finding fault with. He says, "Your sacrifices are fine, but where are your hearts?"

Far Removed

The second thing I see wrong with the evangelical church is its remoteness. It is far removed from life as it is. It tends to withdraw from the really gut issues of life and will not involve itself where people are bleeding, struggling, fighting, and facing terrible problems. We tend to excuse that by saying, "Well, getting in and helping outwardly doesn't solve anything ultimately." Of course, we are quite right about that. That is not where the real solution lies. But it is wrong for us not to be involved. That remoteness is turning off many young people today from the evangelical church. We do not want to touch anyone, like the Levite in the parable of the Good Samaritan, who gathered his robe about him and crossed over to the other side leaving the wounded man without help. So God is judging His people. He is saying, "You observe the form but there is something missing."

What Is Missing?

Then He speaks very clearly and tells us what is missing.

> *Offer to God a sacrifice of thanksgiving,*
>   *and pay your vows to the Most High;*
> *and call upon me in the day of trouble;*
>   *I will deliver you, and you shall glorify me*
> (vv. 14,15).

What does God want from us today? Well, He does not want more hymn singing, although that is fine. Nor does He want only prayer, although that too is fine. He does not simply want our church attendance, although that is good. What He wants is first a thankful heart. Each one of us is to offer to Him the sacrifice of thanksgiving. A sacrifice is something we put effort into, it costs us.

God Wants Thankfulness

Have you ever asked yourself, why do the Scriptures stress thanksgiving so much? Both in the Old and New Testaments you find emphasis that above everything else God wants thankfulness. "In everything," says the apostle Paul, "give thanks, for this is the will of God in Christ Jesus concerning you" (see 1 Thess. 5:18). Why is this? Well, it is because thanksgiving only comes as a result of having received something. You only say, "Thank you" when somebody has given you something that you did not have yourself. It all comes from someone else. Therefore, thanksgiving is the proper expression of Christianity because to be a Christian is to be constantly receiving something from God.

Of course, if you have not received anything from God

then you have nothing to thank Him for. When you go to church in a critical, complaining, griping, grumbling mood, then no matter how many hymns you sing or prayers you recite, you are not worshiping God. It is better that you do not go, really, because worship is for those who have received something. God is a realist. He does not want fake thanksgiving.

I know there are certain people (and they are awfully hard to live with) who think that Christianity consists of pretending to be thankful. They think it means screwing a smile on your face and going around pretending that troubles do not bother you. That is a most painful form of Christianity. God does not want people to go around shouting, "Hallelujah! I've got cancer!" But there is something about having cancer to be thankful for. That is what He wants you to see. There are aspects of it that no one can possibly enjoy, but there are other aspects that reveal purpose, meaning, and reason. God wants you to be thankful for what He can do with that situation.

God Wants Obedience

The first thing He wants in worship is a thankful heart. The second thing is an obedient will. "Pay your vows to the Most High." Notice the kind of obedience it is. It is not something forced upon you; it is something you have chosen for yourself. A vow is something you decide to give, a promise you make because of truth you have seen. You say, "I never saw it like that before. I really ought to do something about it. God helping me, I'm going to do such and such." That is a vow. God says, "I'm not asking you to do things you have not yet learned are important. But when you have vowed something, then do it. Act on it. Obey it." That's the name of the game of Christianity—obeying truth.

God Wants a Prayerful Spirit

The third thing God wants is a prayerful spirit. "Call upon me in the day of trouble; I will deliver you, and you shall glorify me." He wants us to recognize where the source of power is. Power comes from Him. The opening words of Psalm 27 declare: "The Lord is my light and my salvation;

GOD is a devouring fire and He wants to burn out of us the trash, the garbage, the waste of our life.

---

whom shall I fear?" I can see the psalmist thrusting his chest out and saying, "I've got the Lord; of whom shall I be afraid?" That was the spirit in which David met Goliath. Here was Goliath, nine feet tall, clad in his armor, his spear like a weaver's beam, threatening and frightening the armies of Israel, rendering them absolutely helpless and hopeless in their fear. But little David comes along and says, "Who is this uncircumcised giant who dares defy the armies of the living God? Who does he think he is? Why, he's nothing!" (see 1 Sam. 17:26). "The Lord is the stronghold of my life; of whom shall I be afraid?" (Psalm 27:1)

How different David is from us. But God is in the midst of His people , pointing these truths out to us. God is a devouring fire and He wants to burn out of us the trash, the garbage, the waste of our life.

A Second Class of People

A second class of people is mentioned in verses 16 and on.
But to the wicked God says:
"What right have you to recite my statutes,

or take my covenant on your lips?
For you hate discipline,
    and you cast my words behind you.
If you see a thief, you are a friend of his;
    and you keep company with adulterers.
You give your mouth free rein for evil,
    and your tongue frames deceit.
You sit and speak against your brother;
    you slander your own mother's son" (vv. 16-20).

In every congregation there are not only the superficial who need to be rebuked and challenged to be real, there are also some who are essentially false, hypocrites who use all the right words and frame their lives in Christian form, but are basically ungodly, or to use the term here, wicked. That is what wickedness is. It is forgetting that God lives and exists. It is to rule Him out of your life, to be ungodly and so, wicked. The Judge sees these also. He knows the heart of every person.

They Hate Discipline

Three characteristics identify the wicked. First, they hate discipline. They want only their own way. They hate discipline and therefore reject truth. They do not want to hear what is true. They do not recognize any absolutes in life. They want to believe that everything is relative, that you can do whatever you like. They want, basically, their own way at all costs, and they resent any form of restraint or criticism.

They Admire Evil

Second, they admire evil and they enjoy the friendship of those who do evil. This is exactly the charge that Paul levels against some in Romans 1. They not only admire evil themselves but they "approve those who practice" evil things (see v. 32). That is what God describes here in the psalm. "If you see a thief," He says, "you think he is clever. You admire a man who can cheat someone and get away with it. To you he is a clever man. You want to be with him and to imitate him. You see an adulterer, someone who lives in open, flagrant, sexual immorality, and you say he's free, and seek him out. You think he is better off than you are, living under certain restraints. You admire this person who seems to be so free, who has kicked over all the traces, and you want to be like him."

They Possess Ungoverned Tongues

Then, third, the wicked possesses an ungoverned tongue; he says whatever he feels like saying. He has a tongue that lies, frames deceit, and cuts down others, slicing away, jabbing at another's reputation. "You do this," says God, "even to your own brother or sister, or anyone in the family. That" God says, "reveals that you are wicked, that you do not own God in your life. You are essentially ungodly, there has been no redemptive change in you, but you try to cover your wickedness by a religious glaze."

Christians or Christianeers?

Today we have not only Christians, but also what we might call Christianeers: those who subscribe to the outward forms of Christianity much as they would adopt a political slogan. In every congregation there are Christians and there are Christianeers. Sometimes it is hard to tell them apart, but God knows. God is judging. He is in our midst and He sees. He says, "You, you're a Christianeer, you're not real." You may believe you even have God fooled, but listen to what He says.

"These things you have done and I have been silent;

> *you thought that I was one like yourself.*
> *But now I rebuke you,*
> *and lay the charge before you.*
> *Mark this, then, you who forget God,*
>   *lest I rend, and there be none to deliver!"*
> (vv. 21,22).

God is saying, "Now don't fool yourself. I am patient. I do not always act immediately. I do not always strike people with judgment the minute they do anything wrong." Surely it is well for us to remember that. Sometimes we hear people say, "Why doesn't God kill the atheistic leaders of Communist countries and get rid of them?" But what we need to ask is, "Why didn't God cause my hand to shrivel when I took something that didn't belong to me yesterday? Why didn't He cut off my tongue when I said that sharp and caustic word to my friend this morning? Why didn't He blind my eyes when I let them dwell on something I shouldn't have, and played with lust in my mind?" You see, if God is going to judge He must judge all.

"I am patient," God counsels us. "Remember, friend, that I have let you go on because I want to reach you. I don't want you to be this way. I want to change you, I want to redeem you, I want to call you back from this. But do not misread my patience as indifference. You thought I was like you, that I didn't give a fig for these things. But friend, there comes a time when I must lay the charge clearly before you, put the cards right on the table. You can't go on this way. I offer you redemption, salvation. And remember, if you refuse it, there will come a time when I must become your enemy. And if I, God, who wants to be your friend, ultimately am made your enemy by the way you act toward me, then tell me, who will be your friend in that day?"

God has a thousand ways of leveling accounts, of settling up issues, and who can defend against Him? Who can take on God? Who can outwit His purposes? God is an utter realist. We must get that into our minds. He is not fooled by anything or anyone. He sees us exactly as we are. And He is no mere pimple-squeezer, either. He is not dealing with superficial things; he goes right for the jugular, right to the issues of life.

The Salvation of God

Now the closing word is one of promise.

> *"He who brings thanksgiving as his sacrifice*
> *honors me;*
> *to him who orders his way aright*
> *I will show the salvation of God!"* (v. 23).

Such a man is not always able to follow through as he desires, God know that. But to the one who wants to, who "orders his way aright," God says, "I will show the salvation of God." That word *salvation* is a great word. It is a word that gathers up all God wants to do for us, in us, through us, and by us.

God wants men and women, boys and girls, who have found strength in the only place where anyone can find it— in the God who provides salvation for them. God wants to show us how it can be done. There is where we start— whenever we want to take the offer.

Oh, Father, help us to understand how real you are, how realistic you are, and to know, Lord, that we cannot fool you about anything. So keep us, Lord, from trying to fool ourselves. We ask in your name, Amen.

CHAPTER 12 / PSALM 51

How to Handle a Bad Conscience

A London psychologist once told Billy Graham that 70 percent of the people in mental hospitals in England could be released if they could find forgiveness. Their problem was a bad conscience and they could gain no relief from the guilt and pressure under which they lived.

I read once of a man who wrote a letter to the Bureau of Internal Revenue saying, "I haven't been able to sleep because last year, when I filled out my income tax report, I deliberately misrepresented my income. I am enclosing a check for $150.00, and if I still can't sleep, I'll send you the rest." That is one way of handling a bad conscience but I can predict that it will not work. The only way that works is the way set forth in this fifty-first Psalm.

Adultery and Murder

This is one of the few psalms where we are given the historical background from which it arose. The inscription reads, "A Psalm of David, when Nathan the prophet came to him, after he had gone in to Bathsheba." That identifies clearly for us the incident out of which this psalm arose.

It was the time when David became involved in the double sin of adultery and murder while he was king. He had walked with God for many years. He was widely known as the Sweet Singer of Israel; he had gained a reputation as a prophet, a man who understood the deep things of God; and he had established himself as the long time spiritual leader of his people. Then suddenly, toward the end of his reign, he plunged into this terrible double sin.

The interesting thing is that David himself records this sin for us. It must have been a painfully humiliating experience to the king. You remember the account. He was on his palace roof one day when the army had gone out to battle and he saw a beautiful woman bathing herself. His passion was aroused and he sent over messengers and ordered her to be brought up to him. He entered into an adulterous relationship with her, for she was a married woman. Her husband, a soldier in David's army, was away fighting for his king.

Trying to Cover Up

Later, when David learned that she was expecting a child, he panicked and tried to cover up. He ordered the husband home from battle and sent him down to his home, hoping that he would sleep with his wife and the child would then be accepted as his own. But Uriah was a soldier committed to battle, and though he came home at the king's orders, he would not go down to his own house but slept with the soldiers at the palace and returned to the battle the next day.

David knew that ultimately his sin would be found out so he took another step. This is always what sin does—it leads us on deeper and deeper, farther than we ever intended to go. Before the king knew it he found himself forced into a desperate attempt to cover up his evil. He ordered Uriah, the husband, to be put in the forefront of the battle where he would most certainly be killed. When news of Uriah's death reached the king he felt he had safely covered his sin.

In Psalm 32 David records how he felt during that terrible time when he was trying to cover up his sin. "When I kept silence," he says, "my bones grew old through my groaning all day long" (see v. 3). For a year he tried to live with a bad conscience. But, as the story records, God sent a prophet to David. God loved this king, loved him too well to let him go on covering up and thus damaging himself and his entire kingdom by this hidden sin. So God sent the prophet Nathan to David.

Confronted with Sin

Because David was king, Nathan knew he would have to approach him subtly, for his own life was in danger if he blatantly accused the king. So Nathan told him a story. He said that while he was abroad in the kingdom a certain incident occurred, which he felt should be brought to the king for judgment. There was a certain rich man who owned a flock of sheep and a traveler came by to whom he wanted to show hospitality. But instead of taking one of his own sheep and offering it for food, he went to his poor neighbor who owned one little ewe lamb. He took that lamb and prepared it for the man who had come to him. When David heard this he was indignant and cried out, "Such a man ought to be made to restore four-fold what he has taken and then be killed himself."

In a most dramatic moment the prophet Nathan pointed a long, bony finger at the king and said, "You are the man!" David knew then that his sin was uncovered (see 2 Sam. 12:1-15). He fell on his face before God and out of that experience of confession comes this beautiful fifty-first Psalm, which traces for us the proper way to handle a bad conscience. It opens with a prayer for forgiveness.

Seeking Forgiveness

Have mercy on me, O God,
*   according to thy steadfast love;*
according to thy abundant mercy
*   blot out my transgressions.*
Wash me thoroughly from my iniquity,
*   and cleanse me from my sin!* (vv. 1,2).

What a marvelous understanding of the nature of sin and the character of God's forgiveness is found in those verses! There are three things David asks for. First, he understands that sin is like a crime. If a criminal is going to be delivered from the effects of his crime he needs not justice but mercy. Sin is an illegal act, a violation of justice, an act of lawlessness, of rebellion, and therefore requires mercy. David asks for that.

Then he says, "Blot out my transgressions," and thereby reveals that he understands sin is like a debt. It is something owed, an account that has accumulated and needs to be erased.

Finally he cries, "Wash me thoroughly, and cleanse me." He understands that sin is like an ugly stain, a defilement upon the soul. Even though the act fades into the past, the dirty, defiling stain remains as a stigma upon the heart. So he cries out to be delivered from his crime, his debt, and his stain.

Clearly David understands well the basis for forgiveness. He asks on the basis of two things: first, "according to thy steadfast love." He understands that he deserves nothing from God and that God is not bound to forgive him. Some people are never able to obtain forgiveness because they think they deserve it, that God owes it to them. But David knows better. He realizes that only because of God's love does he have any right even to ask. On the basis of that unqualified acceptance, that marvelous continuing love-that-will-not-let-me-go, he says to God, "I am coming to you and asking now for this."

Second, "according to thy abundant mercy," indicates his understanding of the character of God. God is not a penny pincher; He does not dole out bits of mercy, drop by drop. No, He pours it out. His are "abundant" mercies. When God forgives, He forgives beyond our utmost imaginings. Here are a few of the figures of speech that are used in the Old Testament to depict the forgiveness of God. "As far as the east is from the west, so far does he remove our transgressions from us" (Psalm 103:12). How far is that? Well, how far do you have to go east before you start going west? You never come to "west." Then God says He will "cast all our sins into the depths of the sea" (Micah 7:19). Someone has added that He puts up a sign that reads **NO FISHING**. Do not go down there and try to fish old sins out once God has dealt with them. What relief comes when we understand this fulness of God's forgiveness.

Finding Forgiveness

Then David goes on to point out the way to lay hold of forgiveness.

> *For I know my transgressions, and my sin is ever*
> *   before me.*
> *Against thee, thee only, have I sinned,*
> *   and done that which is evil in thy sight,*
> *so that thou art justified in thy sentence*
> *   and blameless in thy judgment* (vv. 3,4).

Here is a frank and full acknowledgement of sin. He says, "I know my sins, I'm not trying to cover them up. They are always before me, this double act of adultery and murder. I am guilty." He does not try to cover them or blame God for them. He says, "It's not your fault, God; it's mine." That is another reason many cannot find forgiveness for sin. They suffer for years with a guilty conscience because they are not willing to come to the place where they acknowledge their sin. They will not call it what God calls it. We all tend to cover up sin and make it sound nicer than it is. We use pleasant names to describe it.

Naming Our Sins

Is it not interesting that we have one list of terms to describe sin in us, but an entirely different list to describe the same sin in someone else? Others have prejudices; we have convictions. Others have a foul temper; we are seized with righteous indignation. Thus, we try to cover over our sins. But we can never be forgiven while we do this, for the first step in the process of forgiveness is an acknowledgment of sin.

There is a verse of an old hymn, which says:

> *"If I have wounded any soul today,*
> *If I have caused one foot to go astray,*
> *If I have walked in my own willful way,*
> *Dear Lord, forgive."*[1]

There is no confession in that! It is saying, "Well, Lord, there is a slight possibility that I might have done some of these evil things, although it is not very likely. So if I have, then forgive them." That kind of "confession" can never lay hold of the forgiveness of God.

IF we do not defend ourselves, then we have an Advocate with the Father, Jesus Christ the Righteous. He will defend us and His defense is perfectly acceptable to God.

An Advocate with the Father

If we are going to defend ourselves, the apostle John argues in his first letter, then we cannot have the defense of that heavenly-appointed Advocate at the Father's right hand who stands ready to defend us. If we defend ourselves, if we say it is not our fault because this happened, or someone did this or that other thing, then the Lord Jesus Christ cannot defend us. But if we do not defend ourselves, then we have an Advocate with the Father, Jesus Christ the Righteous. He will defend us and His defense is perfectly acceptable to God.

It is clear that David understands well the need to

acknowledge his guilt, name sin for what it is, and not charge God with the blame. It is all too easy to do the latter. We say, "Well, God, it's the circumstances you put me in. If it weren't for the fact that years ago you allowed me to be married to this woman (or that man), I would never have done this thing. Or, you made me work for this company. Or, it's the people I live with—my neighbor—or someone else." Whenever we blame it on someone else we are ultimately blaming it on God.

Against Thee Only . . .

David says, "Against thee, thee only have I sinned." It is not that he does not understand that others have been damaged by his sin. There is the woman, Bathsheba; her reputation was sullied, her character blasted, her marriage broken, her husband murdered, and her own heart grieved by the death of the child that was born, all because of David's sin. There is the man, Uriah, whose life was brought to a sudden and bloody end because of David's sin.

But David now sees that ultimately sin is an insult and an injury to God. It is God's love that has been wounded. It is the God of grace whom he has injured most. When a person takes that attitude, then God's forgiveness is always present. That is the only way to handle a specific sin and the bad conscience resulting from evil.

Finding Deliverance

However, the problem is not over yet. Notice how David goes on to strike a deeper note in the verses that follow. He now faces the fear of repeating the same sin. How many of us have felt this way? "Oh, Lord, what a fool I was! What an utter fool I've made of myself! When I see how easily I was deceived and how easily I stumbled into this thing, Lord, I wonder about the future. What's to keep me from doing it all over again next week? If I could be deceived so easily, what's to stop it from happening again?" That is what David now brings before us. In this section, we have a different prayer, a prayer for purifying power.

> *Behold, I was brought forth in iniquity,*
> *and in sin did my mother conceive me.*
> *Behold, thou desirest truth in the inward being;*
> *therefore teach me wisdom in my secret heart*
>
> (vv. 5,6).

Conceived in Sin

Here he understands that his sin was not just a happenstance, a combination of unfortunate circumstances that made him do evil; he now recognizes that sin is something that goes much deeper than that. He says, "I now realize that I was brought forth in iniquity, and in sin did my mother conceive me."

Now, do not misunderstand. He does not mean that there is anything wrong with the act by which conception occurred. His mother was not sinning when she conceived David; that is not what he is saying here at all. There are some who read this as though sexual intercourse were in itself some kind of a sin. But in the marriage relationship it is blessed and honored of God and is a delight to the heart of God.

What he *is* saying is that the act of conception introduced him into a sinful humanity, that he was born into a sinful race in which sin was already deeply imbedded. Now there are many today who challenge this. They question the doctrine of original sin, the theological term (though it is not very accurate) for the idea that the whole race is basically fallen.

But if you challenge that I would like you to answer this question: Who taught you to sin? Where did you learn to lie? Did you have to go to school in order to learn how to be dishonest, to lie, or to cheat? Did your parents carefully train you in how to deceive others? No. Every parent knows that children are "doing what comes naturally." This evil shows up in a baby almost as soon as the baby can express itself. There is a rebellious independence, a self-assertiveness that is present in the tiniest infant and it is there right from the very beginning.

That is what David is saying. "I see now," he says, "that sin is not just a surface problem that can be handled lightly; it is a deep problem. It has stained my whole nature. Unless I find some solution for this polluted nature I will never be able to keep from falling back into sin again." So now he begins to pray for help in the inward life, which is where God wants truth to be found.

Grasping the Truth

In these next verses we find outlined an eight-fold path that one must follow to keep from falling back into a repeated pattern of sin. Follow these carefully. Each is important. First, he cries, "Teach me wisdom in my secret heart." "Give me," he says, "an understanding of the facts of life. Show me reality, show me the way things really are." In other words, help me to understand the truth about myself, that I am a fallen being and that this pollution has penetrated my whole nature. Teach me to start there in my secret heart, to accept as fact what is so clearly declared in your Word. I need to understand, Father, the basic facts that reveal reality in life.

Purged with Hyssop

The second thing is:

Purge me with hyssop, and I shall be clean;
wash me, and I shall be whiter than snow (v. 7).

Hyssop is a sponge-like plant that grew in Israel and was used to apply the blood of the offering to the altar, or the doorpost. To be purged with hyssop is a figurative expression that declares the need for a blood sacrifice. Again, many people are troubled about this. Why all this blood in the Old Testament? Why the millions of lambs, bulls, and goats, and the continual flow of blood? Some have even called Judaism a "slaughterhouse" religion because of this. But God makes very clear that these Old Testament sacrifices were pointing toward the one blood sacrifice of the Lord Jesus. His life had to be laid down in death. These were but symbols, pictures, of that ultimate sacrifice.

But now the question comes: Why that? Why did He have to die to forgive our sins? The only answer is: Sin is so deeply imbedded in us that it cannot be cured by anything but death. The old life has to die. God cannot improve it. Even God cannot make it better; He cannot cleanse it or wash it, He can only put it to death. David understands that now. He says to God, "If you are going to deal with this terrible fountain of evil in me, I can see that it must be put to death. It must be purged with hyssop, then I will be clean."

Hearing with Joy and Gladness

Then the third step:

Fill me with joy and gladness;
let the bones which thou has broken rejoice (v. 8).

The Hebrew here, translated *fill*, really means *make to hear*— "Make me to hear joy and gladness." In other words, "Say something to me, God. Not only lay the basis of cleansing in a blood sacrifice, but tell me what it means. Say something to me about it. Let me have your Word about it, and that will make my bones rejoice. If *you* tell me the truth, then I will know it's true."

Blotting Out Iniquity

The fourth step is:

Hide thy face from my sins,
and blot out all my iniquities (v. 9).

Here he is saying, "Father, if I'm going to be able to be free from falling again, then something has got to be done about the past. I can't always be having it thrown up to me forever. That only depresses me and discourages me and if I'm going to have to live with my wretched, miserable past, I will be defeated over and over again. So, God, I'm asking you, hide your face from my sins and blot out my iniquity." Certainly God is ready and willing to do that. David is only asking for what God has said He would do.

A New Heart

Now look at the fifth step:

Create in me a clean heart, O God,
and put a new and right spirit within me (v. 10).

See the progress he is making here? He sees he must deal with this old life, this old heart, his old past, that it must be put to death. "But Lord," he says, "I'm tied to it. If this old life and old heart naturally incline me toward evil, and I, doing what comes naturally, do that which is wrong, then obviously what I desperately need is a new heart, which naturally does good." That is what he is asking for. It is all-important.

The Assurance of His Presence

The sixth step follows:

> *Cast me not away from thy presence,*
> *and take not thy holy Spirit from me* (v. 11).

Some have interpreted this plea to mean that the Old Testament saints could lose their salvation once they possessed it. I do not think it means that. What the psalmist is praying for here is the *assurance* that the Holy Spirit would be with him. It is exactly the assurance given us in Hebrews 13, "Be content with what you have; for he has said, *'I will never fail you nor forsake you'*" (v. 5). David needs and asks for that assurance. He wants to know that God has forgiven him and is still with him.

A Willing Spirit

The seventh step:

> *Restore to me the joy of thy salvation,*
> [That is, believing all this to be true, put

back into my heart that gladness and joy which
comes from being accepted of you.]
   and [finally, Step Number Eight]
uphold me with a willing spirit (v. 12).

He is saying, "Give me a will that wants to do what you
want me to do even though I may struggle at times." It
takes all of these steps to keep on walking free from sin.
Anyone who is acquainted with the New Testament knows
that all this is exactly what God has provided us in Jesus
Christ.

Several years ago, while preparing to preach a sermon
on this psalm, I received an anonymous letter from someone in my congregation saying that he was a Christian, but
was involved in a very serious and continuing moral failure. The letter was an attempt to be honest and tell me
the trouble in his life. I didn't know if the person would be
in the service the next Sunday or not, but I hoped he
would be.

I decided to refer to the letter in my sermon for two
reasons: (1) because it was anonymous and I could quote it
without betraying a confidence; and (2) because the problem was of such a serious nature that I wanted to help the
person if I could. The writer had acknowledged that he
knew his action was wrong, but finally excused himself on
the basis that God had not yet given him the power to
break away from it.

Now that was self-deception. The truth is that God *has*
given us the power to break away from these things.
Peter clearly declares: "His divine power has granted to
us *all* things that pertain to life and godliness" (2 Peter
1:3, italics added). The very life of Jesus Christ in us *is* the
power that it takes to break away from habits of sin! No
person will ever be free from the awful grip of evil upon his

or her life until he understands that he already has from God all that it takes to be free, if he will but use it.

David is asking for help. "Lord, give me this willing spirit," he says, and God immediately gives it. Then it must be acted on. That is the point. Do not wait for a feeling to come that you are forgiven. God has said you are forgiven. Do not wait for a feeling of power to possess you. God has declared He has already given you the power. As you believe Him (and that is what faith is) you can do what you need to do and what God wants you to do.

That is what happened with David, and that is what happened with the anonymous letter writer. After preaching that sermon, I found out the person had been in that service, because later he wrote a second anonymous letter. This time he shared how God had used that message to deliver him from the grip of the evil relationship he had described before.

A Ministry of Teaching

Finally, David outlines for us the ministry that follows one who has found this kind of forgiveness. First, there is the ministry of teaching.

> *Then I will teach transgressors thy ways,*
> *and sinners will return to thee* (v. 13).

Here is the reason why many people do not become Christians today. Their teachers are not teaching out of experience. Instead of talking about forgiveness as an academic subject, those who have really been forgiven ought to be sharing how wonderful it is to be set free. Many are struggling along in guilt because they have never seen what a relief, what a glory it is, to have God refuse to hold one's transgressions against him. Teaching others should always follow the experience of forgiveness.

Praise and Thanksgiving

Then comes praise.

> *Deliver me from bloodguiltiness, O God,*
> *thou God of my salvation,*
> *and my tongue will sing aloud*
> *of thy deliverance.*
> *O Lord, open thou my lips,*
> *and my mouth shall show forth thy praise.*
> *For thou hast no delight in sacrifice;*
> *were I to give a burnt offering,*
> *thou wouldst not be pleased.*
> *The sacrifice acceptable to God is a broken spirit;*
> *a broken and contrite heart, O God,*
> *thou wilt not despise* (vv. 14-17).

What a wonderful understanding these men and women of the Old Testament had of the nature and character of God! They knew that He was not interested in burnt offerings and animals. They saw beyond all that. This man says, "I will praise you, God, for two things: (1) you have taken my guilt away, you have delivered me from bloodguiltiness; and (2) you have broken my willful spirit. That broken spirit, that contrite heart before you, is all the sacrifice you are looking for. So I can praise you, God, for having broken my stubborn will and brought me to the end of myself."

Healing for the People

Then David, as king, realizes that he has affected his whole kingdom by his sin, and so he concludes with the words of verses 18 and 19:

> *Do good to Zion in thy good pleasure;*
> *rebuild the walls of Jerusalem* (v. 18).

As the king he has caused his whole nation to be in jeopardy because of his sin. The very walls of the city (a symbol of its security) are under attack because of the evil that he has done. So now he says, "Lord, in your greatness, in your goodness, and by your forgiving grace, build it all up again. Heal the hurt to my people and to my kingdom."

Realistic Worship

> *Then wilt thou delight in right sacrifices,*
> *in burnt offerings and whole burnt offerings;*
> *then bulls will be offered on thy altar* (v. 19).

Then worship will be realistic. It will not be a mere form; it will be real. Every song sung, every psalm read, every prayer uttered will not be a mechanical, perfunctory repetition of words but the healthy articulation of a heart that has been cleansed and set free.

Do you know that the Bible says every person is a king over a kingdom? Each one holds a certain area of influence. Our family, our friends, our loved ones are in a sense a kingdom over which we have much influence as a king. What happens to your kingdom when sin reigns unchallenged in your life? It falls apart. You know that, do you not? But God offers to restore that kingdom, to build it up again, to make it real this time, to heal the relationships and build them on a right basis.

Surely our society is suffering as perhaps it has never suffered in the past history of America from the sins of adultery and sexual immorality, which have destroyed the fabric of society. How we ought to be praying that God will answer this prayer for America: "Do good to Zion in thy good pleasure and rebuild the walls of Jerusalem" that have been destroyed by the sin of our hearts. Then we shall see God restore that kingdom to us, as David did.

Our Father, we ask you to heal the hurt of our hearts. You have broken them, Lord, you have caused us to see that we are damaging the very ones we love, and damaging ourselves; destroying, doing terrible hurt to each other and ourselves by clinging to our evil. Now, Father, help us to praise you as David praised you for sending to him that faithful prophet who pointed the finger and told him that he was the man, he was the troubler of Israel. We sense your love, Lord, in pointing out to us things in our own hearts and lives that are wrong and doing damage. Help us, in the words of this psalm, to confess it, to acknowledge our guilt and to receive from you the cleansing that is your delight to give. We ask in Jesus' name, Amen.

1. Author unknown, public domain.

A Song of Confession

Many people, when they first become Christians, have a feeling that becoming a child of God ought to make life easier for them. Now they are the object of a heavenly Father's love and care. But it doesn't happen that way. Instead, they often find things becoming worse! They finally grow frustrated and depressed, especially when, by contrast, they see that ungodly people around them are often enjoying life to the full. There are many Christians who struggle with such a dilemma. It is this problem that is brought before us in Psalm 73.

This is the introductory psalm to the third book of the Psalms, which corresponds to the book of Leviticus. Do you remember Leviticus, where you ground to a halt after you had determined to read the Bible through? Usually that happens because we fail to understand the symbolism of Leviticus. We get bogged down in its detail, which tells of the building of the Tabernacle and of Israel's sacrifices to God. It consists by and large of rules and regulations, and thus is difficult for us to read unless we understand that these are all pictures of God's provision to dwell among His people and become available to them personally.

The key to the book of Leviticus is the Tabernacle, the sanctuary, which is a detailed picture of the person of Jesus Christ and His work. As such, it is also a picture of man as God intended man to be. I have long thought that the most revealing book on human psychology is the book of Leviticus. It corresponds closely to the book of Hebrews; in fact, the two should be read together.

The Prosperity of the Wicked

In this third book of the Psalms, the sanctuary is mentioned many times. Psalm 73 describes an Old Testament believer struggling with a problem that had almost wrecked his faith, and then tells of the solution he found by going into the sanctuary. The problem is stated for us in these opening verses:

> *Truly God is good to the upright,*
> *to those who are pure in heart.*
> *But as for me, my feet had almost*
> *stumbled,*
> *my steps had well nigh slipped.*
> *For I was envious of the arrogant,*
> *when I saw the prosperity of the*
> *wicked* (vv. 1-3).

This man was bothered by the apparent contradiction between what he had been taught in the Scripture—that God was good to the upright and to those who were pure in heart—and his experience in life. He was envious, he said, of the arrogant, and disturbed by the prosperity of the wicked. That prosperity seemed to him a direct contradiction of what he had learned about God. He had been told that if you were to lay hold of the righteousness that God provides and were cleansed by His grace, then God would be good to you, take care of you, and watch over you.

However, this man was finding his own situation to be difficult and discouraging, while the wicked around him, the ungodly (that is always the meaning of "wicked" in the psalms), were seeming to prosper and everything was going well with them. This had bothered him so terribly that it created a deep resentment and envy in his heart. The envy became such a threat to his faith that ultimately he found himself facing a complete loss of faith. His feet had almost slipped, he had almost stumbled, he had almost come to the place where he was ready to renounce his faith.

Here is one of the great values of the psalms to us. As we have seen before, these wonderful songs of faith reflect our own experiences. They are an enactment of what most of us are going through, have gone through, or will go through, in the walk of faith. Many Christians today have felt like this man felt. They see the seemingly logical argument of the infidel or atheist, who says, "How can your God be both a God of love and power? If He's a God of love then presumably He cares for what happens to people in their troubles and their difficulties. But if He cares, why doesn't He do something about it? He must not be a God of power, though He may be a God of love. If

He's a God of power, as you Christians say He is, and can do all things, then He cannot be a God of love or He would do something to correct injustices."

New Christians are oftentimes tremendously affected by this argument and become discouraged and frightened as they face the apparent logic of it. How can God be both a God of love and of power, and yet allow His own to suffer so terribly at times while the unrighteous seem to prosper and everything goes well with them? That was the problem this man was facing.

Description of the Ungodly

In verses 4 to 9 he describes his impression of the ungodly in their seemingly untroubled lives.

> *For they have no pangs;*
>   *their bodies are sound and sleek.*
> *They are not in trouble as other men are;*
>   *they are not stricken like other men.*
> *Therefore pride is their necklace;*
>   *violence covers them as a garment.*
> *Their eyes swell out with fatness,*
>   *their hearts overflow with follies.*
> *They scoff and speak with malice;*
>   *loftily they threaten oppression.*
> *They set their mouths against the*
>   *heavens,*
> *and their tongue struts through*
>   *the earth.*

What an accurate description that is of "a man of the world" who never seems to have any troubles. He is well fed, well clothed, even expensively dressed; pride is like an ornament to his life. His bearing is one of self-assurance and authority. He appears never to have any difficulty. If he is crossed he is quick to retaliate. He is given to self-indulgence in food and pleasure. As the writer says, "Their eyes swell out with fatness, their hearts overflow with follies." They boast in their abilities and throw their weight around by threats and ostentatious displays of influence and connections in the "right" places.

Trials of the Believer

Then he goes on to list the results that follow this kind of life,

> Therefore the people turn and praise them;
>   and find no fault in them.
> And they [the ungodly] say, "How can God know?
>   Is there knowledge in the Most High?"
> Behold, these are the wicked;
>   always at ease,
>   they increase in riches.
> All in vain have I kept my heart clean
>   and washed my hands in innocence.
> For all the day long I have been stricken,
>   and chastened every morning (vv. 10-14).

He has noticed that people treat with utmost respect these ungodly men and women, who may even be gangsters, hoodlums, or murderers. Because they are so well treated the wicked say, "Look at how good life is to us, how all the breaks come our way. If there is a God, He doesn't care about the way we live." They become so used to living without reference to God that they actually forget

He is there. They treat Him as though He were nonexistent.

A Christian man once told me about an experience on the golf course. He was with certain businessmen who weren't Christians and one of them said to him, "You know, something strange happened to me the other day. A man came up to me and said, 'Are you a Jehovah's Witness?' Why would he ask me a thing like that? Why, I hadn't even seen the accident!" He was utterly unaware of who Jehovah was, and was completely puzzled by the question.

That is what bothers this man in the psalm. He asks, "How can people live like this? How can they be so unconcerned about God and give Him no place whatsoever in their lives, and yet everything goes so well. Yet here am I, washing my hands in innocence, trying to keep my heart clean, but God puts me through trials, discouragements, and depressions every day, and I don't understand why."

Have you ever felt that way? Who of us has not? The comparison hurts him. He is almost ready to give up: "My feet had almost stumbled, my steps had well nigh slipped." There is a record in the New Testament of a young man named Demas who accompanied the apostle Paul. He surely must have felt this way and eventually the logic of it got to him. His feet stumbled, he slipped back, and Paul had to record of him, "Demas has forsaken me, having loved this present world" (see 2 Tim. 4:10).

Many feel this way. They say, "What's the use of being a Christian? There's no advantage to it. You read the Bible, go to church, and try to obey the Lord and seek fellowship with Him, but what happens? Everything goes wrong. Nothing good happens at all."

The purpose of the psalm is to tell us how this man solved his problem, so that when we get into similar difficulties we can solve it the same way. We must now trace briefly how he solved his dilemma in seven steps. Each step is important.

Don't Be a Stumbling Block

The first step is in verses 15 and 16.

> *If I had said, "I will speak thus,"*
> *I would have been untrue to the generation*
> *of thy children.*
> *But when I thought how to understand this,*
> *it seemed to me a wearisome task.*

Here he is filled with doubts and despair and almost ready to give up. What arrested his despair was the feeling, "If I utter my doubts, if I speak out of my discouraged, envious heart, I will put a stumbling block in somebody else's path. If I did that I would be untrue to the generation of God's children. So, rather than discourage them with my doubts, I'd rather not say anything at all." Surely this is a low motivation but it is something. He was unwilling to overthrow or even to threaten the faith of others by expressing doubts that he was not at all sure of yet. Rather than spread his unbelief, he decided to keep his mouth shut and not threaten someone else.

Seeing from God's Point of View

The second step followed immediately:

> *Until I went into the sanctuary of God;*
> *then I perceived their end* (v. 17).

By going "into the sanctuary," he came before the presence of God. He went into the Temple where God had made provision to meet with His people. When he did that, he began to see things from God's point of view. This is the most vital part of this psalm in many ways. This is where he began to change. He began to shift from natural thinking to spiritual thinking. He had been thinking like a natural man, within the limits of this life, considering only the visible things of earth. Now, in the sanctuary, he begins to think from God's point of view and that's when he starts to understand or perceive. When you go to church or read the Scriptures, you are not trying merely to find something to soothe you a bit; you are going so that you might have your eyes opened, that you might see things as they really are, and thus begin to understand life.

There are many people who are content to use the Bible only to soothe their feelings when they get upset. They like its beauty or its language. But the Bible is not given to us for its beauty and language. Rather, it is provided that we might understand what is happening to us in every aspect of life.

The trouble with natural thinking is that it centers our attention on ourselves. It makes us slaves to our feelings, our moods, our emotional reactions to circumstances. When that happens your range of vision is narrowed down to only those factors that are troubling you. You cannot think beyond them. When our feelings govern us, they always limit us, make us prejudiced. Prejudice is simply a narrow limited range of vision that has only one fact in view. That is what was troubling this man.

When he comes into the sanctuary, into the presence of God, he begins to think spiritually. Spiritual thinking is centered on God. The mind is in control and not the feelings. Then you are not being governed by emotions but by thoughts relating to facts. Thus your vision is broadened and you can see other things besides what is disturbing your emotions. You can see the whole range and scope of your problem only when you "enter the sanctuary."

How do we enter the sanctuary today? According to the New Testament, we ourselves are the sanctuary. God lives in us. We enter the sanctuary by exposing ourselves to His truth in Scripture, or by fellowshiping with other Christians who help us face truth that we may have forgotten, or by praying directly to God. That's how we can change our attitudes from natural thinking to spiritual thinking.

Perceiving the End

The third step follows, in verses 18-20. What did he learn in the sanctuary? He says, "I perceived their end."

> *Truly thou dost set them in slippery places;*
> *thou dost make them fall to ruin.*
> *How they are destroyed in a moment,*
> *swept away utterly by terrors!*
> *They are like a dream when one awakes,*
> *on awaking you despise their phantoms.*

Here he begins to see additional facts that he had not seen before. He had forgotten the end of the ungodly. This obviously refers to the end of their life, but it is not limited entirely to that. It includes also the end of the processes by which they are living. We come to many ends in our experiences of life. This man failed to take into consideration what was happening within the inner lives of these people whom he had so envied. What he found changed his whole way of thinking.

He discovered, first of all, that without God men cannot have inner strength. God has set them, he says, "in slippery places," and makes them "fall to ruin." This explains why we so frequently read of some prominent person, like a movie star, whom everyone is acclaiming, suddenly and unexpectedly committing suicide. Why? Because inside they had been set in slippery places. There was nothing to hold on to. Though outwardly they maintained a facade of happiness, inwardly they began to fall apart and at last they come to an end. They could no longer stand life; they could no longer stand themselves. Those who have maintained an outward facade of prosperity and carefree living are inwardly torn up, despairing, and suddenly come to an end.

Plagued by Fears and Terrors

Then this man learned that without God the ungodly are plagued by fears and terrors—"how they are destroyed in a moment, swept away utterly by terrors!" I have had people who were not Christians tell me that, though they appeared to be composed and at ease, they were often gripped inside by terrible fears. They have learned to hide these, to keep them from showing on their faces, but to a private counselor they freely admit how frightened they are.

William Randolph Hearst, who built the great Hearst Castle near Morro Bay on the Central California coast searched the world for beautiful objets d'art with which to fill it. But he had a standing rule that no guest in his home could ever mention the word *death*. Each night he was afraid to go to sleep because he was tormented by the fear of death. This psalmist had not faced all the facts about the ones who troubled him. Let us remember the same facts as we look at the apparent prosperity of the ungodly today.

Then the psalmist learned that the ultimate end of these people is to be forgotten. "They are like a dream when one awakes, and on awaking you despise their phantoms." We all know how this is. We have a bad dream, frightening and terrible. Perhaps you are being pursued by a monster, or you are running down the street naked. It is a frightening dream that seems so real; you are upset by it, your emotions are so stirred that it actually wakes you up. You lie there palpitating, sweating, but in a few moments it is all gone. As soon as you awake you forget the dream; it is only a vague memory.

That, says the psalmist, is like the ungodly, those men and women who persist in rejecting God's love and grace. What happens to them? They make a splash for the moment of their lives, but after that they are gone and soon forgotten. Many of us remember how the world stood in awe of Hitler. He had the whole world frightened and hanging on his every word. But already he is almost forgotten. Young people hardly know who you mean when you mention him. He is but a name out of the past, and the fearsomeness of his character and his threat to the world is gone like a dream in the night.

Not an Enviable Position

Thus, this man began to take note of certain other facts. He now comes to the place where he has cleared up his thinking about the ungodly, and about God. He sees that God is ruling over the affairs of men and that the ungodly are not in such an envious spot, after all. In fact, who would want to change places with them in view of their end?

I remember once reading to some young people the story of our Lord's parable of the rich man and Lazarus. I read to them how Lazarus lay at the gate of the rich man, the dogs licking his sores, while the rich man ate in splendor in his house. I said to them, "Which would you rather be, the rich man or Lazarus?"

They said, "Oh, we would rather be the rich man."

Then I read on to where they both died and the rich man was in torment but Lazarus was carried to the bosom of Abraham. I said to them, "Now, which would you rather be?"

They said, "Oh, we'd much rather be Lazarus; we don't want to be the rich man." That is also what the psalmist saw.

Getting out of a Rut

But he did not stop there. Notice what he did next. This fourth step is very important.

> *When my soul was embittered,*
> *when I was pricked in heart,*
> *I was stupid and ignorant,*
> *I was like a beast toward thee* (vv. 21,22).

He did not stop with correcting his thinking; he went on to re-evaluate himself and his problem and to see just how he got into the mess in the first place. He honestly faced himself. Now, this is a difficult thing to do. We do not like doing this. We do not mind working our way through our problem, but the minute we get relief we want to stop right there. We do not go on to face up to what caused us to come to wrong conclusions. That is why we keep going through the same problems over and over again. This man probably never relived this experience because he worked it through so thoroughly here that he never had to face it again.

I often think of the story of the woman who had been teaching school for 25 years. A job opened that she wanted and she applied for it, but another person who had only been a teacher for one year got the position. The older teacher was incensed and went to the principal. "I don't understand," she said, "why you would give this job to an inexperienced person when I've had 25 years' experience!"

The principal said to her, "No, I'm sorry. You haven't had 25 years of experience; you've had one year's experience 25 times."

Mountains out of Molehills

That is often what happens to us. We go through the same problems, the same difficulties, year after year. It is because we never stop to find out what made us act this way and to confess before God the condition that led us into a position of unbelief.

But that is what this man does. He saw three things that led him to doubt. He saw that he had been stupid, that he had worked this all up himself. There was not any real problem, but he had simply allowed his feelings to get hold of him to the point that he had worked himself up into a frenzy. The minute his feelings were corrected by the facts, the problem disappeared. There was no real problem at all. His distress was not caused by the outside circumstances, but was something he himself had produced.

I have been in this very state myself where I suddenly realized I had allowed my feelings to grasp me and to work me up into a frantic state of mind. I have had to realize, like this man, how stupid it was to build mountains out of molehills, to make big issues out of trivial things.

Like an Animal

The second thing he learned was that he was ignorant. There were things that he obviously did not know, but could have known.

He ignored the fact that God loved him. He began to distrust God when he failed to realize that a Father's loving heart is behind each trial that a believer goes through. As Hebrews tells us, if God did not love us He would not chasten us. It is *because* He loves us that He chastens us. He was ignorant of the record of the Scriptures that tells us these things.

Finally, he realized that he was like an animal, reacting instinctively, concerned only with himself, loving to be petted and taken care of but not wanting any kind of discipline at all. So he thinks again, he repents, and bowing before God he says, "How stupid I was, how ignorant I've been, how like an animal I've been before thee."

"Nevertheless"

When he reaches that place, look what happens next, the fifth step.

> *Nevertheless I am continually with thee;*
> *thou dost hold my right hand.*
> *Thou dost guide me with thy counsel, and*
> *afterward thou wilt receive me to glory* (vv. 23,24).

The minute he comes to this low place before God there comes an instant reassurance. He realizes that God still loves him, God has not cast him aside. All the marvel of the grace of God is poured into that one word, "Nevertheless." Suddenly there comes to his understanding the fact that, though he is confessing his stupidity and his ignorance before God, God has not cast him away; He is still with him, He still loves him, He still holds him and supports him. The wonder of that breaks afresh upon the psalmist's heart, and he cries out in astonishment, "Nevertheless, I am continually with thee."

Accepting His Forgiveness

At a Bible school I had an interview with a certain young lady who came to me after I had spoken on the subject, "How to Live in a Sexually Inflamed Society." She told me how disturbed she was by her past. Not long before coming to school she had been guilty of sexual immorality. She described how terrible it made her feel, especially in this school where she felt that the other young people had lived clean lives in that respect. She said, "I feel so dirty, I feel so guilty, and I can't get rid of this feeling. I know God has forgiven me but I can't forgive myself."

As we talked she said, "You know, there is one thing though that really strikes me. Since I've been here God has been so good to me. There are so many wonderful things that He's given me and shown me while I've been here."

I said to her, "Doesn't that tell you something? Doesn't that tell you that God loves you yet and that He has forgiven you? Do you think a Holy God would let you stand in His presence unclean, as you feel yourself to be, and not cast you out? The very fact that He loves you and takes care of you and does wonderful things for you is His way of telling you you've been cleansed, forgiven." Then I reminded her of the Lord's words to Peter when he refused to eat unclean animals, "What I have cleansed, don't you dare call unclean" (see Acts 10:15).

When I said that her face brightened, and she said, "Oh, that's right, that's right. God *has* cleansed me. It's an insult to Him to say I'm unclean."

His Restraining Hand

That is what this psalmist found: first, forgiveness; second, God's restraining hand. He says, "Thou dost hold me by my right hand." What is it, after all, that drew him back, that stopped him from going over the brink? He sees now that it was the hand of God. It was God Himself who put into his mind to go into the sanctuary, and thus stopped him and turned him around. God had been holding him with His right hand.

His Guidance

Third, he saw that God would guide him for the rest of his life. "Thou dost guide me all the way." The Word of God is there to unfold reality, dispel illusion, and guide him safely through the snares and the problems. Finally, he cries, "Afterward thou wilt receive me to glory." That is the end of the Christian. He had seen the end of the ungodly; now he sees the end of the Christian. It is glory.

The Utter Adequacy of God

That leads inevitably to the sixth step.

> *Whom have I in heaven but thee?*
> *And there is nothing upon earth*
> *that I desire besides thee.*
> *My flesh and my heart may fail,*
> *but God is the strength of my*
> *heart and my portion for ever* (vv. 25, 26).

Sometimes we say that New Testament Christians, having the Holy Spirit indwelling us, are much better off than Old Testament saints. But let me ask you this: Can you say what this psalmist said? Have you come to the place where you can say, "God is the strength of my heart and my portion for ever. Whom have I in heaven but thee? And there is nothing upon earth that I desire besides thee." Here is a man who has seen the utter adequacy of God. God can meet your need in loneliness, in despair, in frustration, in disappointment, in sorrow, in life, and in death. In every situation or condition of life God is able to meet you and to supply all that you need. No one else can do this, the psalmist says. So he cries out, "What I want is God Himself."

Resting on the Rock

Now that had been his problem. He had been thinking that he needed other things than God, that he needed things the ungodly had. But now he comes to realize that all he needs is God Himself. If he has God and the fellowship of God, then nothing else is needed. So he concludes with this resolution, which is a most wonderful statement.

> For lo, those who are far from thee shall
>   perish;
> thou dost put an end to those who are false
>   to thee.
> But for me it is good to be near God;
>   I have made the Lord God my refuge, that
>   I may tell of all thy works (vv. 27,28).

His conclusion is, God does keep His word. God does exactly what He says He will do. He is good to those who are upright and to those who have found purity of heart in Him. He keeps them. Those who are far from Him shall perish; but those who draw nigh to God are established and kept. So His resolve is, "to be near God; . . . that I may tell of all thy works."

Do you remember how James puts that same truth, "Draw near to God and he will draw near to you" (James 4:8). When you begin to search for God, to seek His mind in the Scriptures or in the fellowship of others, to expose yourself to the teaching of the Word of God, or to pray before God, then you are drawing near to God. God promises that if you take one step toward Him, He will take a dozen toward you. That is what will keep you through any difficulty of life. The psalmist concludes with that. God, he says, is my rock—that is the meaning of the word "strength." Resting on this rock, he can take anything life can throw at him.

Father, teach us this same truth. These are turbulent days in which we live, days in which there are many pressures, many problems. Keep us from being envious of the ungodly, but help us to hunger, Father, to reach them and to see them delivered as we have been delivered. Make us to trust, Lord, in thy greatness and thy power. In Christ's name, Amen.

The Living God

You will notice in the inscription to Psalm 84 that, like Psalm 8, it is "according to The Gittith," which, as I have pointed out in connection with the eighth Psalm, is an eight-stringed instrument very much like our modern guitar. This psalm, too, is designed to be accompanied by the music of a guitar. In our modern day we have come full circle and have come back to singing with a guitar accompaniment as in the days of David.

Fellowship with the Living God

The theme of this wonderful little psalm is the advantages that accrue to one who is in touch with the living God, the advantages that belong to the life of faith, the life of fellowship with a living God. The psalm divides very simply into three parts marked off by the little word *Selah*, which, in Hebrew, means "think of that"—pause and think of what has just been said. In the first four verses, the psalmist is setting before us the advantages of life with God—God at home within His people.

> How lovely is thy dwelling place,
>   O Lord of hosts!
> My soul longs, yea, faints
>   for the courts of the Lord;
> my heart and flesh sing for joy
>   to the living God (vv. 1,2).

What a wonderful expression that is of the excitement produced by the presence of God. Now, of course, when these psalmists talked about the dwelling place of God, they meant the Temple, the building *in* Jerusalem where God's Shekinah glory was manifest. In the holy of holies within the Temple was a strange and mysterious light, which marked the presence of God. No Israelite was permitted to enter that holy place except the high priest and he could go in only once a year under the most rigorous of rituals. When the Israelites came into the Temple, though they could not physically enter the holy of holies to be in the presence of God there, nevertheless, in their hearts and minds, as they appreciated and understood the truth pictured by their sacrifices, they entered in spirit into the holy of holies. That is what the psalmist is now singing about.

But when we as Christians talk about the dwelling place of God, we learn from the New Testament that we are talking about our bodies. Paul says in 1 Corinthians 6 that our bodies are the "temples" of the Holy Spirit who lives within us. Therefore, we can read the words of this psalm and take them as an expression of the excitement that comes to us because of the presence of God in our bodies.

The Beauty of His Presence

The psalmist shares three reasons why he's excited about being in the presence of God. The first is the inner beauty God creates by His presence. "How *lovely* is your dwelling place, O God." The place where God lives, the heart where God dwells, becomes a lovely place, a beautiful spot. The apostle Paul, in Ephesians, prays that Christ may make His home in your heart by faith because that heart will then always be a lovely place. The character of that heart is changed. In practice that means that you will be a lot easier to get along with. You will be less prickly and difficult when God is living in you. You will become a beautiful person in the truest sense.

Longing for His Glory

The second reason is that God's presence arouses in the psalmist a compelling hunger. "My soul longs, yea, faints for the courts of the Lord." Have you ever felt this way? Have you known a deep-seated longing to have more of the glory of God, more of the sense of His presence in your life? Have you fed upon His Word and been satisfied, and yet as you went away, felt a hunger for more? We sing this sometimes in a hymn:

We taste Thee, O Thou living Bread,
And long to feast upon Thee still;
We drink of Thee, the Fountainhead,
And thirst our soul from Thee to fill. [1]

It is a strange paradox, this wonderful ability God has to satisfy us and at the same time make us hungry for more.

Joyful Vitality

Then the third reason is the joyful vitality that the presence of God gives. "My heart and flesh sing for joy to the living God." That is exactly what God has meant life to be. You may have been a Christian for many years but if you have not yet found this kind of excitement you haven't yet touched the possibilities and resources of a Christian life. This is not an artificial excitement. It is not something put on like a mask, it is the real thing. This psalmist is struggling to set before us the reality of the joy of God's presence.

A young man once wrote me a letter, which said something like this. "I'm a janitor and my work is boring to me. I do the same old things over and over. What can you suggest that will help me in this problem of boredom?"

Now that is a perfectly proper question to address to a pastor. If your relationship with God does not help you with that kind of a problem, then it is not much of a relationship. I answered him by pointing out that the secret to the relief of boredom, in my judgment, was given to us in the fourth chapter of John's Gospel. There the Lord meets with a jaded, bored woman who came to a well. She had run through several experiences of marriage already (having had five husbands), trying vainly to find something to satisfy her. Life for her had grown tedious and dull and boring.

Jesus said to her, "Whoever drinks of the water that I shall give him will never thirst; the water that I shall give him will become in him a spring of water welling up to eternal life" (John 4:14). By that "spring," He was referring to

Himself. He would enter her heart and become to her a spring from which she could drink at any time.

Years ago I learned the practical secret of that. Whenever my outward circumstances get boring, I drink from that which is within. I take a good long drink of the living God who lives within; a drink of the refreshing character of His being. I remind myself of who He is and of my relationship with Him, and that He is continually there. I have never done that but what my spirit has been refreshed and I have come back to my work—the same old work—with a new attitude. That is what the psalmist is speaking of here.

Peace in His Presence

The next two verses describe the contentment that the presence of God brings.

> *Even the sparrow finds a home, and the swallow*
> *a nest for herself, where she may lay her*
> *young,*
> *at thy altars, O Lord of hosts,*
> *my King and my God.*
> *Blessed are those who dwell in thy house,*
> *ever singing thy praise! Selah* (vv. 3,4).

A Sense of Purpose

He mentions here two birds frequently found in Scripture. First, is a sparrow. Do you remember when the Lord Jesus, speaking to His disciples, referred to sparrows? "Not one of them will fall to the ground without your father's will," He said. "You are of more value than many sparrows" (see Matt. 10:29,31). He also said, "Are not five sparrows sold for two pennies?" (Luke 12:6). By

these statements he recognized that a sparrow is a popular symbol for insignificance. Sparrows represent those
who feel they are not worth anything. Now, says this
psalmist, even the man or woman who feels insignificant
finds in God a home, a place of warmth and security, a
place where life is fulfilled. You may feel terribly useless,

---

IT is usually to those who have a deep
sense of failure that the call of God
comes, for they can understand how others feel.

---

but when you come to God you will find through Him a wonderful sense of purpose.

I am impressed as I read the Scriptures how many times
God passes over the proud, the haughty, the powerful, and
the ostentatious, and selects some insignificant, obscure
individual and uses him to accomplish his purposes. Gideon
was that kind of a man. He was so sure he didn't amount to
anything that he protested when God called him to deliver
Israel. Moses did the same thing. He had been a king's son
in the courts of Pharaoh with all the possibilities of power at
his command, but he felt he had blown it when he killed an
Egyptian and had to flee to the backside of the desert. He
thought he had wrecked his life—that there was no more
chance for him.

But it wasn't all over in God's scheme; all that had happened was only part of the training course. When Moses had
reached the place where God could work through him, God
picked him up in his insignificance and began to use him
mightily. God never uses anyone continuously until he has
put them through that kind of training. It is usually to those

who have a deep sense of failure that the call of God comes, for they can understand how others feel.

When did the Lord Jesus say to Peter, "Feed my lambs"? Was it after Peter had come to Him in all his boastfulness and said, "Lord, look at these other fellows; you can't count on them. But Lord, you can count on me. I'll see you through to the end, Lord." Did the Lord then say to him, "Very well, Peter, very well spoken. I can count on you. Feed my lambs"? No. It wasn't until Peter had denied his Lord and had gone out to weep bitterly in the streets of Jerusalem that the Lord Jesus called him and said to him, "Peter, feed my lambs" (see John 21:15). Yes, even the sparrow will find a place of usefulness, a home in God.

Rest for the Soul

So, too, has the swallow. Where I once lived, in northern Minnesota, we had many swallows. Every evening you could see them darting about. They are the swiftest of birds and exemplify restless activity. They are used that way also in the Scriptures. The swallow represents those people who are restless, who are forever looking for something new. They settle down and try this and that but it doesn't work. They are rolling stones, ever on the move. But even the swallow, says the psalmist, can find in God a home, a place to build a nest and to raise young, a place of purpose and fulfillment.

Through 30 years of observation I can tell you that is the only place the restless will ever find rest—in God. They will find in Him that rest of which Jesus spoke, "Come to me, all who labor and are heavy laden, and I will give you rest. Take my yoke upon you, and learn from me; for I am gentle and lowly in heart, and you will find rest for your souls" (Matt. 11:28,29). Those are not mere words. It is not just beautiful language designed to stir your spirit a bit on Sunday mornings. Those words are designed for life. If you are restless, there is a message in them for you. God is speaking to you. God wants to give you rest. You won't find it in circumstances; you won't find it in adventure. These things will pall on you. You will find it only, as the psalmist tells us, "at thy altars, O Lord of hosts, my king and my God."

Everything to Everyone
I love that phrasing. He puts together two concepts of God that seem contradictory. It is done two or three times in this psalm. First, he refers to God as "O Lord of hosts." What does that mean? Well, that means the Lord of the multitudes; the Lord of the many; Lord of the great crowds; the One on whom all the creatures of earth depend for a living; One mighty in power who is able to meet the needs of thousands and thousands everywhere. Then he adds to this, "my king and my God." That is a personal note, set in contrast to the Lord of Hosts. One of the glories of God is this wonderful fact, that He is able to do what none of us can do. He is able to give Himself wholly to me as an individual. At the same time He is doing it also to you and to everyone else all over the world.

I wish I had that power. I sometimes feel stretched in 15 different directions. Everyone seems to want to be my friend and I wish I could be their friend. I'd love to, but I can't. But God can! "My king and my God." No wonder he says, "Blessed are those who dwell in thy house, ever singing thy praise! Selah." What a marvelous concept that is!

Highways in Our Hearts

Then in the next section he sets before us a description of

what happens when God is at work in our hearts.

> *Blessed are the men whose strength is in thee,*
> *in whose heart are the highways to Zion.*
> *As they go through the valley of Baca*
> *they make it a place of springs; the early*
> *rain also covers it with pools.*
> *They go from strength to strength;*
> *the God of gods will be seen in Zion.*
> *O Lord God of hosts, hear my prayer;*
> *give ear, O God of Jacob! Selah* (vv. 5-8).

Where Is Your Strength?

Here the secret of usefulness is set forth. "Blessed are the men whose strength is in thee." Now I want to ask you something. Many of you have been Christians for a long time. When you get in difficulties or troubles or pressures, where is your strength? Have you found that your strength is in God, that He is the One who makes a difference?

One Saturday night I came home after a day away from my church responsibilities and I was tired, very tired. My wife told me some of the things that had been happening, some of the pressures that had come that day from the church and the family. They were the kind of things I would normally want to lay before the Lord and pray about. But I didn't feel like praying. I was tired and I wanted to go to bed. I thought to myself, "What's the use of praying, anyway? I'm so tired that my prayers wouldn't have any power."

Then it struck me; what a thing to say! What difference does it make how I feel? My reliance isn't upon my prayers but upon God's power. It always bothers me to hear Christians talk about "the power of prayer." There isn't any power in prayer. There is power in the God who answers prayer. I was rebuked in my own spirit by the remembrance that it makes no difference how tired I happen to be. So I prayed—very short, because the power of prayer doesn't lie in the length of it, either. Charles Spurgeon used to speak of those who had the idea that the power of ministry lay in the lungs of the preacher. But it doesn't lie there, either. Power lies in the God who is behind prayer. "Blessed are the men—and women—whose strength is in thee."

Power all Around
Some years ago I was trying to sell my car. Intending to put an ad in the paper, I read through several car ads to learn how to phrase it. I noticed a phrase that appeared again and again throughout the ads. It said, "Power all around." At first I didn't know what that meant, and then I realized it meant power steering, power brakes, power transmission, power windows, power seats, and, in the case of a convertible, a power top. Power all around! All this power is designed to take the terrible strain out of driving so that all you need to do is sit there and push little buttons and things will happen. What a great description of the Christian life! Power all around! "God did not give us a spirit of timidity but a spirit of power and love and self-control" (2 Tim. 1:7).

Someone has suggested that when you get into difficult places where it is hard to know what decision to make, you try power steering. "Your ears shall hear a word behind you, saying, 'This is the way, walk in it,' when you turn to the right or when you turn to the left" (Isa. 30:21) Are you having trouble with a stubborn habit? Well, try power brakes. "In all these things we are more than conquerors through him who loved us" (Rom. 8:37). Are you bothered by moodiness and discouragement? Try power windows. "And the peace of God, which passes all understanding, will keep your hearts and your minds in Christ Jesus" (Phil. 4:7). For a satisfying life, try power unlimited. "You shall receive power when the Holy Spirit has come upon you; and you shall be my witnesses" (Acts 1:8). Says the psalmist, these are the men who have their strength in God.

Travel in Blessing

Then he adds, "in whose heart are the highways." Cross out the words "to Zion" because they are not in the original Hebrew. What kind of men are these, with highways in their hearts? All through the Scripture you will find references to the highways, and they always refer to what men do in their lives to prepare the way for God, to give God access to all areas of their life.

You remember, when John the Baptist came preaching before Christ, it was said that he fulfilled the words of Isaiah 40, "A voice cries: 'In the wilderness prepare the way of the Lord, make straight in the desert a highway for our God'" (v. 3). The prophet also described how it would be done: "Every valley shall be lifted up, and every mountain and hill be made low; the uneven ground shall become level, and the rough places a plain" (v. 4).

That is what is described in Psalm 84: men and women who know how to build in their hearts a highway for God. How is that done? Well, when you get into the valleys, you bring them up to level by trust in God. "Every valley shall be exalted." And when you get on a mountain of difficulty, or you find yourself lifted up in pride and self-conceit, you judge it in the light of the Word, and bring it low. "Every mountain shall be brought low." When you find things in your life that are crooked, you make them straight, and if there are rough spots you work on smoothing them out. Thus you make a highway for God to travel in blessing, not only to your heart but to others. Blessed are the men who have learned this secret of usefulness. Their strength is in God, and they have made a highway by which God can work in the valleys and the mountains.

A Place of Springs

Then the psalmist refers to what follows: "As they go through the valley of Baca they make it a place of springs; the early rain also covers it with pools."

The valley of Baca is the valley of weeping. This refers to the ministry that men and women who know how to make a highway for God will have in the lives of others. They will come into the place of sorrowing, of despair, of discouragement, and by their radiant faith and their cheerful outlook, turn it into a place of fountains, of refreshment, of satisfaction. They will do it by means of the Holy Spirit. The early rain is a picture of the Holy Spirit.

This beautiful, picturesque language of Scripture lends itself to exact interpretation if you understand how these symbols are used in other places. Here is a reference to the early rain and in the prophets there is also a reference to the latter rain. The early and the latter rain is a symbol of the outpouring of the Holy Spirit, as the prophet Joel makes clear (see 2:23-29). Pentecost was such an occasion—the pouring out of the Holy Spirit—and that is what is referred to here. These men and women are able to turn sorrow into joy by means of the Holy Spirit, who fills their lives with pools of blessing and springs (permanent fountains) of joy. Do you know people like that? What wonderful people they are. It is refreshing to have people who come into your life and, with but a word, change your whole outlook.

I have a good friend, Dr. Jack Mitchell of Portland, Oregon. He is in his 90s as this is written and is a dear man of God. What a blessing he is when he comes to minister in our church, for whenever he comes he opens the windows of God and helps us see again the glory of the Lord Jesus. An incident that took place one week when he was visiting our church provides a particularly clear illustration of the ministry in the valley of Baca.

In the services on the day when Dr. Mitchell spoke was a young man who had been struggling with some very difficult problems in his life. He had come under an awful load of defeat and depression. In the morning service he was so taken by what Dr. Mitchell said that he came back for the evening service.

That evening Dr. Mitchell brought forth most beautifully the forgiveness of God and the way the grace of God sets us free. This young man sat in the second row, his face fastened on Dr. Mitchell, drinking in every word. At the end of the service he said to one of his friends, "What a burden of guilt has been lifted from my life!"

The following Tuesday he met with one of our pastors to have lunch together and talk over his difficulties. As they were riding in the pastor's Volkswagen, they stopped at a red light. They were engrossed in their talk when suddenly around the corner—and through the red light—came a huge, loaded moving van. The van hit the front of the Volkswagen, the door on the right side was forced open and the young man fell out into the street where he was killed instantly. The pastor was left unhurt, with hardly a scratch.

It was a shocking thing to him and to us, for our staff had been praying for that young man just that morning.

When the pastor came back, he said, "The boy we prayed for this morning is dead." Though we were shaken and shocked by what happened, I thought immediately of the comfort that had been brought him as Dr. Mitchell had passed through his valley of Baca and had made it a place of springs instead of tears.

From Strength to Strength

The psalmist points out the effect that building these "highways" has on the persons who do it. "They go from strength to strength" (v. 7). They get better and better as they experience God's grace until, ultimately, "the God of gods will be seen in Zion" (v. 7). The face of the invisible God becomes visible through the lives of people like that. When I read this psalm I feel like praying exactly what this psalmist prays in verse 8:

Learn Where Our Strength Lies

O Lord God of hosts, hear my prayer,
give ear, O God of Jacob! Selah (v. 8).

He asks, in effect, "Make me this kind of a man; help me to learn where my strength lies and to build in my heart highways for God so that I can go through the valley of weeping and make it a place of springs and so go from strength to strength until the God of gods is seen." Is that not also what you want?

Behold Our Shield

Then let us give ear to this prayer as it is set forth in the closing section, "Behold our shields, O God," or more literally, "O shield, behold!" It is God who is the shield. The writer is now addressing God and he says:

> *Behold our shield, O God; look upon the face*
> *of thine anointed!* (v. 9).

It is a cry for a personal application of these great truths. This is perfectly proper. The psalmist says, "Lord, I see your blessing and power in the lives of others and I want this. Give it to me as well!" It is perfectly right to pray that way. It is never wrong to ask God to do for you what He wants to do for you. It is right to pray, "Lord, I want to find the way into this!"

Better than Anything Else

Then the psalmist gives two reasons why he wants this kind of life, set forth by the "for's" of verses 10 and 11.

> *For a day in thy courts is better*
> *than a thousand elsewhere.*
> *I would rather be a doorkeeper in the*
> *house of my God than dwell in the*
> *tents of wickedness* (v. 10).

The first reason he wants this is because life with God is incomparably better that anything else. There is no other place to go. One day lived in fellowship with God is the equivalent of almost three years (1000 days) without him. That is worth something, is it not? This man has evidently discovered how rich God can be and, remembering it, he says, "If every day could be like that, what a difference there would be in my life! Lord, this is what I want. A day with you is worth 1000 elsewhere. I'd rather be a humble doorkeeper in your house than to have everything else without you, to live in the tents of wickedness. Life with you is incomparably better."

All We'll Ever Need

Second, it is inexhaustibly complete.

> *For the Lord God is a sun and shield;*
> *he bestows favor and honor.*
> *No good thing does the Lord withhold*
> *from those who walk uprightly* (v. 11).

If I need a sun, if I am in darkness, if I do not know where I am going and I do not know what lies ahead of me, then God can be to me a sun. He is wonderfully adaptable to my need. If I need protection, then He is a shield around me, guarding me, guiding me. Whatever I need, He is. That is the good news of the gospel. I love the acrostic that is built around the name of Jesus:

J   just
E   exactly
S   suits
U   us
S   sinners

Is that not right? Jesus exactly suits us sinners! He is designed for us. He is a sun and a shield, and gives grace and glory. Grace is for pressures. It is His power to keep the heart at peace within. That is the inner gift. Glory is the outward expression. God gives grace in order to bring us to glory, not only in heaven, but *now*.

God is constantly giving grace and glory. He does not take us out of the pressures, but He gives us grace in the midst of them in order that He might bring us to glory (thanksgiving, joy and gladness). This is to be the repeated pattern of the Christian life. If you are going through a time of pressure, thank God for it and ask for grace. He will give it and it will lead you on to glory. Our problem is that we are always wanting it to happen NOW. We want glory all the time. But God knows that is not good for us. So He gives us grace first, and then glory.

The Secret of Life

This writer sums it all up in verse 12:

> *O Lord of hosts,*
> *blessed is the man who trust in thee!*

Happy is the man who trusts God, who has learned that life lived with God has tremendous advantages. This is for the problems you are now facing. You young people, this is for you at school, to help you with the longings and yearnings of your heart. This is for you in business. You older people, retired, facing loneliness, this is for you. Blessed is the man who trusts in God. That is the secret of life.

Heavenly Father, keep us from taking these words artificially or mechanically. Help us to know they are a testimony given to us to make us see that our lives can be rich and full. Teach us patience in this, Lord. We want richness overnight. Help us to realize that your process is to drop a seed and let it grow, to come at last to fruition. Teach us then to wait, Lord, upon you, and to know that you will bring us to a glory and a richness that is beyond our wildest dreams, more than we can ever express. We ask in your name, Amen.

1. These words were written by Bernard (1090-1153), abbot of the monastery of Clairvaux, France.

A Song of Realities

We come now to Psalm 90, which introduces the fourth book of the Psalms. You may be interested to learn that this is the oldest of the psalms and probably the pattern psalm upon which others are based. According to the inscription Psalm 90 was written by Moses and is one of possibly two psalms Moses wrote. Some scholars feel he also wrote Psalm 91, which ties in somewhat with Psalm 90.

The fourth book of the Psalms corresponds to the book of Numbers in the Pentateuch. Numbers is the book of wilderness wanderings, the story of the failure of man. It is very likely that Moses wrote this psalm at the end of the wilderness wanderings, just before he died. This is, in my judgment, one of the greatest of the psalms. In its scope, range of thought, and vastness of concept, it is a marvelous statement of divine glory.

The Greatness of God

It opens with a powerful declaration of the greatness of God.

> Lord, thou hast been our dwelling place
>> in all generations.
> Before the mountains were brought forth,
>> or ever thou hadst formed
>> the earth and the world,
> from everlasting to everlasting
>> thou art God (vv. 1,2).

In that brief statement are three great facts that mark the greatness of God. The psalmist begins by declaring that God has been the dwelling place of man in all generations. What is a dwelling place? Well, it is where you live. It is your home. This statement declares that God has been man's home ever since man has been on the earth. In all the generations of man it is where he continually lives. This is the same truth Paul uttered when he addressed the Athenians on Mars Hill. He said to them: God is not far away from any of us (even pagans, he points out), for "in him we live and move and have our being" (Acts 17:28). God exists as a home for man.

That is a wonderful thought, is it not? Here Moses is looking back over the course of human history and declaring that God is great because He is the God of history. Moses had seen the Pharaohs live and die. Perhaps he had often crossed the Nile River and gone over to the Valley of the Kings, which tourists now visit and where the tombs of the Pharaohs are located. There he could have noted the many who, throughout past history, had been laid to rest. Yet, despite the passing centuries, there is no change in the relationship of man to God. He has been the home of man for all generations.

The God of Creation
Then the psalmist points out that God is the God of creation. "Before the mountains were brought forth, or ever thou hadst formed the earth and the world." Notice the order of events here. He is beginning with the latest geological fact: the mountains were formed after the earth itself had been created. They are more recent in the geological record. Moses here is looking back across that record and saying, "Before the mountains were formed, God was."

Even before forming the mountains, He "formed the earth and the world." Now, to us the "earth and the world" are the same thing, but in the Hebrew it is literally, "the earth and the land." God formed the earth first and then later brought out the land from the waters, as the book of Genesis makes clear. The land emerged from waters that covered the earth. So Moses is gradually moving back in time from the formation of the mountains to the emergence of the land and, finally, to the creation of the earth itself. Before all this, God was.

From Everlasting to Everlasting
Then he takes a longer leap into timelessness and says, "From everlasting to everlasting thou art God." Surely here is the greatness of God. He is the God of history. He is the God of creation. But beyond all that, He is the God eternity. He is beyond and above His creation. He is greater than the universe He produced and, before it

existed, He was. The Hebrew here is again very interesting. It suggests the translation "From the vanishing point in the past to the vanishing point in the future." How great He is!

This is far different from any pagan concept of God. Plato, the great Greek philosopher, was the only one of whom we have record in the ancient world who held some concept of the timelessness of God. In the eyes of others, the pagan gods all had a beginning. Read the pagan myths and you will find that all the gods started somewhere. But here is a God who never begins, a timeless, endless God who is beyond and above His creation, and beyond and above all the events of history. That mighty God, that tremendous Being so far different, above and "other" than ourselves, is now brought close to us in the rest of the psalm.

God's Sovereign Control

The psalmist now examines the relationship of God to man. That is the theme of this psalm. How do you and I relate to the greatness of God? Again he gives us three great facts, beginning with verse 3.

> Thou turnest man back to the dust,
>   and sayest "Turn back, O children of men!"
> For a thousand years in thy sight
>   are but as yesterday when it is past,
>   or as a watch in the night.
> Thou dost sweep men away; they are like a dream,
>   like grass which is renewed in the morning:
> in the morning it flourishes and is renewed;
>   in the evening it fades and withers (vv. 3-6).

The Limits of Knowledge

Three things about God mark the limits of life for man. These are the three greatest facts of human existence. First, we must live within the sovereignty of God. It is God who controls human life. As the psalmist points out, "Thou turnest man back to the dust, and sayest, 'Turn back, O children of men!'" God sets the limits to life.

There are certain things He will not let us do. Some years ago, when space exploration was in its infancy, many people asked, "Is it right for man to explore space? Is it right for us to go up to the moon? Is this a proper activity of man?" The answer is "Yes." If it were not, God would simply say, "Turn back, O children of men," and that would be as far as we could get. What He has allowed is something He obviously permits. The very fact that man is exploring space makes it clear that this is within the limits of God for man. We could never explore what God does not permit us to explore.

But through the Bible we find two or three things reserved from man's knowledge. The understanding of time is one. Jesus says, "The times and the seasons are not for you to know" (see Acts 1:7). Again and again He hints that time is a mystery that man will never understand. The nature of the occult world is another secret hidden from man. Thus God sets certain limits to human life.

He says to man, "Turn back to the dust for you came from the dust" (see Gen. 3:19). To each individual, at some time or another, God says, "Go back to the dust." A little girl once learned in Sunday School that man came from the dust and eventually returns to the dust. She looked under her bed one morning and said, "Mother, Mother, come! There's someone under my bed, but I don't know if he's coming or going!" That is a child's way of underscoring this great truth. God sets limits to life. Man comes from the dust and he must return to the dust.

The Limits of Age

Verse 4 suggests the thought that God had originally intended a greater span of life for man. In connection with His Word about the limits of life, the psalmist says, "For a thousand years in thy sight are but as yesterday when it is past, or as a watch in the night." In reading that I have often wondered if 1000 years was God's originally intended limit for the life of man. That is, incidentally, the length of the Millennium. According to Revelation 20 the coming Golden Age of earth will be 1000 years long (see vv. 2,3).

The truth of this suggestion is strengthened by the fact that early man, as recorded in Genesis, lived almost 1000 years. The oldest man who ever lived, Methuselah, was 969 years old when he died. Before sin began to spread through the earth, it is quite likely that God intended man to live 1000 years. But even 1000 years, even the longest possible lifetime of man compared with the greatness of God, is "but yesterday when it is past, or as a watch in the night."

The Limits of Time

Then the psalmist points out that man also is suddenly taken from the earth. "Thou dost sweep men away; they are like a dream" (v. 5). Again it is clear that we live within the sovereignty of God. We have no control over how long we are to live. History confirms to us the fact that men can very suddenly disappear from the scene.

Many of us remember that in the early '60s it looked as though the Kennedy family would be prominent in politics in the United States for many years to come. When John

F. Kennedy was elected President, news of the Kennedy tribe filled the papers. But how suddenly the picture changed. "Thou dost sweep men away," says the psalmist.

Even if men are not swept away suddenly, they are but as grass, which is renewed in the morning: "In the morning it flourishes and is renewed; in the evening it fades and withers" (v.6).

THE course of history has been the story of the rise and fall of men who appear for a brief time and then disappear, exactly as the psalmist says.

The normal span of life is one of gradually increasing decay and deterioration until, like the grass, it is there in the morning, but gone in the evening. This is a picture, he says, of the life of man.

Again, history confirms this. I think of Ho Chi Minh, in the '60s, and how he dominated the scene in Vietnam. Now he is gone, his life has deteriorated. The same is true of great men like Winston Churchill, Dwight Eisenhower, Franklin Roosevelt. The course of history has been the story of the rise and fall of men who appear for a brief time and then disappear, exactly as the psalmist says. So man lives within one great fact about God: His sovereign control over all.

The Wrath of God

There is another aspect of man's relationship to God that concerns the psalmist—God's wrath.

For we are consumed by thy anger;
by thy wrath we are overwhelmed.
Thou hast set our iniquities before thee,
our secret sins in the light of thy countenance.
For all our days pass away under thy wrath,
our years come to an end like a sigh (vv. 7-9).

Here the psalmist, in all honesty, is facing a reality that many of us try to avoid. He is dealing with what we might call the tragic sense of life: the fact that every moment of enjoyment is tinged with something sorrowful, tragic, or unhappy. There is a bittersweet quality about life, which these psalmists face realistically. They are quite ready to come to grips with the problem of evil. Why is human life tinged with a dark side? Why do we have these tragedies, irritations, injustices, and the catastrophes that strike both innocent and guilty alike?

Is It Fair?

Some years ago I succumbed to family pressure and a long standing personal interest by buying a small motor boat to use for water skiing, fishing, and other things. Of course I couldn't wait to see how the boat would run. I took it down to the Palo Alto Boat Harbor and launched it in the bay. My wife and youngest daughter were aboard as we went out for a spin. We took right off and headed for the Dumbarton Bridge. But out in the middle of the bay, almost directly under the bridge, we ran aground. The motor hit bottom and, before I could lift it up, the shear pin had severed and there we were, powerless in the middle of the bay.

Fortunately I had taken along a couple of paddles, which belonged to a little rubber boat we had. But when I fully realized that we were adrift in the middle of the bay, I was a bit concerned as I didn't know which way the tide was running and I had read stories in the paper about people who spent the night on the mudflats.

The thought then crossed my mind: Is this really fair? Should a thing like this happen to the pastor of the Peninsula Bible Church? The longer I paddled toward the disappearing shore, the more convinced I was that it was unfair treatment. We eventually landed at the only place on the lower western side of the bay where there was a telephone and some people, so we didn't spend the night on the bay. But it served to underscore to me the fact the psalmist is facing here.

A Dark Side to Life

There is a dark side to life. There come sudden occurrences that cast a cloud over the sunshine. Sometimes they are much more serious than my boat incident. A family grieves over the loss of a little eight-year-old girl, apparently the kidnap victim of some sex deviate. The wife of a young minister, married only a month, disappears one Sunday morning; no trace is ever found of her. A friend is killed instantly in a motorcycle accident. We all know how frequently these things happen. What is the reason for them?

The psalmist says it is because of the wrath of God. He ascribes them directly to God. Surely this phrase, "the wrath of God," is greatly misunderstood by many people. Many think invariably of some sort of peeved deity, a kind of cosmic, terrible-tempered Mr. Bang, who indulges in violent and uncontrolled displays of temper when we human beings do not do what we ought to do. But such a concept only reveals the limitations of our understanding.

The Bible never deals with the wrath of God that way.

A Result of Sin

According to the Scriptures, the wrath of God is God's moral integrity. When a man refuses to yield himself to God, he creates certain conditions (not only for himself but for others as well), which God has ordained for harm. It is God who makes evil result in sorrow, heartache, injustice and despair. It is God's way of saying to man, "Look, you must face the truth. You were made for me. If you, in the dignity of human choice that I have given you, decide that you don't want me, then I will leave. But you will have to bear the consequences." The absence of God is destructive to human life. That absence is God's wrath and God cannot withhold it. In His moral integrity God insists that evil things should occur as a result of man's choice.

See how the psalmist links these two together. He sets man's sin and God's wrath within the same frame. "Thou hast set our iniquities before thee, our secret sins in the light of thy countenance." The cause of God's wrath then is always human sin. The manifestation of God's wrath would never be apparent were it not for the secret sins that are set in the light of God's countenance. God knows our inner sins, our secret inner thoughts.

The Scriptures never teach that a passing thought is a sin. A thought that comes to your mind unbidden and remains there for a moment tempting you to do something wrong is only a normal exposure to temptation. Even the Lord Jesus experienced it. But here the psalmist refers to thoughts that we harbor, that we mull over and play with, that we take great pleasure in and often summon up ourselves if they do not come to us unbidden. God is aware of these inner defilements of life, and they are all contributing to the tragic events of life.

The Exercise of His Love

It is amazing how blind we are in this area. Every now and again someone will ask the question, "Why doesn't God kill the devil? If it's the devil that is doing all this to us, why doesn't God get rid of him?" That same question appears often concerning a human being. "Why didn't God kill Hitler? Look at all the terrible things Hitler did and the awful bloodbath to which he subjected the world. Why didn't God kill him before he could do this?"

We ask such questions with great ease, but when we ask a question like that we should also ask, "Why didn't God paralyze my hand when I filled out my income tax and put down a wrong figure?" We should ask, "Why didn't God strike me dumb when I yelled at my wife or my children?" And, "Why didn't He send a stroke when I said that catty thing over the phone to my neighbor? Why didn't He paralyze my tongue?"

If God is going to deal with sin, He must deal with it in everyone, not just the Hitlers, and not only in its extreme forms. The psalmist faces the fact that God allows His wrath, His moral integrity against sin, to be manifest precisely because it affords Him opportunity for the exercise of His love.

Filled with Trouble

Then he goes on to consider the universality of this.

> *The years of our life are threescore and ten,*
> *or even by reason of strength fourscore;*
> *yet their span is but toil and trouble;*
> *they are soon gone, and we fly away* (v. 10).

Here is a statement of the length of life to which man is reduced under sin. At best we live to 70 years of age, and if by reason of strength we reach 80, still it is filled with trouble. This was written by Moses, remember, and Moses himself lived to be 120 years of age. Surely that was a remarkable extension of time, beyond the ordinary life span of his own day. It is striking that 2000 years the other side of Calvary, man's span of life was only 70, or at most, 80 years. We really have not made much progress, have we? All our vaunted achievements in medical science have not brought the average span of life for man today beyond this figure. But no matter how long man lives, his days are still filled with trouble and the tragic quality of life that marks the presence of the wrath of God. So the psalmist closes this section with a question.

A Heart of Wisdom

Who considers the power of thy anger,
*   and thy wrath according to the fear of thee?*
So teach us to number our days
*   that we may get a heart of wisdom* (vv. 11,12).

Now he is facing the strange indifference of man. Why do we ignore the fact of the wrath of God? Why do we try to pretend it does not exist? Why don't we face up to these great facts, the sovereignty of God over man and the ever present justice of God working in human society? Why do we struggle so to evade other conditions in human life, or to put the blame everywhere but where it belongs, with ourselves?

In answer, the psalmist prays, "Lord, help me to number my days (that is, to be aware of the limitations of life), that I might get a heart of wisdom." What is a heart of wisdom? Well, it is a realistic outlook on life. It is facing life the way it is, and fully reckoning with the relationships of man to God.

God's Love for Man

In the last section the psalmist moves to the third of these relationships. It is a declaration of God's love for man. This is rather unexpected, is it not? Most of us think of man's relationships to God only in terms of God's justice and God's wrath. He is the great Law Giver watching over us, and we are responsible to fulfill His law—or else. But here is a closing section in which the psalmist speaks of the love of God. It begins with a cry for a personal God.

> *Return, O Lord! How long?*
>   *Have pity on thy servants!*
> *Satisfy us in the morning with thy steadfast*
>   *love,*
> *that we may rejoice and be glad all*
> *our days* (vv. 13,14).

You cannot experience the love of God unless you are ready to cry out like this for a personal relationship to God. "Return, O Lord! This great and mighty God who rules the universe, may He come back to me," says the psalmist. "Enter my heart and have pity upon me, thy servant." That cry for a "personal relationship is the key to the results that follow, as set forth in the following verses.

Suppose now you have come to a relationship with God personally. You know Him, He has returned to your spirit where He was intended to dwell. What has really happened, of course, is that you have returned to Him. From our human point of view we think that God has come to us. We cry out for Him to come to us, when all the time He is saying to us, "Come unto me."

If this has happened in your life, what can you expect? First, you can expect to know a satisfying love. "Satisfy us in the morning with thy steadfast love, that we may rejoice and be glad all our days." You will notice that all through the psalms the RSV gives repeated reference to the "steadfast love" of God. In the King James Version, it is translated, "lovingkindness." I admit I have an emotional preference for the term *lovingkindness*. I often think of the little boy in Sunday School who was asked to describe lovingkindness. He said to the teacher, "Well, teacher, if I ask my mother for a piece of bread and butter, and she gives it to me, that's kindness. But if she puts jam on it, that's lovingkindness." That is striking very closely to what the word really means.

The revisers are quite right in noting the time quality of this love. It is continuous love. It is love that does not change. It is, in other words, unqualified acceptance. It is a love that does not depend on whether I am good or bad, but is ready to receive me and forgive me and set me back on my feet again. God shows unqualified love, love that has already dealt with our behavior, already dealt with our misdemeanors and our rebellion—and still loves. We sing the hymn, "O love that will not let me go." It is that kind of love that the psalmist is talking about. That is satisfying love.

Recompensing Joy

Then he speaks of recompensing joy.

*Make us glad as many days as thou hast
afflicted us,*

and as many years as we have seen evil (v. 15).

There is a joy that makes up for the past, a joy that will restore to you the "years which the swarming locust has eaten" (Joel 2:25), to use the beautiful phrasing of one of the Minor Prophets. Man looks out upon the field of life and sees it eaten by locusts, all its value gone, all its worth ended. Then he sees God coming in and restoring, planting a new crop, bringing it to fruition and to harvest, so that one may look out across a full field blowing in the wind, every head laden with grain, and rejoice over the fact that God has restored the years that the locusts have eaten.

One of the greatest joys of my Christian life is to look back upon the wasted moments and years of my past and set in contrast to it the fruitfulness of my present experience. God is continually correcting what once looked like a hopeless situation, restoring to me the years that the locusts have eaten. A recompensing joy, that is part of the glory of God's love.

Hereditary Healing

Then the third element the psalmist sees is in verse 16:

Let thy work be manifest to thy servants,
and thy glorious power
to their children.

This is an amazing request. It envisions what I would call hereditary healing. We moderns are inclined to see life out of focus. We seldom think of ourselves as being part of a bundle of life that goes back to the very beginning.

Americans, particularly, are very individualistic. We like to think of ourselves as individuals almost as though we were the first men and women in the world. It is part of the American dream to feel we are starting all over. We think we can correct all the mistakes of the past. We think we can change everything within our lifetime.

But the Bible never takes that view. The Bible recognizes the fact that man is tied to his past and he is affecting the immediate future. God Himself stated it in the giving of the Law, in Exodus 20. "I the Lord your God am a jealous God, visiting the iniquity of the fathers upon the children to the third and the fourth generation of those who hate me, but showing steadfast love to thousands of those who love me and keep my commandments" (Exod. 20:5,6).

Something in human life persists from one generation to another. Though you or I may become a Christian and God begins to heal our personal life, we will never experience the full effect of that healing in our lifetime. But our children may! That is what the psalmist is saying here. Notice how he puts it. "Let thy work be manifest to thy servants"—his own generation—"and thy glorious power to their children." Let me understand how you work, Lord, give me an understanding of your methods in society and life. Then let the effect of that understanding be evidenced in my children. That is what often happens.

I have seen young men and women beginning a family, as new Christians. They are discovering for themselves the healing power of God to change a wretched, miserable, wasted life, and they experience much of the loving grace, kindness, and restoration of God. But their children go on to even greater and richer experiences than the parents had. They are benefiting from the change and understanding that has come into the lives of their parents. That benefit can be passed on, say the Scriptures, to the third and fourth generations. That is why, oftentimes, children are either much worse or much better than their parents.

The Beauty of Truth and Love

Then the fourth thing. Here I would like to revert to the *King James Version*; it is much better.

> *Let the beauty of the Lord our God be upon us* (v. 17).

This is a prayer for the visible manifestation of God's beauty. It is what the New Testament calls "godlikeness" or godliness. What is the beauty of God? God is beautiful because He is two things: truth and love. Truth is always necessary to beauty. You can never have anything beautiful that is not true. And love is warmth, graciousness, and attractiveness, which, added to truth, constitutes beauty.

A man or woman, boy or girl, whose life is characterized by truth and love is a beautiful person. We hear much about beautiful people today. The world uses that term. What does it mean? Basically it means to them, "someone who pleases me," "someone I like." But in the understanding of life that the Scriptures represent, beauty is the manifestation of truth and love. The only place you can get those, in the ultimate sense, is from God. So Moses prays for such beauty.

Meaningful Labor

> *And establish thou the work of our hands upon us,*
> *yea, the work of our hands establish*
> *thou it* (v. 17).

What does this mean? The last result of God's love is to make our labor, our work, meaningful, valuable, and enduring. It will not be something wasted or frantic and frenetic, spent in a moment. The work of our hands becomes an enduring thing, impressive, affecting others, having in itself great value.

Who does not long for this? In everyone's heart, is there not a longing that your life will be worthwhile, that you will be the kind of person who will be worth something, that others will value you and your life? Well, that is the great promise of God's love. That love is available to any who are ready to say, as this psalmist says, "Return, O Lord! How long?" Come back, O God. Come back into my life and work through me. God is ready to produce in you that kind of love.

Here, then, are the three great facts that relate to God and man: *God's sovereignty*, within the limits of which we all live, whether we like it or not; *God's wrath* which we all experience, whether innocent or guilty, because we are living in a world in which God is allowing man's sin to have its full expression. But in the midst of all this is the glory and wonder of *God's love*, manifesting itself to us in terms of these qualities of satisfying love, recompensing joy, hereditary healing, visible beauty, and meaningful labor. All is available to those who love Him.

We never fail, father, to be awed and humbled by the words of Scripture. When we think that Moses, so many long centuries ago, understood these great facts about you, we are inclined to cry with him, "O Lord, thou hast been our dwelling place throughout all generations!" Thou art the same God, the eternal, unchangeable God, the Rock upon which any life may be built. Lord, we pray that none of us will be so foolish as to try to build on any other rock, but that each of us will give ourselves to establishing our life upon Thee, our rock and our strength. We ask in your name, Amen.

How to Worship

Psalms 95 is one of a series of psalms that the Israelites sang together as they went up to the Temple in Jerusalem to worship. The series begins with the ninety-third Psalm and concludes with the one-hundredth Psalm. Each of these is a demonstration and exhortation on how to worship. They are not only magnificent poetry, but they are also instructions on what worship is and how it is to be done.

Singing and Prayer

Two appeals are made in the ninety-fifth Psalm, two exhortations to join in worship. One is in the very first line, and the other is in verse 6.

O come, let us sing to the Lord;
let us make a joyful noise to the rock
of our salvation! (v. 1).
O come, let us worship and bow down,
let us kneel before the Lord, our Maker! (v. 6).

As we look at these together we shall see that they are two invitations to two separate expressions of worship. One is an invitation to sing and the other is an invitation to pray. Thus, in the opening passage of this psalm, we are immediately made aware that congregational worship largely consists of singing and prayer. If you are regularly in attendance at any church, you know that this is almost invariably the pattern that united worship follows in our day. It is proper that we should worship in this way, for even in the days of Israel, under David, it was the pattern of worship.

Thanksgiving and Praise

Now, there is special reason why worship involves singing together. Notice that the exhortation in verse 2 is to let that singing be an expression of thanksgiving and praise.

Let us come into his presence with thanksgiving;
let us make a joyful noise to him with songs
of praise! (v. 2).

Thanksgiving and praise are to be the major elements expressed in our singing. It is possible to give thanks and to praise God individually, but if any congregation took time to let everyone do that, it would take all day just for the preliminaries. Singing is something we can do together. So through the ages the believers in God, both of the Old and New Testament, have sung their praises and thanksgivings. This is very important. It is the reason we should be careful not to sing in a desultory manner. There is nothing more conducive to dullness in a service than halfhearted singing. So the exhortation here is most appropriate. "O come, let us sing to the Lord; let us make a joyful noise to the rock of our salvation!"

Perhaps in this present generation it is necessary for me to point out that, though the word *rock* is linked with singing, it does not have the meaning that youth apply to it today. In this case *rock* means a large stone. It is not a form of music. It means the Lord is the strength from which we draw, the rock upon which we rest. The motivation, therefore, for singing thanksgiving and praise is that we recognize the source of our strength.

Our Maker and Our Creator

As we read on we learn that the reason for thanksgiving and praise is because we are related to God in creation. He is our Maker and our Creator.

For the Lord is a great God, and a great King
above all gods.
In his hand are the depths of the earth; the
heights of the mountains are his also.
The sea is his, for he made it; for his hands
formed the dry land (vv. 3-5).

Do you see what the psalmist is doing? He is giving the basic reasons why everyone should give thanksgiving and praise to God. They apply not only to those of us who are believers, but to all men. Each one has a responsibility to praise God, for all are creatures of His hands. In the first chapter of Romans the apostle Paul points out that one of the charges God brings against men is that "when they knew God they glorified Him not as God, neither were thankful" (see v. 21). They did not care to recognize their relationship to Him.

I am constantly amazed that men can be so blind to the fact that they are not, as they often imagine themselves to be, independent creatures making their own way through life. We accept as perfectly natural to us all the forces that keep us alive, and boastfully talk about being self-made men. We strut through life as if we needed to recognize no one else as the source of our strength and power.

Like Irrational Animals

Dr. H. A. Ironside, a long-time pastor of the Chicago church founded by D. L. Moody, used to tell of an experience he once had at a restaurant. He ordered his meal and, just as he was about to eat, a man walked up to his table and said, "Do you mind if I sit down with you?" Dr. Ironside said no, it was quite all right, so the man sat down. As was his custom Dr. Ironside bowed his head and said a silent word of thanksgiving to the Lord before he ate.

When he lifted up his head, the man said to him, "Do you have a headache?"

Ironside said, "No, I don't."

The man said, "Well, is there anything wrong with your food?"

Ironside said, "No, why?"

"Well," the man said, "I saw you sitting there with your head down and I thought you must be sick or there was something wrong with your food."

Ironside replied, "No, I was simply returning thanks to God as I always do before I eat."

The man said, "Oh, you're one of those, are you? Well, I want you to know I never give thanks. I earn my money by the sweat of my brow and I don't have to give thanks to anybody when I eat, I just start right in!"

Dr. Ironside said, "Yes, you're just like my dog. That's what he does, too!"

That little story quite properly suggests that when

E VEN those who deny the existence of God have gods whom they worship and to whom they give their allegiance and loyalty.

---

men, who are rational creatures of God, will not give thanks to God, they are acting like irrational animals. They become bestial and are already losing their humanity. Such is the basis of this appeal by the psalmist: no matter how we may feel, or what may be our attitude toward God, we are bound, as creatures dependent upon His love and grace, at least to give thanks to Him as our Creator.

The Glory Due His Name

Psalm 96, verse 8, says, "Ascribe to the Lord *the glory due his name*" (italics added). God is worthy of thanksgiving. It would doubtless make a great difference in our worship if we would remember that praise is not something that merely reflects our transient feelings. It is what we ought to do simply because God made us and we cannot live a moment without Him. The glory due unto His name should bring us together for worship.

Ironically, some people use God's gifts of intelligence and free will to try to persuade others that God does not exist! So the psalmist reminds us that we are related to Him as creatures to the Creator.

Supreme Over All Forces

He calls two things to our attention in this relationship. One is that God is supreme over all the forces that affect our lives. "The Lord is a great God, and a great King above all gods." He is certainly not suggesting that there are other gods; it is only that men think there are. Pagans erect idols and call them gods. Even those who deny the existence of God have gods whom they worship and to whom they give their allegiance and loyalty. No man is without a god. I have never yet met an irreligious man, although I have met many who claimed to be so. All men have gods. Man is inherently and necessarily a worshiping being. If nothing else, he will worship a projection of himself. Man becomes his own god. The psalmist declares, "No matter what your idea of a god may be, the true God is above all such ideas."

Even false gods derive their strength and influence from God Himself. There are, as the New Testament reminds us, demonic powers behind the idols of the pagans. They are genuine spirit beings, but they exercise their power under God. He is a great King over all gods.

This is important to bear in mind today when we are facing a revival of interest in astrology, horoscopes, seances, and so forth. For a Christian to give himself to these is to deny the Fatherhood of God and the fatherly care of God over him. If you think your life is run by the stars and you give allegiance and loyalty to what the stars decree, then you have ruled out the fatherly care of God. the two cannot be held together. That is why the Bible faithfully warns against getting involved in practices like these. Even the devil is ultimately under God. The devil and God do not constitute a bad god and a good God, opposed to each other; the devil is under God and derives his power and his authority from God. We must always remember that.

Worship, then, is to recognize the over-arching authority and supremacy of God over all the forces that bear upon our lives.

In God's Hands

Then the psalmist reminds us that in God's hands are all the things that challenge men, that make life exciting.

> *In his hand are the depths of the earth;*
> *the heights of the mountains are his also.*
> *The sea is his, for he made it;*
> *for his hands formed the dry land* (vv. 4,5).

Here we have the depths of the earth, the heights of the mountains, the breadth of the sea, and the dry land; these are the things that challenge men, that hold forth promise of adventure, excitement, fascination, and mystery. We are still trying to plumb the depths of the earth, and only in recent years did man finally scale the heights of the mountains in the climbing of Mt. Everest. We are still exploring the mysteries of the sea. We are trying to solve the problems of the dry land and discover its resources.

The psalmist is simply reminding us that all these things that hold forth to us challenge, mystery, excitement, and adventure are from God. He has planned them, He has put them there. Let us thank God, not just because He is in charge of all the forces that sustain our lives, but also because He is behind the mystery, the adventure, the excitement of life, the things that give it flavor and enticement, and make it worth living. All men are exhorted to worship and praise God for these things. Not only are we to sing together, but we are to pray together.

Our Shepherd-God

> *O come, let us worship and bow down,*
> *let us kneel before the Lord, our Maker!*
> *For he is our God,*
> *and we are the people of his pasture,*
> *and the sheep of his hand* (vv. 6,7).

What does that last sentence mean? Notice that the relationship has changed. It is now no longer God our Creator who is in view, but rather God our Redeemer, our Savior. We are the people of His pasture and the sheep of His hand. He is our Shepherd-God. We have entered into a personal relationship with Him and the proper expression of it is one of awe and humility: "Let us worship and bow down."

The Amazing Love of God

Think of what the Word of God reveals to us of the amazing love of God and how that love has pursued us and won us. Despite the obstacles we have raised against Him and the resistance we have shown Him, nevertheless His love has kept after us, has broken down our reserves, and won us. There is not one of us who has not fought against God, who has not tried to resist His love's attempt to win us and to change us. Therefore, we have nothing to praise in ourselves. We have not added anything to our salvation.

We are all like stubborn, stupid sheep, who go according to their own ways. As Isaiah accurately puts it, "All we like sheep have gone astray; we have turned everyone to his own way" (Isa. 53:6). Ask any shepherd if that is not the way of sheep. They love to go astray. But God has pursued us, found us, and brought us back. Thus, out of a sense of our relationship to him as Redeemer, as Savior, we kneel before the Lord our God and thank Him for the amazing love He has bestowed upon us.

"Amazing grace! how sweet the sound,
That saved a wretch like me!
I once was lost, but now am found,
Was blind, but now I see"
(John Newton, Public Domain).

In worship we offer praise and thanksgiving to God for the personal knowledge we have of Him. He is our God, He is our Maker. We have also come out of a distant relationship into a personal relationship with our God. That ought to awaken the love of our heart. We have experienced His Shepherd's care over us as the sheep of His hand, the people of His pasture. That constitutes worship: singing and praying, not artificially, nor perfunctorily, but genuinely expressing praise unto God.

Hearken to His Voice

In the latter part of the psalm, beginning with the closing sentence of verse 7, there is a change of voice. The first part has been man exhorting other men to worship God. The psalmist has cried out, "Let us sing together, let us worship and bow down together." But now the voice of God Himself sounds, preceded by this admonition, "O that today you would hearken to his voice!" (v. 7). God now speaks to us, to tell us what it is that He essentially wants in worship, what makes worship true worship. What He wants is that we would listen to His voice! It is commendable for people to go to worship services, but the value of going soon vanishes if all they do is sit while their thoughts are elsewhere. To worship is to listen to the Word and the voice of God.

That is why the exposition of Scripture must be the central thing in public worship. Those churches that have departed from this, and that come together to go through certain formal, liturgical rites, or where a man gets up to give his opinion on certain current events of the day are making a travesty of worship. There is no true worship there at all. Worship must include listening to the voice of God, hearing what He has to say, and letting His Word correct our attitudes and our reactions.

As a pastor, I wish it were possible for all who attend services to go up on the platform and watch people during the hour of worship. Externally it looks as though they are all paying attention. They sit there quietly, with rapt, turn-up faces, their eyes open and staring straight ahead, apparently attracted by what the Word of God is saying. But having sat there myself, I know it is not always true. Some are playing golf. Others are rehearsing a business deal. Some are planning a trip. Some are going over a conversation they had two days ago. Some are doing other things. It would be fascinating at the end of a service to know where everybody had been!

But God is desirous that, whatever else you may do in a service, when His Word is speaking, listen! And not only listen, but hearken! *Hearken* means to heed the Word, to do something about it, to let it really change you. God is infinitely concerned that our coming to worship should do something to us. "O that today you would hearken to his voice!"

Harden Not Your Hearts

Then he puts the same thing negatively,

> *Harden not your hearts, as at Meribah,*
> *as on the day at Massah in the wilderness,*
> *when your fathers tested me, and put me to the*
> *proof, though they had seen my work* (vv. 8,9).

The exhortation of God to His people is: When you are worshiping together, listen to my voice, and while listening, do not harden your hearts. Hardening the heart is the exact opposite of hearkening to His voice. If you hearken to His voice you are not hardening your heart. If you harden your heart you are not hearkening to His voice. The two are mutually exclusive.

Putting Him to the Proof

He gives us an example of what He means by hardening the heart. God Himself refers us to the incident we read of in the seventeenth chapter of Exodus. It occurred shortly after the Israelites had come through the Red Sea and had journeyed only a week or two into the wilderness beyond. They came to a place where there was no water, and they all became thirsty. They hardly had time to become very thirsty before the leaders of the people came to Moses and began to complain. "What are you doing? Leading us out into this wilderness to perish? Where is this God that is supposed to be taking care of us? Why hasn't He provided water for us?" They demanded that God prove Himself again. They put Him to the test.

Moses came to God and said, "Lord, what shall I do? Here are these people murmuring and complaining till they're about to stone me! What shall I do?"

Then God said, "Lead them out to the rock and in their presence strike the rock with the rod with which you struck the Nile, and out of the rock will come water." Moses did that, and there came out a gushing stream; not just a trickle but a full stream, plenty to satisfy all the people (600,000 men, besides women and children, and all their cattle and sheep). The thing that vexed God about this situation was not that they asked for help in their time of need. God never scolds His people for that. But He says, "They put me to the proof, *though they had seen my work*" (see vv. 1-7).

This event occurred only a few days after the Israelites had experienced the miraculous deliverance from Egypt. They had seen the marvelous provision of God during the days of Moses' contest with Pharaoh when the plagues of Egypt had fallen and God had driven Pharaoh into a corner. Eventually, after the slaying of the firstborn throughout the land of Egypt, Pharaoh had been forced to let God's people go. Then, when the Israelites reached the Red Sea, He had parted the waters before them, they had walked through on dry ground, and had seen the waters crash down behind them and cover the pursuing Egyptians. There Israel sang a great song of triumph. Yet, in spite of such a magnificent demonstration of the power of God, they immediately fell to murmuring and complaining because they were a little thirsty.

Worship Effects Change

That, says God, is what it means to harden your heart. It indicates that you have not learned anything from God. God is concerned that none of us should worship Him endlessly, yet remain unchanged. He desires that worship should stabilize us, steady us, establish us so that, the more we see God at work, the harder it is to fall back into unbelief. The Lord Jesus was constantly dealing with His disciples about this.

Remember how often He said to them, "O ye of little faith." He only said that after they had seen a tremendous demonstration of His power. Immediately after He multiplied the loaves and fishes and fed 5,000 men and their families, the disciples were on the sea and a storm came

---

IT disturbs God when people hear stirring and glowing reports of what He is doing in many lives, when they observe those whose lives have been miraculously changed, when they sense the release and freedom that He is bringing about in many hearts, and yet, the minute anything goes wrong in their own lives, they are ready to fall apart.

---

up. In a panic they came to Him and said, "Lord, wake up! We're going to perish!" And the Lord arose and rebuked the storm. Then He turned to them and said, "O ye of little faith [that is, why don't you learn something? Why don't you grow in your faith? Why don't you advance?]" (see Matt. 8:23-27, KJV).

This is the problem God has with us. It disturbs God when people hear stirring and glowing reports of what He is doing in many lives, when they observe those whose lives have been miraculously changed, when they sense the release and freedom that He is bringing about in many hearts, and yet, the minute anything goes wrong in their own lives, they are ready to fall apart.

The Patience of God

In verse 10 God gives His reaction to this. He says, "For forty years I loathed that generation." What a revelation of the patience of God! He dones not immediately condemn them because of their unbelief. He works patiently with them for 40 years. For 40 years He cries, "O that today you would hearken to my voice!" He makes possible their existence by taking care of them throughout that entire period. But all the time, He says, they consistently vexed Him. *Loathe* is perhaps too strong. It does not mean that God felt revulsion or disgust. What it means is that He was grieved by these people who never seemed to catch on. He analyzed their problem in two ways.

> *For forty years I loathed* [was grieved with]
>   *that generation and said, "They are a people*
>   *who err in heart, and they do not regard*
>   *my ways"* (v. 10).

Set on the Wrong Things

First their hearts were set on the wrong things. They were not looking for the really important things. Read the account and you can see what He meant. This was a generation that kept harking back to Egypt. They wanted to return to Egypt and kept longing for the melons, the leeks, garlic, and onions of Egypt. Why would they want onions, leeks and garlic? I don't know. All three are foods which, when you eat them in private, everyone in public knows it. Since they thought only of their bellies, God says they were wrong in their hearts.

In Colossians God says to us, through the apostle, "Set your affections on things above, where Christ sits at the right hand of God, and not on things of earth" (see Col.

3:2). That does not mean to go around thinking of heaven all the time. The "things above" are the important matters of life: the things of truth, honor, and justice; the demonstration of patience, tolerance, and grace toward one another in our personal relationships. Those are the things that Christ, seated at the right hand of the Father, is ready to minister to us in these days.

Let me show you from the letter to the Colossians itself what Paul had in mind. In the first chapter the apostle prays for his people. "May you be strengthened with all power, according to his glorious might" (Col. 1:11). Doesn't that sound thrilling? Is that not what we all want? Would you like to have Paul pray for you that way—that you "may be strengthened with all power, according to his glorious might"? For what? Well, "for all endurance and patience with joy." That is why you need power.

You do not need power to go about moving mountains and other spectacular demonstrations; you need power to be patient, to have joy in the midst of your trial, to endure to the end. That power comes from the right hand of God through Jesus Christ, who ministers it to us now. Set your mind on things that are above, not on things that are on earth.

The Israelites were looking at the wrong things and desiring foolish trifles instead of enduring realities. Somebody has described "keeping up with the Joneses" as "using money you don't have to buy things you don't need to impress people you don't like." How futile it is to have your heart set on the wrong things!

Not Regarding His Ways
Then God puts His finger on their second problem: "They do not regard my ways"—they do not understand how God works. It is important to understand how God works,

for God's ways are not our ways and His thoughts are not our thoughts. His ways are higher than our ways as the heavens are higher than the earth. That means that God does not always behave the way we expect Him to. That is one of the "aggravating" things about God. He never seems to do what we want Him to do. We have a goal in mind and, in prayer, we outline the process to God of how He can bring it about. But He is so "stubborn." He will not do it our way at all. So we get upset with Him.

Entering His Rest

God is saying that the Israelites hardened their hearts because they would not consider that He had His way of doing things. So, He said,

> *Therefore I swore in my anger*
> *that they should not enter my rest* (v. 11).

The supreme thing in worship is to learn how to rest in God. To rest means to depend upon God's activity and not our own. The writer of Hebrews says, "Whoever enters God's rest also ceases from his labors." (Hebrews 4:10). Rest is really mental health, peace of heart, peace of mind, a sense of living out of adequacy instead of inadequacy. God wants us to be adequate, to be able to cope with whatever may come. That adequacy will come to us only as we hearken to His Word. But if we do not hearken to His words, we can worship for 40 years and, at the end of it, we shall have so hardened our hearts that God may finally say, "You shall not enter into my rest."

There is no other way. No drug you can take will give you that rest. No pursuit you follow, no book you read will bring you peace of heart. There is simply no alternative.

You cannot come into rest if you will not hearken to His Word.

That is why it is so important that, when we worship together, we listen to the Word of God and let it correct us. Let us sit under the judgment of the Word. Let it search us and find us out and change us, and thus we shall glorify the God who made us and give unto Him the glory due His name.

Our Father, perhaps there is even now some evident duty we should be performing; some proper appeal made to us that we are rejecting; some hurtful relationship we are defending; something that we need to do that you are now correcting. Perhaps there is something we need to do positively, something we need to do to draw near to you. Lord, we pray that you will help us to hearken, to not be like the fathers of old who resisted you, vexed you, and grieved you for 40 years. We ask it in Jesus' name, Amen.

A Song of Restoration

O give thanks to the Lord, for he is good;
for his steadfast love endures for ever!

This recurrent them of Psalm 107 introduces the fifth book of the Psalms, which corresponds to the book of Deuteronomy in the Pentateuch. *Deutero* means "second"; *nomos* is "law": the second law. The First law is the law of sin and death, the law that condemns, the law that destroys, the law that makes us feel guilty and brings us under a sense of fear and condemnation. But the Second Law, says the apostle Paul, is the law of the spirit of life in Christ Jesus, which sets us free from the law of sin and death (see Rom. 8:2). It is the way God finally redeems His people. He buys them back (redeems them) by the operation of the Second Law, of which this psalm speaks.

The psalmist speaks of the steadfast love of God. In Hebrew, the word for the steadfast love means "an eager and ardent desire," and refers to the fact that God's love never gives up. We sing about it in the hymn, "O Love that wilt not let me go, I rest my weary soul in Thee." What finally gets to us, breaks the back of our rebellion, and sets us free from our emotional hang-ups? It is always that unqualified love of God that never lets us go.

The term "unqualified acceptance" might be more easily understood in our day. God's love accepts us without reserve. What is acceptance? A writer in *Eternity* magazine gives the following analysis.

"Acceptance means you are valuable just as you are. It allows you to be the real you. You aren't forced into someone else's idea of who you really are. It means your ideas are taken seriously since they reflect you. You can talk about how you feel inside and why you feel that way, and someone really cares.

"Acceptance means you can try out your ideas without being shot down. You can even express heretical thoughts and discuss them with intelligent questioning. You feel safe. No one will pronounce judgment on you even though they don't agree with you. It doesn't mean you will never be corrected or shown to be wrong; it simply means it's safe to be you and no one will destroy you out of prejudice." ("That's No Generation Gap!," *Eternity* Magazine, October 1969.)

This kind of acceptance is what the psalmist calls "the steadfast love of God." God accepts us as we are and then sets about to make us what we ourselves are longing to be.

The psalm is very simple in its structure. It is divided into two major parts after the opening introductory sentence.

O give thanks to the Lord, for he is good;
  for his steadfast love endures for ever!
Let the redeemed of the Lord say so,
  whom he has redeemed from trouble
and gathered in from the lands,
  from the east and from the west,
  from the north and from the south (vv. 1-3).

A City to Dwell In

In two following sections the psalmist describes first the works of God and then the ways of God; that is, how God proceeds in His wonderful demonstration of loving acceptance. The psalmist uses a very modern yet ancient technique for this—he asks for testimonies. We have all been in testimony meetings where people stand and tell what the Lord has done for them. In these next verses, beginning with verse 4 and on through verse 32, there are four testimonies of how God delivered people from circumstances and difficulties, which are very much like the ones we go through today. The first description is found in verses 4 to 9.

Some wandered in desert wastes,
  finding no way to a city to dwell in;
hungry and thirsty,
  their soul fainted within them (vv. 4,5).

The Restless Ones

Who are these? They are what we might call "the restless ones." They are the ones who wander about from place to place or from job to job or from marriage to marriage, filled with questions and seeking to find where the answer lies: There are a lot of them today. They are looking for something but they cannot find it. They keep wandering from place to place and from experience to experience, trying to find something to satisfy.

The psalmist says they are looking for "a city to dwell in." Those of us who live in a twentieth-century city, choked with fumes, crowded on the freeways, fighting taxes, crime, and crabgrass, wonder why on earth anyone would want to live in a city; it is the country that is attractive to us. But the Bible indicates that God has designed that man should ultimately live in cities. It says of Abraham, in Hebrews 11, that he was looking for the city "which has foundations, whose builder and maker is God" (see v. 10).

Excitement and Security

A city always has two qualities about it: excitement and security. Excitement is created whenever people gather together where the action is. Cities are also a place of security. If you are going to meet trouble, it is better to have others around. If you need defense, you want to be where others are. Defense is more easily possible in a city if an attack comes. So the people described here are looking for the things you can find in a city: excitement and security.

Excitement is a quality we need in life. There is nothing worse than a life filled with boredom and dullness. What a drag! How difficult it is to live when everything is dull! Youth today are demanding excitement even at the price of their health or sometimes their lives. But God never intended life to be dull; He intended it to be exciting.

A city is also intended to be secure, to afford a place where you feel at home, at rest, relaxed. But these people cannot find it. They are hungry and thirsty, the psalmist says. That means their cravings have not been satisfied.

By a Straight Way

Then we are told how they find satisfaction.

> *Then they cried to the Lord in their trouble,*
> *and he delivered them from their distress;*
> *he led them by a straight way,*
> *till they reached a city to dwell in* (vv. 6,7).

Some of you have had this experience. You too were restless, you were uncertain, wandering, you were hungry and thirsty for life but you could never find it. You tried everything. Finally, when you reached the bottom, you cried to the Lord in your trouble. When you did, He heard you. Not suddenly or instantaneously, but gradually He began to set you free. He began to lead you "by a straight way." God delivers those who have been wandering circuitously, deviously; now they start going straight. That is the way described in the Scripture. It is a straight way, right through the middle of life. God leads them until they find a city to dwell in, until they reach the place of excitement and security. It does not happen overnight. Sometimes it takes awhile.

Let Them Thank the Lord

Some of us are finding this true in our lives. Gradually, step by step, as we walk in the straight way, God is leading us to a place of excitement and security, of adequacy, of power. Those who have found this way then have a responsibility, says the psalmist.

> *Let them thank the Lord for his steadfast love,*
> *for his wonderful works to the sons of men!*
> *For he satisfies him who is thirsty,*
> *and the hungry he fills with good things* (vv. 8,9).

Let them thank the Lord for His steadfast love because the factor that reached and held them was God's unqualified acceptance. Those who have come from this background ought to praise God. They ought publicly to give thanks for this one quality by which God has led them to contentment and satisfaction.

In Darkness and in Gloom

Now here is another problem:

> *Some sat in darkness and in gloom,*
> *prisoners in affliction and in irons,*
> *for they had rebelled against the words of God,*
> *and spurned the counsel of the Most High.*
> *Their hearts were bowed down with hard labor;*
> *they fell down, with none to help* (vv. 10-12).

These we might call the hostile, the rebellious ones. Notice their condition. They sit in darkness and gloom. That is always the figure in the Bible for hopeless ignorance. They cannot figure out what is wrong with them. Their lives are filled with gloom, they have no hope, but they do not know what is wrong.

Put in Chains
More than that, they are afflicted and in irons. That means they are held by something, they are as men put in chains.

They are held prisoner by certain habits, by ideas, by thoughts, by attitudes that hold them in an iron grip. No matter how hard they try, they cannot break the grip, despite the misery it causes.

Many things can do this. Drugs can do it. It is no longer unusual to read in the newspaper how some youth gets into the grip of drugs, finds to his dismay that he cannot break loose and, finally, takes his life. His body scarred with needle marks tells an all-too-familiar story. Wrongful sex can also do it. I have seen young people (and old people too) so given over to sexual promiscuity that they could not break the habit. They were wrecking their homes, but they could not stop. A bitter attitude can do it, too. There are people who never give way to sex or drugs or alcohol but who, nevertheless, are bound in irons because of a bitter, resentful, critical spirit. A whole family can be ruined when the father and mother both have a critical spirit from which they cannot seem to break loose. The children grow up afraid of life because they have been affected by this negative, bitter attitude. These are conditions the psalmist is describing here.

Bowed Down with Hard Labor

The cause is clearly revealed to us. It is, first, because they "rebelled against the words of God." In other words, they did not like what God said about life. They disagreed and they chose to act on what they felt. They did not realize that God was telling them the truth, and they rebelled against reality. Second, they "spurned the counsel of the Most High." Since they did not like what God said, they decided not to follow what He advised. They turned aside from it and, thus, found themselves "bowed down with hard labor."

Do you know why "hard labor" inevitably follows disobedience? Because if you will not follow God, who is intended to be the strength of man, you have only one other place to go—your own resources. The man who tries to do everything by himself is already in trouble. It is a hard, hard life.

Remember when the Lord Jesus appeared to Saul on the Damascus Road, He said to him, "Saul, it is hard for you to kick against the pricks" (see Acts 9:5, *KJV*). Working up excitement and security out of your own resources is agonizing, exhausting labor. It will drag you down every time. So, no matter how long it might take, these who rebelled against and spurned the counsel of the Most High turned to their own resources, fell down, and there was no one to help them. Thus they literally ended up prisoners, bound by their own weakness.

He Broke Their Bonds Asunder

Yet, God does not leave them there. That is the glory of this. He does not say, "All right, you've made your bed; now lie in it. Tough! You made your own decision, you took your own course, now it's too late. You will have to reap the results." No, that is not God's way.

Then they cried to the Lord in their trouble,
and he delivered them from their distress;
he brought them out of darkness and gloom,
and broke their bonds asunder (vv.13,14).

That was the first step. He opened their eyes to show them that what they were rebelling against was reality, that the words of the Most High are not an artificial standard that God has imposed in order to give man a bad time. God is not a peeved deity, enjoying the struggles of men. His words are a revelation of the way things are.

So, having dispelled their ignorance, He "broke their bonds asunder." That means that, when these people cried to God, they found a power to act that they never had before. It means that, though they were in the grip of vicious things (drugs, sex, alcohol, bitterness, whatever it might be), they finally brought their problems to the Lord and laid them at His feet. Then they rose up with a new kind of power, suddenly, just like that.

IF you are struggling with habits you have not been able to break, there is a power that can do what no psychologist or psychiatrist, no social worker or any other well-intentioned person can do for you: it can set you free.

It does not mean they did not have a struggle, but the struggle was on different terms from then on. It was no longer a struggle to break free, but to keep from sliding back again. They fought on a wholly different basis. Some of you have had this experience. You know what the psalmist is talking about here. You can sing with Charles Wesley, "He breaks the power of canceled sin, He sets the prisoner free; His blood can make the foulest clean; His blood availed for me."

A Responsibility to Praise Him

When this happens their responsibility is to give thanks, and to give thanks with a special note. They are to thank

God for His shattering power, His ability to deliver suddenly and instantaneously.

> *For he shatters the doors of bronze,*
> *and cuts in two the bars of iron* (v. 16).

If you are struggling with habits you have not been able to break, there is a power that can do what no psychologist or psychiatrist, no social worker or any other well-intentioned person can do for you: it can set you free. Once you experience it you ought to spend the rest of your life talking about it.

Near to the Gates of Death

Now the next condition:

> *Some were sick through their sinful ways,*
> *and because of their iniquities suffered*
> *affliction;*
> *they loathed any kind of food,*
> *and they drew near to the gates of death* (vv.17,18).

Here are the neurotics. They are sick people, either physically or emotionally sick. How many millions are like this today! Their first characteristic is to loathe food. Now, food is what the body requires and, figuratively, it is what the soul requires. It is that which ministers health and strength. But these neurotic people do not want healthy things. They do not want good food. They do not want the plain fare of meat, potatoes, and gravy; they want whipped cream and caramel sauce. They do not want to read good books; they want highly spiced literature that sets them a-tingling and panders to their lust. That is all they will eat. That is all they will read. That is all they want to live. Therefore they get worse and worse. "They draw near to the gates of death." Here are sick people, neurotic people, who are unable to handle life. They are fearful, nervous, anxious, afraid to go out and face life as it is.

No Peace to the Wicked

The cause of this sad condition is given to us. It is because of their "sinful ways" and "their iniquities." As a pastor I have met with scores of this kind. They never like to be told that their ways are sinful because they never think of themselves as sinful. Yet they cannot be helped until they see that sin is their basic problem. Dr. Henry Brandt, a Christian psychologist, once told of a woman who came to him in deep emotional difficulty. He watched her as she talked for a half hour or more. Finally he said to her, "You're not a very peaceful woman, are you?"

She said, "Why do you say that?"

He said, "Well, I've been noticing you chewing on the edge of your handkerchief, upset and distraught, and you tell me all these terrible things that happen to you all the time. Even though you're a Christian, you are not very peaceful, are you?"

She wanted to know what that had to do with it. He said, "You know, in Isaiah it says, 'There is no peace,' saith my God, 'to the wicked'" (see 48:22).

She sat up straight and said, "Are you calling me wicked?"

Various Degrees of Wickedness

He said, "Well, you know, there are various degrees of wickedness. It's wicked for a man to take a gun and go into a bank and rob it of $100,000; but if a little boy takes a nickel out of his mother's purse when she isn't looking, that is wicked, too. It is wicked to take a knife and plunge it into someone's heart and, thus, murder him; but it is wicked also to use your tongue to shatter, destroy, and murder the reputation of another. It is the same kind of wickedness, but of a different degree. But in each case, there is no peace to the wicked. If you do not have any peace, it is because you are wicked."

Little by little he began to show this woman that her troubles came from sinful ways of which she was not aware, things that she was doing to herself and to others that were wrong. She did not mean to do these, but this was what was destroying her and making her sick and neurotic.

And He Delivered Them

Then what happens?

> *Then they cried to the Lord in their trouble,*
> *and he delivered them from their distress;*
> *he sent forth his word, and healed them,*
> *and delivered them from destruction* (vv. 19,20).

"They cried to the Lord." It is when a man gets into trouble that he cries to the Lord. "And he delivered them." How? "He sent his word, and healed them," and thus delivered them from destruction. I like that phrase, "He sent his word, and healed them." When the psalmist says, "He sent his word," it does not mean God gave them a Bible to read; it means He identified with them. The Lord Jesus is called the Word of God, the Living Word, the Logos. We read of that Word, "He became flesh and dwelt among us" (see John 1:14). He came to live where we live.

Thus, when it says that God sent His Word and healed

them, it means that in some way He moved right in where they were. He did not reject these neurotic people because they were difficult to live with. He moved right in beside them, put an arm around their shoulder, and said, "I understand; let me show you what's causing this." With His Word He healed them and set them free. Jesus said, "If you continue in my word, . . . you will know the truth, and the truth will make you free" (John 8:31,32). How many have been set free as they have begun to understand the truth about themselves and about life through the Word!

Sacrifices of Thanksgiving

These kinds of people have a special responsibility to praise the Lord.

> *Let them thank the Lord for his steadfast love,*
> *for his wonderful works to the sons of men!*
> *And let them offer sacrifices of thanksgiving,*
> *and tell of his deeds in songs of joy!* (vv. 21,22).

Joyful service is their response. Sacrifice always pictures costly service. But it is service that is done with joy, with gladness, with cheerfulness. That is the way to say thank you to a God who has set you free from neurosis.

At Their Wits' End

Let us look now at the next testimony:

> *Some went down to the sea in ships,*
> *doing business on the great waters;*
> *they saw the deeds of the Lord,*

his wondrous works in the deep.
For he commanded, and raised the stormy wind,
which lifted up the waves of the sea.
They mounted up to heaven,
they went down to the depths;
their courage melted away in their
evil plight;
they reeled and staggered like drunken men,
and were at their wits' end (vv. 23-27).

Through the Christian centuries, some have actually been saved through this sort of circumstance. John Newton was a slave trader and owner of a ship running slaves from Africa to England. He was converted when he ran into a great storm. In the midst of that storm, fearing for

---

THOSE who are delivered from storms have a responsibility to thank the Lord for His steadfast love and for His wonderful works to the sons of men, and to do it publicly.

---

his very life, John Newton cried out to God and God changed that man's heart right there. He became a great preacher and wrote many songs, which have helped people ever since.

It is easy to get into trouble at sea. A friend told me once of a man who went out on a sailboat for the first time. When the owner of the boat, the only one aboard who knew how to handle it, fell overboard, this man was confronted with some strategic decisions. But since he didn't know anything, he turned the helm in the wrong direction and promptly capsized the boat. He, too, was "at his wits' end." That is exactly the kind of hopeless predicament the psalmist is talking about here.

This passage can also be taken figuratively. The Scriptures often picture life as like the sea. A man goes out to work in the great waters of the business world. He conducts his business ventures on the sea of life in a normal fashion. But suddenly he is confronted with a crisis. It is interesting that the psalmist says God sent that crisis, "he commanded and raised the stormy wind," which lifted up the waves of the sea.

Free at Last!

Then they cry to the Lord in their trouble and now God delivers the fearful from their distress.

> *He made the storm be still,*
> *and the waves of the sea were hushed.*
> *Then they were glad because they had quiet,*
> *and he brought them to their desired haven.*
> *Let them thank the Lord for his steadfast love,*
> *for his wonderful works to the sons of men!*
> *Let them extol him in the congregation of the*
> *people,*
> *and praise him in the assembly of the elders*
> (vv. 29-32).

Those who are delivered from storms have a responsibility to thank the Lord for His steadfast love and for His wonderful works to the sons of men, and to do it publicly.

These, then, are the works of God. He delivers the restless, the neurotic, the hostile, the fearful; those who are sick, who are wandering, and who are unsatisfied. He delivers them by that unqualified love that keeps after them and will never let them go. This is what sets them free.

God Uses Adversity

We will go briefly through the latter part of the psalm. It describes God's methods.

> *He turns rivers into a desert,*
> *   springs of water into thirsty ground,*
> *a fruitful land into a salty waste,*
> *   because of the wickedness*
> *   of its inhabitants* (vv. 33,34).

To accomplish His purposes, God uses adversity. At times He deliberately sends into our pathway trouble and disaster, because it is the only way He can get our attention. You know that you never had time to listen to the voice of God when you were well or trouble-free. But when trouble loomed, then you had time to listen to what God was saying. C. S. Lewis put it well, "God whispers to us in our pleasures, speaks to us in our work, but shouts at us in our pain. Pain is his megaphone to reach a deaf world."

God Uses Prosperity

Then God can use prosperity.

> *He turns a desert into pools of water,*
> *   a parched land into springs of water.*
> *And there he lets the hungry dwell,*
> *   and they establish a city to live in;*
> *they sow fields, and plant vineyards,*

> *and get a fruitful yield.*
> *By his blessing they multiply greatly;*
> *and he does not let their cattle decrease* (vv. 35-38).

When you take God at His word, to walk in the fulness of His strength and supply, and you begin to fellowship with Him and enjoy His presence, He rewards you. He sends you the very thing you are looking for. He meets your needs, satisfies your heart, and fills you with good things. Your prayers do not go unanswered, for God moves to meet your need and to protect you.

. . . to Accomplish His Work

When they are diminished and brought low
*   through oppression, trouble, and sorrow,*
he pours contempt upon princes [your enemies]
*   and makes them wander in trackless wastes;*
but he raises up the needy out of affliction,
*   and makes their families like flocks* (vv. 39-41).

God uses both adversity and prosperity to accomplish His work.

Fair and Just in What He Does

Then in closing we learn the reaction of men to the ways God works.

> *The upright see it and are glad;*
> *and all wickedness stops its mouth* (v. 42).

As the godly man works his way through life and sees how God works, he rejoices. But when ungodly men

become aware of how God acts, they simply have nothing
to say. They are reduced to silence. It becomes evident
that God is fair and just in what He does, and no man can
complain. That was the reaction of the Pharisees when
they questioned Jesus. They tried to trap Him, but when
He answered they were reduced to silence.

Take Heed and Consider!

So the last word is one of admonition.

> *Whoever is wise, let him give heed to these*
> *things;*
> *let men consider the steadfast love of the Lord* (v. 43).

That means, think about all this! How does this relate
to you? Ask yourself that. You may have been going
through one or more of these difficult situations. Are you
wandering, restless, hostile, or bitter? Are you held prisoner by some attitude, outlook, or habit: or are you sick,
neurotic, emotionally upset? Perhaps you are fearful, troubled by a crisis into which you have come.

Stop and think about how God accepts you, how He
loves you, how He is deeply concerned about you and will
meet you right where you are and take you just as you are.
His love does not change a bit whether you are a failure or
a success. It does not make any difference to Him how you
appear in the eyes of men. God loves you, He is concerned about you and has already received you, already
given you all that He can give in Jesus Christ.

Your first step should be to rejoice in that fact. You will
then find that love will set you free, so that you can act
upon the power and liberty God gives.

Then think about your relationship to others. Give

heed to these things. Have you ever tried unqualified acceptance to these things. Have you ever tried unqualified acceptance on your boss? Or your mother-in-law? Or the kid next door who is so mean and difficult? Have you ever tried unqualified acceptance with your children who are giving you so much trouble, your teenagers who make you mad every time you come in the door? Have you ever tried unqualified acceptance with your parents who are always on your back and never seem to give you a break? Have you ever tried unqualified acceptance with those who are difficult or demanding of you? That is what this psalmist is suggesting. "Whoever is wise, let him give heed to these things; let men consider the unqualified acceptance of the Lord."

Our Father, we ask you to help us with this. We are beginning to catch on to the wonderful way you work. How different it is than the way the world around us acts. Father, how wonderful to see that your unqualified love is designed for life and the situations in which we find ourselves right now. We ask you to set us free by love that we might sing this wonderful song of deliverance. In Christ's name, Amen.

When You Are Falsely Accused

Psalm 109 reflects a common problem that we all have experienced. The psalm describes the reactions of a man who has been unjustly accused, wrongly treated. He has been set upon by those who are attempting to destroy him, yet without a cause. This is also a problem psalm. One need only read it to be troubled about this psalm. Why should this strange, extravagant language of hostility against another human being be included in the book of Psalms? We shall attempt an answer to that as we go through the exposition of this psalm.

Notice that it is a psalm of David and therefore reflects an experience that David went through. It is difficult to tell exactly which of his recorded experiences is referred to here. Personally, I think it probably is the time when he was railed upon by Nabal, the husband of Abigail, as recorded in 1 Samuel 25. Later, God judged Nabal and took him in death, and David married Abigail. I think this psalm best fits that occasion. It is clearly a psalm of someone who is deeply, deeply disturbed.

Under Attack

The opening words set before us the problem this man faces.

> *Be not silent, O God of my praise!*
> *For wicked and deceitful mouths*
> *are opened against me,*
> *speaking against me with lying tongues.*
> *They beset me with words of hate,*
> *and attack me without cause* (vv.1-3).

Here is a man who is under attack from rather unscrupulous persons. Those who attack him so bitterly are obviously not to be trusted. "They are deceitful," he says, "they are wicked." They are determined upon evil, they do not care what they say or what they do. With lying tongues they are out to destroy.

Perhaps some of you have had this experience. You have been unjustly accused by someone who has deliberately sought to slander you, to besmirch your character or ruin your reputation, and you know just how this man felt. Furthermore, these people are wholly unjustified in this attack. He says they do this "without a cause," at least as far as the psalmist can see, and we take him to be an honest man. He sees absolutely no reason for their accusations. They are afflicting him, upsetting him, and attacking him without any reason to do so.

What to Do Next?

In verses 4 and 5 it is apparent that this man has tried to remedy the situation, but it has come to a place where it is humanly hopeless. He has tried to answer these people in the right way. He says,

> *In return for my love they accuse me,*
> *even as I make prayer for them.*
> *So they reward me evil for good,*
> *and hatred for my love.*

This man understands that "a soft answer turns away wrath" (Prov. 15:1), and he has tried that with them. He has followed the New Testament standard of praying for those who hate him and despitefully use him. It is remarkable, is it not, that here in the Old Testament you find such a clear demonstration of the fulfillment of the New Testament requirement to pray for our enemies? We are to bless those who persecute us and try to do good toward them. This man has done that, yet it has not altered the situation. His enemies have not ceased their attack; they are just as vicious, just as malicious, just a fiercely hostile as they were before, and now he does not know what to do next.

Cursing and Damning

Now, according to the next verses, it sounds as though he gives up. His response resembles this interpretation of the Sermon on the Mount: "If someone smites you on the right cheek, turn to him the other cheek—and then, POW, let him have it!" Listen to the vitriol that pours out!

Appoint a wicked man against him;
  let an accuser bring him to trial.
When he is tried, let him come forth guilty;
  let his prayer be counted as sin!
May his days be few;
  may another seize his goods!
May his children be fatherless,
  and his wife a widow!
May his children wander about and beg; may they
  be driven out of the ruins they inhabit!
May the creditor seize all that he has; may
  strangers plunder the fruits of his toil!
Let there be none to extend kindness to him,
  nor any to pity his fatherless children!
May his posterity be cut off; may his name be
  blotted out in the second generation!
May the iniquity of his fathers be remembered
  before the Lord, and let not the sin of his mother
be blotted out!
Let them be before the Lord continually;
  and may his memory be cut off from the earth! (vv.
6-15).

What strong language! What hostility! How fierce is
the invective here! This passage has raised the problem of
so-called "imprecatory psalms," these psalms which seem
to heap imprecations, maledictions, against people. Many
have been troubled by these, and this is the worst of them
all. There is no stronger language in the Psalms. We have
chosen to deal with the toughest one of all.

Who Is Speaking?
How do you explain language like this in the Psalms? Well,

it seems to me that the clearest and simplest answer is that this is not one of the imprecatory psalms at all. In these verses this man is not quoting himself, but is quoting what his enemies say about him. In Hebrew there are no quotation marks, so the psalmist simply has to run on. But there are several clues that indicate these are not his own words. In verse 5 he says, "They reward me evil for good, and hatred for my love." Then in verse 6 he says, "Appoint a wicked man against him; let an accuser bring him to trial." It seems incredible that a man should so suddenly turn from an attitude of love and warmth to one of such violent and appalling invective. So the first clue is a remarkable and immediate change of attitude which seems unlikely to happen.

Second, a change of number occurs. Notice that in verses 1 through 5 you have his enemies referred to in the plural— "them," "they"; but in verse 6 it becomes "he." If the psalmist is going on to describe what he wants to have happen to his enemies, it is difficult to explain this sudden change of number. But if he is quoting what *they* say about *him*, it makes perfect sense.

That the harsh words fit best in the mouths of the psalmist's accusers is further confirmed at the end of this quoted portion in the Jewish version of the Old Testament. Verse 20, instead of reading "May this be the reward of my accusers from the Lord," says, "This is the reward which my accusers seek from the Lord, those who speak evil against my life!" Thus the psalmist seems to sum up what his enemies are saying.

It is reasonable, therefore, that this entire portion from verse 6 through verse 19 should be put in quotation marks. You might like to mark your own Bible that way. By revealing what these people have said about him, and by quoting *verbatim* some of their fierce and unrelenting language, he has given us a vivid glimpse of the intense hatred that had so distressed him.

A Clever Strategy
Verses 6 through 15 reveal the strategy they have devised against him. Notice what they are after. First, they want to rig a false trial. They want to get him before the law on a false charge and arrange a false witness to accuse him and thus gain a legal condemnation. Note the cleverness of these people. They are not going to waylay him and murder him; they would be open to charges themselves if they did that, but they are going to destroy him legally. They have figured out a way by which they can rig the trial and get him condemned, and do it all legally. They want it all to end with a death sentence. "May his days be few; . . . May his children be fatherless, and his wife a widow! May his children wander about and beg . . . " (vv. 8,9).

Then they want to take everything he has. Their hatred is so terrible that they want to leave nothing for his wife and children, but wish to destroy them as well. "May the creditor seize all that he has; . . . Let there be none to extend kindness to him, nor any to pity his fatherless children!" (vv. 11,12).

A Fierce Revenge
Finally, so fierce, so appalling is their revenge that they even want to carry it on before God Himself. The attempt is made on their part to seek his eternal damnation. Their prayer is, "May his posterity be cut off; may his name be blotted out in the second generation! May the iniquity of his fathers be remembered before the Lord, . . . Let them be before the Lord continually; and may his memory be cut off from the earth!" (vv. 13-15).

To put it bluntly, they are asking God to damn this

man. They are saying, "God, damn him!" Isn't it rather revealing that this is the most common oath heard today. When hatred rises in the heart, the easiest thing for men to say is "God, damn him!" Hatred seeks the ultimate destruction, even the eternal destruction of an individual. The ultimate wish of hate is that God would damn.

Cursing, though men do it rather lightly, has a terrible reality about it. There is really such a thing as being cursed. There is such a thing as being damned. What makes cursing so terrible is that men take it upon themselves to pronounce this sentence of damnation and they do it in the lightest way, as though it were nothing. When you hear someone say, "God damn you!" remember that it is a terrible malediction, an awful thing, which only God has the right to say.

A Twisted Reasoning

Now the psalmist lists the reasons his enemies give for this abuse. What has this man done to make them so vindictive, so filled with fierce hatred? He lists the two reasons they set forth. First,

For he did not remember to show kindness,
but pursued the poor and needy
and the brokenhearted to their death (v. 16).

That was the way it looked from the viewpoint of his enemies. You can see here a strange twisting of reason that occurs when we act defensively. These men were blaming the writer for crimes that they themselves had committed. It was that same rationalizing that we do when we see ourselves as the victims of injustice when we may, in fact, be getting exactly what we deserve.

How prevalent this is in human nature! In San Mateo, California, years ago a man was on trial for his life. He was charged with the rape and murder of a young woman who had stopped at his service station late one night to get the lights on her car fixed. In a very cruel and terrible manner,

---

THERE is this strange reaction in humanity that blames another for the things we ourselves have caused.

---

he had destroyed this woman. All the ugly facts were revealed at the trial, and the jury concluded that he was guilty. The judge then sentenced him to death. According to the papers, when the sentence was pronounced, the parents of this man stood up and shook their fists at the judge and the jury and threatened them, charging them with injustice, although the man was caught red-handed in his guilt. There is this strange reaction in humanity that blames another for the things we ourselves have caused.

Seeking Justification

The second reason for his enemies' hatred is like the first. They said of him,

> He loved to curse; let curses come on him!
> He did not like blessing; may it be far from
> him!
> He clothed himself with cursing as his coat (vv. 17,18).

Again they are blaming him to justify their own cursing. They have just said, "May God damn you!" But to justify it they say, "Well, that's what he said to us!" Again, this is human nature, is it not? I remember seeing two children fighting, one of whom happened to be my own. I broke up the quarrel and said to them, "Who started this?" The boy said, "She did! She hit me back!" How true that is to our nature. We love to blame the other. We accuse others of the very things for which we are guilty. That is what is happening here.

Hatred and Malevolence

Notice how they intensify this.

> *May it* [these curses] *soak into his body like*
>   *water,*
> *like oil into his bones!*
> *May it be like a garment which he wraps round him,*
>   *like a belt with which he daily girds himself!* (vv. 18,19).

So terrible is their hatred, so malevolent is their fierce reaction that they intensify language to the ultimate refinement of malice. They pour out invective upon him to justify their own hate.

Reference to Judas?

Before we go on to look at the psalmist's reaction, we should note one further thing in this section. In verse 8 are words that are taken by the Holy Spirit and applied in the New Testament to Judas Iscariot. "May his days be few; may another seize his goods!" or literally, "May another take his office!" The first chapter of Acts tells how the 11 apostles gathered together to appoint a successor to Judas. Peter quoted from two of the psalms to justify that appointment. One of them was Psalm 69, which stated, "May his habitation become desolate" (see v. 25), and the other is this verse from Psalm 109, "May another take his office!"

This has raised the suggestion that perhaps this whole passage applied to Judas, that it is all a prediction of the terrible fate that would await Judas Iscariot; his wife and children would be left desolate and he himself would be damned of God. Perhaps that view is justified in the light of Jesus' own words, "Woe to that man by whom the Son of man is betrayed! It would have been better for that man if he had not been born" (Matt. 26:24).

A Cry to the Lord

Now let us look at the psalmist's reaction. Here he is in this terrible situation with his enemies attempting to take his life. He has tried to react the right way but it does not seem to work. He does not know what to do now. He cries before God, in the literal rendering of verse 20:

> *This is the reward my accusers seek from*
> *the Lord,*
> *those who speak evil against my life.*

An Appeal to the Lord

What he finally does is beautiful. He commits the whole matter to the Lord in prayer. This closing prayer of the psalm is a marvelous picture of the right attitude, the right reaction, the right way to handle this kind of situation.

> *But thou, O God my Lord,*
> *deal on my behalf for thy name's sake;*

> *because thy steadfast love is good,*
> *deliver me!* (v. 21).

Notice that the first thing he does is to commit the cause to God. "Thou, O God of my life, deal on my behalf for thy name's sake!" Here is a man who understands the nature of reality. He knows the truth behind the admonition of Scripture, both in the Old and New Testament, "Vengeance is mine, says the Lord; I will repay" (see Rom. 12:19). Vengeance is God's! Don't try to get even. If you do you'll only make the matter worse. You will perpetuate a feud that may go on for years, even centuries, destroying, wrecking, damaging others and creating all kinds of difficulties both for them and for you. No, no! "Vengeance is mine," says the Lord. "I am the only one who has adequate wisdom for handling this kind of a problem."

God's Name Involved

The writer also understands something else. He understands that God's name is involved in all this. When God's people are being persecuted, then God is also being persecuted. It is up to God to defend that name, not man. When Saul of Tarsus was converted on the Damascus road and the Lord Jesus appeared to him in light brighter than the sun, Saul cried out to Him and said, "Lord, who are you?" Jesus said, "I am Jesus whom you are persecuting" (see Acts 9:5). Saul was persecuting the Christians, but when he was persecuting them, he was also persecuting the Lord.

God is involved in what happens to His own. The psalmist, understanding this, commits the whole cause to God and says, "God, you deal with it. It's your problem. Your name is involved; you handle it on my behalf for your name's sake." Is that not a thoroughly Christian reaction? Peter shows us that this was exactly the reaction of the Lord Jesus Himself. "He committed no sin; no guile was found on his lips. When he was reviled, he did not revile in return; when he suffered, he did not threaten; but *he trusted to him who judges justly*" (1 Pet. 2:22,23, italics added). Jesus has left us an example to follow. He trusted Himself to Him, the Father, who always judges justly.

Leave Vindication to God

Dr, F. B. Meyer, beloved English pastor, has said, "We make a mistake in trying always to clear ourselves. We should be wiser to go straight on, humbly doing the next thing, and leaving God to vindicate us. 'He shall bring forth thy righteousness as the light, and thy judgment as the noon day' [see Ps. 37:6]. There may come hours in our lives when we shall be misunderstood, slandered, falsely accused. At such times it is very difficult not to act on the policy of the men around us in the world. They at once appeal to law and force and public opinion. But the believer takes his case into a higher court and lays it before his God."

Seeking Strength

Now the psalmist cries out for strength. He himself is in need.

> *For I am poor and needy,*
> *and my heart is stricken within me.*
> *I am gone, like a shadow at evening;*
> *I am shaken off like a locust.*
> *My knees are weak through fasting;*
> *my body has become gaunt.*

> *I am an object of scorn to my accusers;*
> *when they see me, they wag their heads* (vv. 22-25).

Slander is difficult to endure; it does something to you; takes something out of you. When first I read this my reaction was, "Lord, is this what I do to people when I accuse them? Have I made others feel like this? What an awful thing! This man cries out to God for help in his physical weakness, in hishumiliation, and the scorn that he feels heaped upon him.

Seeking Vindication

Then he asks for vindication:

> *Help me, O Lord my God!*
> *Save me according to thy steadfast love!*
> *Let them know that this is thy hand;*
> *thou, O Lord, hast done it!*
> *Let them curse, but do thou bless!* (vv. 26-28).

Again he places the matter in the Lord's hands.

Many English versions put the next two sentences in the optative mood, that is, "may this happen," "let this happen." It should, however, be stated in the indicative as a simple statement of fact:

> *My assailants shall be put to shame,*
> *and thy servant shall be glad!*
> *My accusers shall be clothed with dishonor;*
> *they shall be wrapped in their own shame*
> *as in a mantle!* (vv. 28,29).

Notice what this man is doing. First he asks God to vindicate him, but to do it in such a way as to reveal that

God is doing the vindicating. He says, "Now, Lord, let them curse. I can't stop them, and you may not choose to, but if you let them curse, bless me anyhow so that they will see that you are not cursing me. Give me inner strength, inner blessing, so that I can remain calm, untroubled and undistressed in the midst of the cursing. Then men will see that it is your hand that is holding me up, your hand that is strengthening me."

Second, he says, "Vindicate me in such a way as to make the accusers ashamed of themselves." Now, he does not mean "put to shame" in the sense of heaping scorn and humiliation upon them; he means, let them be ashamed of themselves, let them see the facts in such a light that eventually they'll be sorry for ever attempting anything so unjustified. "Lord," he says, "vindicate me in that way."

Keep Your Conscience Clear
Once again this is exactly in line with the New Testament. In 1 Peter, chapter 3, Peter says, "And keep your conscience clear, so that when you are abused, those who revile your good behavior in Christ may be put to shame" (v. 16).

It is the same thing, you see. If you are in this situation, keep your conscience clear. Don't return in kind. Don't strike back. Don't curse, don't revile, don't attack, don't try to get even, don't avenge yourself; but walk with God. Those who revile your good behavior will be brought to shame, brought at last to the place where they are ashamed of themselves.

Finding Victory
Someone has beautifully expressed that truth this way:
"When you are neglected or snubbed or insulted, and

you're able to thank God for the experience, accepting it as allowed by him for your spiritual development, that is victory.

"When you're seeking to serve him faithfully and you find yourself criticized severely for the way you do it, and you accept the criticism patiently for his sake—that is victory.

"When you are slandered and your motives are impugned and you do not complain but receive it in love and as a measure of the filling up of that which is behind of the afflictions of Christ—that is victory."[1]

Such a victory can only be won in the yieldedness of self to Christ. "Thanks be to God who causes me to triumph through our Lord Jesus Christ!" (see 2 Cor. 2:14).

At the Right Hand of the Needy

The psalm closes on a note of ringing affirmation and confidence in God:

> *With my mouth I will give great thanks*
> *to the Lord;*
> *I will praise him in the midst of the throng.*
> *For he stands at the right hand of the needy,*
> *to save him from those who condemn him to death*
> (vv. 30,31).

Recall that in verse 6 this man's enemies had wanted to appoint an accuser to stand at his right hand and condemn him. But he closes the psalm by saying he realizes that God stands at the right hand of the needy. God makes their cause His own. God knows 1000 ways to work it all out without violence, without the perpetuation of hatred, without the destruction of lives. He is assured that God will bring truth to light and establish the facts in such a way that even the accusers will be ashamed of themselves for ever attempting such a thing. How wise it is to commit our cause to God in times like this.

Our Father, we have all been guilty. We have all felt feelings of resentment rising up within us. We have all wanted to strike back, to pour invective against another. And we have done it, too, at times, Lord. We ask you to forgive us and to teach us from these psalms how to handle such problems. Help us to have confidence in the fact that you, Lord, know how to work these things out, and that we do not need to have our little pound of flesh. Rather it is you, Lord, your great cause and your great name, who needs to be vindicated and justified. Help us to follow the example of this psalmist by turning these issues over to you and quietly going on trusting you, just as the Lord Jesus did, to work all things out for your glory. We ask in your name, Amen.

1. "Victory" from *Our Hope*. (This magazine ceased publication in 1956.)

Who Am I, Lord?

Everywhere today one hears of those who are passing through an identity crisis. That is a fancy way of saying what people have been asking for a long time, "Who am I?" We all ask this question occasionally but perhaps it is asked more frequently today because of the prevailing scientific view of the universe. That view tells us that our earth is but a tiny speck in a vast universe, and we are struggling mortals on an obscure planet located in a second rate galaxy among billions of other galaxies.

Such an outlook tends to make us feel most insignificant. It contrasts sharply with the biblical view of man and especially the view that deals with man in relationship to God. Psalm 139 describes a man who is thinking about himself and his relationship to God. If you are struggling with an identity crisis and you are not sure just who you are, then I suggest you read carefully as we look together at this marvelous psalm.

God Understands Us

It is divided into four paragraphs of six verses each. In each paragraph the psalmist faces a question about himself in relationship to God. In the first paragraph he asks, "How well does God know me?" The first sentence gives us his answer:

O Lord, thou hast searched me and known me! (v. 1).

The Hebrew word for "searched" is the word *to dig*. Literally, what this man is saying is, "O Lord, you dig me!" Now that is how up-to-date the Bible is! The word means, "You dig into me and therefore you know me." It is not surprising that the word *dig* has come to mean in English, "to know or understand." It was a very popular term some years back, and this is the way the psalmist begins: "Lord, you dig me!"

In what way does God understand?

God Knows Our Thoughts

*Thou knowest when I sit down and when I rise up;
thou discernest my thoughts from afar* (v. 2).

That is, "Lord, you understand and know me in my conscious life. You know when I sit down (my passive life) and when I rise up (my active life). When I am resting or when I am active, you know me. And you know me also in my subconscious life—that level of life from which my thoughts arise. You understand them even before they get to the surface. You know how I think and what I think about. You even understand the thoughts that come, unbidden, in a constant flow to my mind."

God Knows Our Ways

Then there follows the awareness of God's knowledge of habits and choices.

> *Thou searchest out my path and my lying down,*
> *and art acquainted with all my ways* (v. 3).

You know the way I choose to go, and you know the habits of my life. "You know me, Lord," says this man, "intimately—inside and out." Then in verses 4 and 5 he contemplates the fact that God is concerned about him.

God Speaks Our Language

> *Even before a word is on my tongue, lo, O Lord,*
> *thou knowest it altogether* (v. 4).

That is, "You understand my language. Every word that I utter you know and understand."

When I was a boy in northern Minnesota I lived for a time in a Swedish settlement. The Swedish Christians used to tease the rest of us, saying, "You know, we Scandinavians are going to have a wonderful time in heaven while all the rest of you are learning the language!" I used to resent that until I discovered that God knows more than Swedish; he also knows English, Afrikaans, Hebrew, and all other languages of earth. That is what impresses the psalmist. "Even before I utter a word, Lord, you know it. You understand my language, you communicate with me."

God Knows Us Best

Then God is active, the psalmist discovers, in his past, his future, and his present.

> *Thou dost beset me behind* [the past] *and before,* [the future],
> > *and layest thy hand upon me* [now, the present].
> *Such knowledge is too wonderful for me;*
> > *it is high, I cannot attain it* (vv. 5,6).

He is simply overwhelmed by the fact that God knows him better than he knows himself, better than anyone else knows him. That is amazing, is it not? God knows me better than I know anyone else, no matter how hard I have tried to communicate to that person and better even than I know myself. For God knows me in the subconscious, the unexplorable part of me life, as well as in the conscious. What a wonderful revelation this is of God's understanding of each individual human being. How desperately we need in this day of depersonalization, to remember that, though science tells us how vast the universe is, and, thus, how great is the power of God, it takes God's self-revelation to tell us how important we are to Him and how well He knows us.

Is God Ever Absent?

In the second paragraph the writer is exploring the question, "How near is God to me?"

> *Whither shall I go from thy Spirit?*
> > *Or whither shall I flee from thy presence?* (v. 7).

How many times we have asked that of ourselves. "Lord, how can I get away from you? Is there any way in my guilt that I can escape?" This is the psalmist's answer.

God Is Always with Us

*If I ascend to heaven, thou art there! If I make
my bed in Sheol, thou art there!* (v. 8).

No destiny can separate me from the fact of God. If I go to heaven, God is there, of course. And even though I go to hell I still will not escape God. Of course, other Scriptures make clear that there is a vast difference between the experience of God for one who is in heaven and for one who is in Sheol, or hell. In heaven we shall experience to the full the love, compassion, glory, and warmth of God—the positives of God. In hell it is the other way around. There men experience the absence of God's love, the dark side of it, the wrath of God— His negatives. But He is still God, that is the point. God owns and runs His universe and there is no escaping His presence.

God Goes Before Us

The presence of God is not a fearful thought. The writer goes on to say that no distance can separate him from God.

*If I take the wings of the morning
and dwell in the uttermost parts of the sea,
even there thy hand shall lead me,
and thy right hand shall hold me* (v. 9,10).

What do you think he means by the "wings of the morning"? This is a beautifully poetic expression. If you have stood and watched the sun come up you will have noticed how the rays of the rising sun shoot across the heavens with the speed of light and reach to the farthest bounds of the horizon. This is what he is describing. "If I could travel with the wings of the morning," that is, with the speed of light; "if I could go with the speed of light and reach to the farthest points of earth (the uttermost parts of the sea), even there," he says, "I would find you, Lord. You have gone before me, have preceded me, and I will find you there as much as here."

When I was about 12 years old, we moved from Minnesota to Montana. The night before we left I got down by my bed and said, "Good-bye, God. We're going to Montana." I was sure I would not find Him there, but when we arrived, there He was. I have found Him everywhere since. That is what this writer is saying.

A young airman of the Royal Canadian Air Force wrote a poem, which ties in beautifully with what the psalmist is saying. Killed at the age of 19, this is the way John Gillespie Magee described his experience of flight.

"Oh! I have slipped the surly bonds of earth
And danced the skies on laughter-silvered wings;
Sunward I've climbed, and joined
    the tumbling mirth
Of sun-split clouds—and done a hundred things
You have not dreamed of—wheeled and soared
    and swung
High in the sunlit silence. Hov'ring there,
I've chased the shouting wind along, and flung
My eager craft through footless halls of air.

Up, up the long delirious, burning blue
I've topped the wind-swept heights

with easy grace
Where never lark, or even eagle flew—
And, while with silent lifting mind I've trod
The high untrespassed sanctity of space,
Put out my hand and touched the face of God."[1]

This pilot had experienced the truth that, "if I take the wings of the morning and dwell in the uttermost parts of the earth," there God has gone before.

God Is but a Touch Away

Finally in this section the psalmist cries that not even darkness can separate him from God.

If I say, "Let only darkness cover me,
and the light about me be night,"
even the darkness is not dark to thee,
and the night is bright as the day;
for darkness is as light with thee (vv. 11,12).

Remember when you were little and had misbehaved, you felt guilty and tried to hide from God by crawling under the covers or hiding under the bed or in the closet? You thought that God could not see you because humans couldn't. There are many grownups who are still trying to do that. They feel that if they do not think about certain things, then God will not think about them either. But He does. No darkness, physical or mental, can hide us from God's presence. He knows us and sees us, no matter how dark it is. Paul reminded the Athenians that God is not far from any one of us. Whether we know Him or not, He is but a touch away.

God Made Us

In the third paragraph the psalmist is telling us *how* he knows all this. Someone might say, "Well, this is certainly beautiful poetry, all this about God's knowing me and being with me, but how do you know it is true?" "All right," says the psalmist, "I'll tell you." First, because of deduction from the design of the body.

> *For thou didst form my inward parts,*
> *thou didst knit me together in my mother's womb.*
> *I praise thee, for I am fearfully and wonderfully*
> *made* [literal Hebrew translation].
> *Wonderful are thy works!* (vv. 13,14).

Here he is examining himself, and he is amazed at the vitality and complexity of the forces in his own body, which are essential to life, but over which he obviously has no control. "That," he says, "shows me there is something outside of man that is regulating and running me. I live within the limits of God."

Have you ever stopped to think how much of your life is dependent upon forces at work in you? If any one of them stopped you would die very quickly. You are dependent on something over which you have no control. Your heart is thumping away right now, and it would be terrible if you had to control it with your mind or will. How would you like to have to keep saying to yourself now as you are reading, "Now, thump. Now, thump. Now, thump." Or if you had to say to your diaphragm, "Now, di, now, phragm. Now, di, now, phragm."

No, it is wonderful, is it not? Someone else is running our lives; that is obvious from the design of our bodies. This is what has struck the psalmist. He says, "Thou didst knit me together in a most amazing way in my mother's womb. I praise thee, for I am fearfully and wonderfully made."

God Designed Us

Then he is struck by the process that is necessary in the forming of a human being.

> *Thou knowest me right well;*
> *my frame was not hidden from thee,*
> *when I was being made in secret, intricately*
> *wrought in the depths of the earth* (vv.14,15).

The frame is the foundation of the body, the bone and muscle system. That is where the body begins to be put together, with the frame. Without a frame we would be but rolling balls of gelatin. (Some of us are getting that way anyhow!)

That phrase "intricately wrought" is one word in the Hebrew. It is really the word for "embroidered." Some of you ladies know what embroidery is, the little fancy stitches that are added to cloth. I don't know how you do it; most of us men never understand embroidery, but it adds beauty and is especially fancy. That is the word used here. It describes the delicate embroidery of the body, the things that tie us together so that one organ supports another. The lungs need the heart, and the heart needs the lungs; the liver needs the kidneys, and the stomach needs both; all the parts are amazingly embroidered together.

This, by the way, raises one of the unanswered questions of evolution: how can an organ, which is only helpful to the body when it functions as a complete and mature organ, develop in stages over a long period of time? Evolutionists have never answered that, yet it is one of the most vital questions to ask. The psalmist simply says, "I am astonished when I consider the fact that my inward parts are knit together and embroidered together, and are necessary one to the other."

God Has *Always* Known Us

Then he uses this phrase, in verse 16,

Thy eyes beheld my unformed substance.

Literally, the word in Hebrew is, "my rolled up substance." It pictures the embryo, all rolled up. People are asking questions today about when life begins. When does an embryo become a human being? When does abortion become murder? The answer of the psalmist is "Thy eyes beheld *me*, not an impersonal collection of cells that wasn't me yet, in my rolled-up embryonic state." The marvel of the human body, even at that stage of growth, has convinced him that God is with him and knows him intimately.

Some of you may remember the Alger Hiss case quite a number of years ago. Alger Hiss was accused of communist conspiracy while he was a functionary of the government. The case brought into prominent view an unknown (at that time) Congressman named Richard Milhous Nixon. A primary participant in that case was a man named Whittaker Chambers, also a member of the Communist Party and a contact of Alger Hiss.

Whittaker Chambers later wrote a book in which he tells how he became a Christian. He describes an incident one day when he was sitting with his little two-year-old daughter on his lap. His eye fell on her ear and it caught his attention. He was struck by the design of that ear. How beautiful, how shell-like it was, and how perfectly designed to catch every sound wave in the air to be translated into sound by the brain. Knowing something of the mechanics of the ear he began to think about it. He was so struck by the impossibility that anything so intricate, so complex, so beautifully designed could ever occur by chance. That led him to other lines of thought and eventually he investigated the Christian position and became a Christian. The argument from design is a great argument and it is what the psalmist uses here.

God Determined Our Lives

But that is not all. In verse 16 he says,

> *Thy eyes beheld my unformed substance;*
>   *in thy book were written, every one of them,*
> *the days that were formed for me,*
>   *when as yet there was none of them* (v. 16).

He is not only impressed by the argument from design, but by the evidence of determination. Evidently, he'd had certain experiences in his life when so many unrelated factors and incidents suddenly tied together that he knew it must have all been brought about by a mind greater than his own. To him this was evidence of the fruition of pre-made plans.

We have all had this feeling. Something that we did not plan nor expect suddenly takes place. Many varied factors all of a sudden fit together, dovetailing beautifully. Then we become aware that Someone else is planning our days and yet allowing us free will in experiencing them. Even before these days occurred they were recorded in the Book of God; He planned them.

This, of course, is the basis for all biblical prophecy.

How is it that an event can occur in the life of our Lord that was predicted by the prophets 500, 600, sometimes 1000 years before—predicted not only by one prophet, but by several? After the passing of years and even centuries there comes a moment when many factors suddenly fall together and our Lord fulfills an event that was foretold

---

EVEN though we have the evidence of design and the evidence of determination, yet apart from this marvelous revelation of the thoughts of God, which fit so perfectly with the design and the determination, we would never understand ourselves.

---

long before. All this impresses the psalmist, and he is made aware of God's knowledge of him.

God Reveals Our Lives

The third thing that convinces him follows.

> *How precious to me are thy thoughts, O God!*
> *How vast is the sum of them!*
> *If I would count them, they are more than the sand.*
> *When I awake, I am still with thee* (vv. 17,18).

An alternate reading says, "Were I to come to the end I would still be with thee." The psalmist is impressed by the abundance of revelation from God. We would never understand our lives if God did not tell us who we are.

Thus, even though we have the evidence of design and the evidence of determination, yet apart from this marvelous revelation of the thoughts of God, which fit so perfectly with the design and the determination, we would never understand ourselves.

How precious are God's thoughts! How vast is the sum of them! How wide is the range of fact that God comments upon in His revelation. Even if you come to the end, says the psalmist, God is still more. No revelation can ever plumb the depths of God. How great, how impossibly great, are His thoughts toward us.

Making Requests of God

The last paragraph seems to take a rather abrupt turn.

> *O that thou wouldst slay the wicked, O God,*
> *and that men of blood would depart from me,*
> *men who maliciously defy thee,*
> *who lift themselves up against thee for evil!*
> *Do I not hate them that hate thee, O Lord?*
> *And do I not loathe them that rise up against*
> *thee?*
> *I hate them with perfect hatred;*
> *I count them my enemies* (vv. 19-22).

Many have asked: Why do these psalmists seem suddenly to interject these bloody thoughts? Why this sudden word of passion, "Lord, kill the wicked!" This has troubled many because it seems so far from the New Testament standard, "Love your enemies; pray for those who despitefully use you; do good to those who injure you" (see Matt. 5:44). How shall we understand these things?

Asking Against His Will

First, we need to recognize that everything that is declared in the Psalms is not necessarily a reflection of God's will. We are listening to the experiences of believers and they do not always reflect God's truth. They honestly mirror man's viewpoint, and we need to understand these passages in the light of their context. The psalmist, having been impressed by his close relationship to God, now naturally comes to the place where he asks God for something. That is also what we do. When we are aware of being near to God, being dear to Him, we tend to ask God for things too.

He asks for two things. First, he asks God to take care of the problem of the wicked. His suggested manner of handling it is rather naive. He says, "Lord, wipe them out," as though such a simple remedy for human ills had never occurred to the Almighty. "Lord, wipe them out, that's all. That will take care of them." Have you ever felt that way? I remember hearing of Mel Trotter, the famous American evangelist, who said, "There are a lot of people I know what are wonderful people. They're going to go to heaven someday, and oh, how I wish they'd hurry up." We have all felt that way, have we not? One of the refreshing things about these psalms is the honesty they reflect.

Short of His Standards

There are several things we need to note about this. For one thing, this psalmist's request falls short even of the Old Testament standard. It is the Old Testament that first says, "Love thy neighbor as thyself." The New Testament and the Old Testament are not opposed to one another in this matter of moral standards, not in the least. But this man has not yet learned this. In his honesty, he says, "Lord, it seems to me the easiest way for you to handle this problem of evil would be to slay the wicked. Why don't you do that?"

Notice he does not say, "Why don't you let me do it?" That is what many are saying today. "Lord, I'll wipe out the wicked; just turn them over to me. I'll take care of them." But this man does not say that. He recognizes that vengeance belongs to God and that if anybody is going to do it, and do it right, God alone must do it. He is saying, "Lord, it's your problem; why don't you do it?"

THE sharpest words Jesus ever spoke were against the religious hypocrisy of the Pharisee, who were using God's name for evil.

We can understand why he is so upset by this, because verse 20 points out he is not concerned about what the wicked do to him but what they do to God. "They maliciously defy thee." In the Hebrew it is even clearer. Literally, he is saying, "They speak of thee for wickedness," that is, "they use your name to carry out their evil designs." "In effect," he says, "they take thy name in vain for evil." These are religious hypocrites, and there is nothing more disgusting than a religious hypocrite. The sharpest words Jesus ever spoke were against the religious hypocrisy of the Pharisee, who were using God's name for evil.

The Way Everlasting

Here is the case of a man who has felt the hatred of God against sin, but not yet the love of God for the sinner. That is why, I think, he concludes with these words.

Search me, O God, and know my heart!
 Try me and know my thoughts!
And see if there be any wicked way in me,
 and lead me in the way everlasting! (v. 23,24).

Is he not saying, "Lord, I don't understand this problem of evil. It appears to me the easiest way is for you to eliminate the evil man. But Lord, I also know that I don't think very clearly and I don't often have the right answer. There can easily be in me a way of grief (that is literally what 'wicked' means). I have often found, Lord, that my thoughts are not right. So, Lord, in case I don't have the right remedy for this problem, let me add this prayer: Search me, O God, and know my heart! Try me and know my thoughts! See if there be any way of grief in me, and lead me in the truth, the way that leads to everlasting life!"

What a wonderful prayer. How often we should pray like this! "Lord, I don't understand what's going on around me and my solutions may be quite inferior, may even be wrong. But Lord, I'll trust you to lead me. Reveal the wickedness that may lie undetected in my own heart, and guide me in the way that leads to fulness of life."

Father, we thank you for this revelation of the humanity of these men of old, and how it fits our own situation today. How desperately we need to be led through the complexities of our age. Help us not to settle for simple yet wrong solutions, but to be willing to let you work out your own purposes, knowing that you have taken all the factors into consideration, for you know us so intimately. We thank you in Jesus' name, Amen.

1. John Gillespie Magee, Jr., "High Flight" *from Sourcebook of Poetry* (Grand Rapids: Zondervan Publishing House, 1968), p. 500.